THE
PACKER
AFFAIR

by the same author

CRICKET IN THREE MOODS

THE PACKER AFFAIR

◆

Henry Blofeld

COLLINS
St James's Place, London
1978

William Collins Sons & Co. Ltd
London · Glasgow · Sydney · Auckland
Toronto · Johannesburg

First published 1978
© Henry Blofeld 1978

ISBN 0 00 216654 2

Set in Monotype Imprint
Made and printed in Great Britain by
William Collins Sons & Co Ltd., Glasgow

Contents

Acknowledgements

First of all I would like to thank Ken Murphy, the *Guardian* librarian, who has been of immense help to me in seeking out the volume of material that has appeared in the press on the whole Packer affair. Michael Davie and Peter McFarline have both given me considerable help as well as allowing me to use their material. The London *Sunday Times*, the *Australian* and the Trinidad *Sunday Express* have likewise allowed me to use material from their pages, and Mike Brearley has allowed me to quote from his book *Return of the Ashes*. Louis Blom-Cooper, QC, generously allowed me to quote from his article in the *Guardian* on the legal aspects of the Packer case; David Austin, sports Editor of the Melbourne *Age*, was extremely helpful to me during the time I spent researching the book in Australia; and Jim Coldham compiled the index with his usual meticulousness. Finally I would like to thank Wendy Wimbush for her help in typing the script, which she did at very short notice and with great care; since she spent the summer of 1977 working closely with the Australian touring team, often typing highly confidential material about World Series Cricket, her work for me must have had its share of ironic moments.

Illustration Credits

Australian Consolidated Press – 1; Melbourne *Age* – 2; Patrick Eagar – 3, 5, 6, 10, 11, 12, 13; Jack Manwaring – 4; *Herald & Weekly Times* – 8; G. W. Sparkes – 7, 9.

Author's Preface

ON THE EVENING of 17 March 1977, I was walking through the beautiful Fitzroy Gardens past Captain Cook's cottage – removed, brick by brick, from its native Yorkshire – on the way back from the Melbourne Cricket Ground after the last day's play in the Centenary Test Match between England and Australia. I could not help wondering what the situation would be at the end of the Bicentenary Test Match in 2077.

They would surely not have had a better game of cricket than the one I had been watching. But would the game have developed or changed as comprehensively as it has during Test cricket's first hundred years? Lillee, Marsh, Randall and company, of course, would be dim figures by then, although not quite so dim as Charles Bannerman, David Gregory, James Lillywhite and those other hirsute characters are today: photographic and television records would see to that. About the only certainty, I concluded, would be that the Bicentenary match would not, like the matches in 1877 and 1977, end in victory for Australia by 45 runs. When Knott was LBW to Lillee in the last hour of the game it was an uncanny coincidence that the margin between the two sides was exactly the same as it had been one hundred years before: a final, perfect seal on a remarkable week.

The organization in Melbourne had been faultless, and almost all the old cricketers still living who had played in a Test Match between the two countries had been brought to see the game. A walk through the lobby of the Hilton Hotel where they were staying on any evening of the match was like taking a stroll through the dusty pages of some old *Wisden*. Almost every Test Match between England and Australia over the last fifty years was re-played. Harold Larwood, Bill Voce, Gubby Allen and Bill Bowes were there, and Bodyline was constantly discussed. Ironically, Larwood and Voce were acclaimed perhaps more than any of the

other old players, English or Australian, and they were cheered to
the echo when, during one of the intervals, they went out together
to inspect the pitch. Voce even handed his coat to Larwood and
marked out his run. To round it all off, on the last day the Queen
watched some of the play.

Australia's win was hardly a surprise, for they were the stronger
side, but in coming so close to victory after being left to score 463
in the final innings England had shown that they could once again
compete with Australia on level terms. This match came at the
end of four months in which England's cricket had improved
dramatically, and it seemed that at last here was the solid basis for
a successful side.

To those of us who had watched England lose fairly consistently
in the last few years the victory in India was as pleasing as it was
to the players themselves. When I am on tour with an England
side I find it almost impossible not to identify with their fortunes –
although I hope I grow better at disguising it. At times India can
be an irritating country, for the journeys are long and aeroplanes
are often late. In the smaller centres the accommodation is simple,
the food often unfamiliar and stomach upsets are a recurring
problem. Against this background the performance of Greig's side
was even more remarkable.

India had been beaten by three matches to one – never an easy
result to achieve on their spinning pitches – some of the young
players were beginning to realize their potential and, as if to under-
line this, in Melbourne Australia had been made to fight to the
utmost to win. The cricket in the Centenary Test could not have
been more intensely contested. There had been no question of the
players treating it as a festival occasion, and English supporters
returning home after the game had reason to expect that the
England side they had seen in action in Melbourne would have a
good chance of avenging their defeat when Australia toured
England in the summer.

Yet even as the Centenary Test Match was under way Kerry
Packer, the younger son of the newspaper tycoon Sir Frank
Packer, was walking through the corridors of the pavilion. Already
most of the players who were to become involved in World Series
Cricket – those from the Australian dressing room, at any rate –
were happily and secretly contemplating his money in their bank
accounts. The biggest player revolution in the history of the game

had begun: the second hundred years of Test cricket was assured of a dramatic start.

When next I walked through the Fitzroy Gardens to the Melbourne Cricket Ground it was the day before the start of the first Super-Test between Packer's World Series Cricket Australian Eleven and his West Indian Eleven at the VFL Park at Waverley, which is about sixteen miles from the centre of Melbourne, out by the Dandenongs Ranges, to the east of the city. Only eight months had passed since the last day of the Centenary Test Match, but in the intervening period the Packer intrusion into cricket had split the game down the middle as had never happened before. As I walked I hoped that in just over a year's time I would once again be passing Captain Cook's cottage on the way to watch the New Year's Test Match between England and Australia at the MCG. But even that was far from certain. It was on 1 December 1977, and at that moment it was impossible to be sure of anything as far as the future of cricket was concerned. By then Packer had signed fifty-five of the world's best cricketers, some of whom were the next day to embark upon his brand of television cricket in unfamiliar surroundings before an unknown audience in a campaign directed at the world's cricket authorities, big business and the entertainment industry. Just the previous week Mr Justice Slade had ruled overwhelmingly against the cricket authorities in the High Court in London, and throughout the world people waited to see how Packer's cricket would be received by the Australian public.

At that point in events, just over six months after news of the Packer circus first became public, most journalists in England were deeply suspicious of Packer's methods and motives. What we could only guess at then, however, was how his own style of cricket would fare in almost direct competition with the established game. By the time I left for Australia at the end of November, Packer had already spent anywhere between four and eight million Australian dollars on his project. I went because I felt that it was important that his early matches should be reported by people who had watched a fair amount of Test cricket and would not be taken in by any gimmickry. I arrived in Australia determined to be fair to the actual end-product, the cricket, though with the strongest misgivings.

It turned out to be extremely dull. It was played between sides which were not representative, and the results and therefore the details did not matter. I was present at the hostile press interviews Packer gave after he heard that he had won in the High Court, I was confronted by the blind faith of the players in Packer and, in many cases, their open contempt for the established authorities.

Packer's intentions became even clearer to me in the next four and a half months. I travelled round Pakistan with the England side, returned to Australia for ten days, rejoined England in New Zealand, and then spent a final five weeks in the West Indies, watching another series completely dominated by Packer.

After all of this I have no doubt that if Packer's revolution is successful the ultimate loser will be the game of cricket, for the present order of the game will be disrupted and the nature of the game will also change. I do not blame the players for being attracted by his money, although I do not think that they should be allowed to return to established cricket at their own convenience when their first loyalties are to a form of cricket set up in direct opposition to it. As it is, Packer's television cricket encourages short-pitched fast bowling which has already been increasing at an alarming rate, it virtually denies the draw and also the innings of, say, eighty made in six hours which has often won a Test Match. And if, as is a distinct possibility, WSC goes to the United States, the form of the game seems bound to change considerably to suit an audience with entirely different tastes to a traditional cricket crowd. They will want constant action.

For all that, there have undoubtedly been beneficial effects from what Packer has done. The financial plight of professional cricketers has been underlined as never before, and Test players in England, Pakistan and the West Indies are already receiving significantly more money – ironically, because of the opposition to Packer. He has forced the authorities to look carefully at themselves and to ask if they are doing the best for the players under their control. They have learned a greater commercial awareness, although there has not yet been time to evaluate night cricket or the white ball.

This book is about the first year of Packer. He will be involved with cricket for some years to come, and I write with much of the story not yet known. But I believe that any future developments will stem from the events of the first twelve months and the implacable positions the two sides took up. Regardless of the outcome, the story of this first year will be highly relevant to all that follows. It is important that the events and attitudes taken up by both sides in this period be set into an immediate perspective.

It is for the reader to make up his own mind about Packer. I make no apology for having come down firmly against him. I have tried nevertheless to be objective throughout, certainly in the sense of trying to see the point of view of all the main participants. But having seen so many of the events at first hand I would have found it dishonest, perhaps even impossible, not to have taken sides – not only to report events but to interpret them too.

◆

CHAPTER I

The Story Breaks

WORLD'S TOP CRICKETERS TURN PIRATE
Headline from the *Daily Mail* front page story by Ian Wooldridge,
9 May 1977

IT IS DIFFICULT to pinpoint the exact moment when the first idea which led to World Series Cricket came into being. Two years before the story first broke, Kerry Packer's Channel Nine television network had carried out an analysis of future marketing trends and had decided that the most exciting potential lay with sports programmes. If these programmes could be made to produce a mass audience, they argued, they would attract huge sponsorship. But in order to achieve this the network had to offer exclusive coverage; otherwise it could not guarantee the advertisers an audience large enough for them to charge the money they needed to buy such rights.

Packer duly wrote off to the Australian Cricket Board of Control, saying that his channel wanted to bid for the exclusive rights to cover the cricket series against the West Indians in Australia in 1975/76. The Board acknowledged his letter but, without giving him the chance to make an offer, sold the rights, which were not exclusive, to the Australian Broadcasting Commission. Packer's next move was to bid half a million Australian dollars for the sole rights of the following year's series against Pakistan, together with the Sheffield Shield matches: this bid too was turned down. The offer was part of a much larger one of two and a half million Australian dollars made in the hope of buying exclusive rights to televise Test cricket in Australia for the next five years. The ABC again won the contract, which was still not exclusive, and at a lower price. Packer left the room saying to one of his colleagues, 'Well, damn, I don't know why we don't put on our own cricket Tests.'

By a coincidence there were two others in Sydney at that time who, for different reasons, had come to a similar conclusion. Some time in November 1976, John Cornell, impresario, television actor and entrepreneur – and also Dennis Lillee's agent – met Austin Robertson, whom he had known in Perth when they were both journalists there. They discussed far into the night how they could find more money for top cricketers, and decided to explore the possibilities of bringing together the best Australian players in a series of one-day matches for television all round Australia, playing against local opposition. In his 'television actor' persona Cornell is the straight guy, 'Strop', for the comic Paul Hogan in his extremely popular television comedy series. With the help of Cornell, Hogan had recently moved over to Channel Nine, and it was a natural move for Cornell to visit Packer and put to him his idea of one-day cricket for television. By coincidence this was just after Packer had been turned down by the Australian Board in his attempt to buy the exclusive rights for the series against Pakistan; his immediate response to Cornell's idea was that they should go the whole way and produce their own Test series.

The contract which an independent television company has to sign with the Australian Government demands that over a quarter of the programmes shown must be home-produced. Cricket was not only a home product but also, on the scale Packer envisaged, it was relatively cheap to put on the air. This was an added attraction for the owner of Channel Nine. The Packer revolution therefore had a threefold beginning. There was Packer's determination, given cricket's money-making potential, to show the best cricket in Australia on his channel; there was his wish to salvage his pride, dented by the Australian Board's refusal to sell him exclusive rights in the Pakistan series; and, finally, there was Cornell and Robertson's determination to find money for the best players which bore more relationship to their entertainment value. To do this they were prepared to try to adapt cricket for television and to commercialize the game in a way which had only been attempted once before and in a much less ambitious way – by Rothman's

International Cavaliers in the 1960s, when a side full of star players took part in one-day matches around England primarily for a television audience.

Probably the biggest surprise about Packer's plans was that such a massive project was kept secret for such a long time. Packer and his main associates had anticipated the hostility they would meet from the established authorities and had gone to great lengths to keep their plans secret. As prospective players or administrators were approached they first had to agree that whether they joined Packer or not everything they had been told was in the strictest confidence.* On the signing of their contracts the players were given sizeable cheques which contained an element of hush money. Successful, even beneficial revolutions can have sordid beginnings: often they would not have been possible without them.

The city of Melbourne could not have given itself more whole-heartedly to the Centenary Test Match, and it was hardly surprising that any hints of the trouble that was to come should have been ignored. In those first three weeks in March there was one oblique indication, however, of what was about to happen. When the Fifth Test Match in Bombay finished the MCC party had embarked upon a month of contrasts which were as strange geographically as they must have been emotionally. They had a relaxed two weeks in Sri Lanka and then, after a hideous plane journey, arrived nearly twelve hours late in Perth where, the next day, they began a three-day match against Western Australia, which they almost lost. This game gave Lillee the chance to show that he was still a marvellous bowler, and also the opportunity of demonstrating how remarkable a recovery he had made from an extremely serious back injury – stress fractures of three of the lower vertebrae – an injury which had revealed itself three years before in the West Indies. Due largely to his personal dedication he had recovered in time to destroy England's batting in 1974/5 – with the help of Jeff Thomson – but it was an injury which needed constant treatment to prevent a recurrence. He bowled noticeably

---

* Ironically, as early as 1975 Packer had approached Bobby Simpson and asked him to captain a special Australian Eleven, but Simpson did not like the idea and suggested that instead Packer approach Ian Chappell, which of course he did. The next time that Simpson and Packer met was in Georgetown on 30 March 1978, with Simpson captain of the official Australian eleven.

well for Western Australia, and then in the Centenary Match took eleven wickets for 165 runs: his fitness seemed beyond doubt. During the Perth match, however, there had been a rumour that he needed to rest his back from the constant strain of bowling, and that he would not be available for the 1977 tour of England. Sure enough, towards the end of the Melbourne match it was officially announced that he would not be coming to England; his doctors had told him that he must rest his back for the next home series in Australia, and that a strenuous tour of England might cause permanent damage. It seemed strange at the time that a man who had bowled as fast and as well as Lillee in the Centenary Test should be so near to being unfit, but in view of his record his reasons were accepted, and in any case, from the England view-point, Australia without Lillee was more beatable than an Australia with him. Englishmen were happy to accept the news. Of course, throughout the publicity that followed the announcement it was reckoned that Lillee's next home series would be against India the following December.

The only other hint that some sort of cricket revolution was in progress came from South Africa about three weeks before the story was to break in England. Lee Irvine, the South African batsman who once played for Essex, said in a speech which was reported in the South African newspapers that a form of exhibition cricket for television was being planned for the following season in Australia. No one imagined that it was other than a series of matches which would be run along the same lines of the Cavaliers. It was thought by some of the Packer players that Barry Richards might have inadvertently let something slip, but he vigorously denied it.

It rained incessantly at the start of the season in England and the Australians found themselves moving from one county ground to another without even changing into white flannel trousers. By the time they arrived in Canterbury to play Kent on Wednesday 4 May the Packer revolution was in an advanced stage. Thirty-five players had signed contracts and, as thirteen of the seventeen touring Australians were among them, it was not surprising that Alan Shiell, a former South Australian player working for the Murdoch group, should have obtained the story from one of the Australian players. Although Shiell was evasive about which one, it was thought to have been David Hookes, who was known to have had serious doubts about the wisdom of signing for Packer and was also the only South Australian in the party who still played for his original State: Greg Chappell and Gary Cosier had both moved to Queensland.

Shiell, who as a player had scored a double century for South Australia against Mike Smith's MCC side in 1966/67, had promised his informant that he would not use the story until he was told he might do so. Peter McFarline of the Melbourne *Age* also heard the details from one of the party, and when they discovered they were both on to the same story they pooled their knowledge.* It was during the Australian side's match against Kent that Shiell and McFarline realized that some members of the British press were close to the story. Not wishing to be scooped, they wrote it for their papers back in Australia where it broke on the Sunday morning.

I had been unaware of what had been going on at Canterbury and drove unsuspectingly into the County Ground at Hove on the morning of Saturday, 7 May, and watched the few overs which rain allowed. During the afternoon I ran into Tony Greig inside the ground and he asked me if I would like to come to a party that evening which he and his wife, Donna, were giving for the Australians at their house in Hove. I already had plans to dine with someone else, and asked if I could leave it open; in the end I thought it was too late to go. It was at that party that Greig and the other Packer players heard that their plans were about to be published in Australia. There were about 150 people in a marquee in Greig's garden and the party was in full swing: according to one of the guests, Alan Lee of the *Sunday Telegraph*, Greig even had a bottle of champagne in his hand when he was told. He was naturally greatly concerned, and the party rapidly developed into a council of war as those involved gathered in whispering groups. Those who did not know what was happening could not understand what was going on, and the night was full of furtive, sidelong glances; by the end it was apparently difficult to distinguish those who knew from those who did not. Because of the time difference of nine hours the Sunday papers had come on to the streets in Sydney while Greig's party was still in progress, and for much of the night the telephone line between Hove and Sydney must have

* McFarline has written about the initial stages of the Packer affair in his book on the Australian tour, *A Game Divided*.

been kept extremely busy as Packer, who was not even a name to most Englishmen at that stage, spoke with his confederates on their tactics.

Play between Sussex and Yorkshire began at Hove at two o'clock on the Sunday, and when I arrived in the press box, still unaware of what had been happening, I was surprised to find nearly all the main cricket correspondents from Fleet Street there. I was soon brought up to date. The facts were slightly garbled and were distorted by endless conjecture and speculation, but even so the main picture was clear, and it did not sound as if it was just an idea of Greig's to raise a little money. I think everyone in the press box that day was staggered by the size of the operation and also by the audacity of attempting to threaten established cricket in this way. The long-term implications were there to be seen, and this proved to be one of the comparatively rare occasions when most of the press predicted accurately the course of events which would follow.

Greig had already been questioned but had refused to comment, beyond saying that he would issue a statement later in the day. Stanley Allen, the Sussex Secretary, delivered copies of a statement to the press box and then read it out:

> There is a massive cricket project involving
> most of the world's top players, due to commence
> in Australia this winter. I am part of it,
> along with a number of English players. Full
> details and implications of the scheme will be
> officially announced in Australia later this
> week.

The detailed story was published the following Wednesday in Sydney in the *Bulletin* magazine which belongs to Packer. Obviously it had gone in at the last moment on Packer's instructions and inevitably spoke in glowing terms of all that had been planned, describing it as the most imaginative and go-ahead project ever to involve cricket.

Greig's statement established beyond doubt the size and importance of the story. He would say nothing more, and I sat in the press box for ten minutes or so in a state of bewilderment trying to grapple with the implications which became larger and more complex by the minute. England's reigning captain was at the centre of Packer's plans, and the morality of his involvement immediately became an issue. According to Shiell's information it had been planned to announce the details in June during or after the First Test Match at Lord's. By then Greig would have been appointed to the England captaincy for the full series against Australia, and with the series under way between an Australian side which contained probably eleven Packer players and an English side which contained three or four, it would have been difficult for the English authorities to have removed Greig from the captaincy and to have taken action against the players.

The press box that afternoon in Hove seemed to move from an initial state of numbness to surprised chatter, as journalists made sure that what they had heard was right and checked the details, and then became one of exhilaration as they realized the magnitude of the story. Sports editors were informed of its importance, with more than one needing convincing, and then it was concentrated work as we all put together our reports, the silence broken every now and then by the ring of a telephone or a question as someone quickly checked a fact.

I rang my sports editor, John Samuel, who soon realized that if all that I told him was right then the implications were immense. John Arlott is the main cricket correspondent of the paper, and it was possible that Samuel would prefer that he should write the story, but as I was at Hove and Arlott was probably already on his way home after broadcasting a Sunday League match on television he thought that I should write it. He rang off, having asked me to ring him back in an hour. I then started to write, and as each detail slotted into place it looked as if I would need at least a thousand words to convey the impact of what had happened. When in Fleet Street parlance a journalist comes on a really 'hot' news story it brings with it a thrill which people unconnected with journalism will be unable to appreciate, and this was one such moment.

When I rang Samuel back he fuelled my enthusiasm by telling me that the news desk wanted it written as a front-page story – and then dampened it by telling me that they only wanted three hundred words. This meant that I had to tear up all that I had written and start again. It was about a quarter past seven when I had telephoned through my report on the match, which by then could scarcely have been of less importance, and my front-page piece which was hopefully an accurate précis of what I had first written. I spoke again with Samuel who was understandably con-

cerned with the authenticity of the story. I did my best to convince him, telling him which journalists were in Hove for the other
papers, and that I had heard most of them put their stories over.

I stayed in Hove that night, for I was watching the Australians
the next day, and when I rang Samuel at about nine o'clock to
check if he and the news desk were happy with what I had written
he again asked me if I was absolutely certain that the details were
correct. He was talking on another line to Arlott, who was doubtful
about its authenticity, because he had not heard a murmur about
Packer, and, as President of the Cricketers' Association, he felt
that he was in a good position to have received some sort of
advance warning. But any doubts that still lingered in Arlott's or
Samuel's minds were dispelled with the publication of the first
editions of the other newspapers: the Packer story was big news.
The best and most complete version was on the front page of the
Daily Mail, written by Ian Wooldridge, who was thought to have
been given the story or at any rate had the details filled in by
Richie Benaud, a close friend and revealed in the article as being
a member of the Packer entourage. My own piece was on the front
page of the *Guardian*, with a brief comment by John Arlott on the
sports page. Only the *Daily Telegraph* failed to mention the story –
they had seen it in the early editions of the other papers and felt
that too much was conjecture – while *The Times* carried just a few
paragraphs from an agency report.

That Monday morning – 9 May – England learnt for the first
time that Packer had thirty-five of the world's leading players
under contract, mostly for a period of three years and for as much
in some instances as £25,000 a year, their duties to play cricket for
him during the Australian summer in a series of international
matches which would be shown on his Channel Nine television
network. The two sides – at this point it looked as if there would
only be two – were to be 'Australia', captained by Ian Chappell,
who had come out of retirement, and 'The Rest of the World',
captained and mostly recruited by Greig. The full list read:
England: Greig, Knott, Snow, Underwood. *Pakistan:* Asif Iqbal,
Majid Khan, Imran Khan, Mushtaq Mohammed. *West Indies:*
Vivian Richards, Lloyd, Holding, Roberts. *South Africa:* Barry
Richards, Proctor, Barlow, Graeme Pollock, Hobson. *Australia:*
Ian Chappell, Greg Chappell, Redpath, Ross Edwards, Lillee,
Thomson, Davis, McCosker, Hookes, Walters, Marsh, Robinson,

O'Keeffe, Gilmour, Walker, Malone, Pascoe, Bright.

The 'Circus', as the players were soon dubbed, were going to play for considerable amounts of prize money on a winner-take-all basis. Appreciating that there would be strong opposition to his plans by the traditional authorities in the game, Packer had already obtained the use of grounds which were outside the jurisdiction of the Australian Cricket Board, and he had taken on a groundsman, John Maley, who used to be in charge of the Woolloongabba in Brisbane. They were going to play fifty-five days' cricket, we were told; and since at the end of 1977 and the beginning of 1978 England were to tour Pakistan and New Zealand, playing three Test Matches in each country; India were to tour Australia and to play five Test Matches; and in late February Australia were planning to visit the West Indies for a five-match series, we could only speculate on the effect that Packer's planned series of matches might have on these tours.

On that Monday newspaper headlines, BBC and ITN television and all the radio news bulletins were full of Packer. Inevitably, as they read and listened, people began to take sides. At first many people outside cricketing circles were extremely interested, feeling that perhaps the journalists had got it wrong and Packer was going to rejuvenate cricket and bring players the rewards which they deserved. This quickly changed to a feeling of anger that Packer was almost trying to rob England of a national heritage. The semi-hysterical beginnings then quietened down and the long-term implications were seen in a more rational light. From the start those always anxious for a stick with which to beat the Establishment found that they had been given a present, but Fleet Street was mainly critical. The 'Street' may be a curious supporter of tradition, but almost all the main cricket writers were able to appreciate the pressures which Packer was putting on the game's administration, and to see the longer-term disruptive effect his plans would have.

In a remarkably short time Kerry Packer had thrown the cricket world into upheaval. Yet all that was known about him was that he had enormous wealth, owned a television station in Australia, and was the son of the man who had been responsible for two out of Australia's first three challenges for the Americas Cup. Two weeks later, on Saturday 23 May, he stepped out of his aeroplane at Heathrow.

◆

CHAPTER 2

Introducing
Mr Packer

'It's unfortunate we Australians inherited the English mentality rather than the American.'
Kerry Packer, in an interview in the *Guardian* on 1 September 1977

KERRY PACKER may dislike the English way of life and have the unwieldy appearance of the typical American businessman, but he has a family background which at times he must find almost embarrassingly English. For ironically, thanks to the efforts of an American cousin, one Grant Donnington Packer, a librarian from Pasadena in California, there is a family tree which runs from the time of Charles I to the present day.

The Packers were staunch Royalists, and Donnington Castle, near Newbury in Berkshire, belonged to John Packer Junior at the beginning of the Civil War when it was garrisoned by Charles I. The castle played an important part in both the first battle of Newbury, in 1643, and in the second three years later. John Packer Junior's father, John Packer Senior (the Junior and the Senior are presumably innovations from Pasadena), became secretary to George Villiers, the first Duke of Buckingham. John Packer Junior was a member of the committee chosen for the 'Visitation and Reformation of the University of Oxford' in 1647. His sons, Robert and Philip, were members of University College, and the Packer coat of arms, a cross Lozengy between four roses argent, decorates one of the windows of the college hall. Robert Packer became MP for Wallingford in Charles I's Long Parliament.

The branch of the Packer family through which Kerry descended remained for generations in Berkshire, living just outside Reading. His great-great-great-grandfather, Charles Packer Senior, was born in Reading in 1747, became a professor of music, and was for many years the organist of St Mary's Minster in that town. Charles Packer Junior was also the organist at St Mary's; he married Amelia Sandys, known locally as the 'beauty of Berkshire', and a direct descendant of the House of Stuart. Kerry's great-great-grandfather, Frederick Alexander Packer, was born in 1814 and became an associate of the Royal Academy of Music, as well as keeping up the family tradition at St Mary's. He married Augusta Gow, the granddaughter of one of Scotland's best-known composers, Neil Gow. Then, in the middle of the nineteenth century, Frederick Alexander Packer and his wife emigrated to Tasmania, where a sizeable colony of well-to-do British emigrants had settled. He died in Hobart in 1862. His son, Arthur Howard Packer, Kerry's great-grandfather, became head of Her Majesty's Customs in Tasmania before he died, also in Hobart, in 1912. Arthur Howard and his wife, Margaret Fitzmaurice Clyde, had three sons – Robert Clyde (Kerry's grandfather), Arthur Patrick Wellesley and John Howard. Robert Clyde Packer was born in Tasmania on 24 July 1879. In 1900 he moved to Sydney where, after working on several provincial newspapers, he was appointed editor of the Sydney *Sunday Times*. On 3 December 1906, Frank Packer, Kerry's father, was born in King's Cross, Sydney.

Grandfather and father were both in their ways extremely successful newspapermen. They were also big, strong, difficult and demanding men who made enemies as easily as friends and who were pioneering a road where one's instinct for survival necessarily had to be strong. Frank Packer had a razor-sharp mind and the ability to make decisions quickly; at times also he could undoubtedly be unscrupulous. Sir John Williams, for a long time Frank Packer's opposite number with Herald Newspapers in Sydney, is quoted in *Sir Frank*, a sympathetic biography of Frank Packer published during Packer's lifetime, as saying of his rival, 'For all his toughness, he can be the most sentimental of men. He is generous with his own money. Waste with business is a cardinal sin. He can spend a dollar easily, but never let a cent slip through his fingers.'

Another of Sir Frank Packer's oldest friends, Jim McLeod, said of him towards the end of his life: 'One of the things I have admired most about Frank is that all through his life he has refused to become very serious about himself. He has just refused to grow up. He is still at times a very dangerous little boy. He has kept this youthful approach and outlook and boyishness right through. Even today he is full of tricks. He plays jokes on people at every opportunity. No matter what he is doing, be it a business deal, be it things he is about to undertake – his racing, sailing or other sport – he goes to tremendous pains in preparing himself. He has extraordinary enthusiasm and application. He gets all the relevant details ready in every matter in which he acts. No detail is too small for him. He has all the facts marshalled before he makes his first move. I feel this is one of the things that has helped towards his great success.'

In some ways, in spite of his unorthodoxy, Frank Packer must also have been a traditionalist. It may have been in conformity with the times, but he insisted that the journalists on his staff should wear a suit and tie to the office on all days except Saturdays, Sundays and public holidays. He dressed quietly and correctly himself, was proud of his conservatism, and was determined to preserve time-honoured institutions. The Sydney *Daily Telegraph*, the first mass-circulation newspaper he owned, adopted suitably conservative policies – although to have been more sympathetic to the Labour cause would have substantially increased the circulation. Sir Robert Menzies was a lifelong friend.

Frank Packer had two children, both sons, the younger being born on 17 December 1937 and christened Kerry Francis Bullmore. Kerry's education began at Cranbrook School, Sydney, and from there he went to Geelong Grammar School in Victoria, the leading public school in Australia. Throughout his early life he was aware that it was his brother, Clyde, born on 22 July 1935, who was being groomed to succeed his father at Australian Consolidated Press Ltd, the parent company for all the many Packer enterprises in newspapers, publishing and television. Yet it was also Clyde who, as a young man, was prepared to challenge and to argue with his father; Kerry, with possibly less to lose, was usually content to agree.

The brothers were at Geelong together and some amusing stories are told about them. Clyde somehow owned a greyhound at school which he kept in training and used to run at the local track. It was called 'Old Vic', after Vic Tunbridge, his housemaster, and one evening Tunbridge went along to the track. He soon spotted Clyde, complete with greyhound. He stole up behind him and whispered in his ear, 'Am I all right for five bob each way this evening?' Clyde's reactions are not recorded, nor is the penalty exacted for keeping a greyhound in training while at school . . .

It was Frank Packer himself who was responsible for perhaps the best-known story about his younger son. While Kerry was still at Geelong he returned to Sydney for the summer holidays having left his tennis racquet behind at school. His father, always mindful of the value of possessions, sent him straight back by train to retrieve it. It was a 1200-mile journey and Kerry had to sit upright all the way. When he reached Melbourne on his way back to Geelong he is said to have wired his parents: ARRIVED MELBOURNE SAFELY STOP NO LOVE KERRY.

When Kerry left school he went into his father's business as a matter of course. He has said that it never occurred to him to do anything else, adding that when he was young he was simply 'too stupid'. Once at the Sydney *Daily Telegraph* he went through every aspect of the production of the paper, and then went to work for eighteen months in Cleveland, Ohio. It was there that he acquired the passion for the American way of life which he has never lost, and which seems to motivate so many of his actions. It was also at about this time that he was involved in a dreadful car accident in which the three people travelling in the other car were killed. He himself smashed up his hip socket, was in traction for three months and spent nearly five months on crutches. Although he glosses over this incident now there can be no doubting the pain he experienced, or his bravery; it was probably one of the main influences in forming his character.

Life was never easy for him at home. His father had been the heavyweight boxing champion of New South Wales and lived a tough, Spartan life (though it was Kerry, not his father, who became a teetotaller). Whenever he disagreed with one of his sons or felt that they should be punished he made an assignation with the son concerned in one of the larger rooms in their Bellevue Hill house: boxing gloves were worn. Kerry admits to having been on the receiving end of his father's punches a number of times, although later he was able to even up the score: he also boxed at school, and won the heavyweight championship. He bears no grudge at his father's treatment and later admitted that he usually got what he deserved – and that there were occasions when he got less than that. Asked to sum up his father he did so in three words: 'strict but magnificent'. His father's biographer, R. S. Whitington, is less epigrammatic. 'It is essential', he wrote, 'to realize that Frank Packer is dominated mainly by three forces. The first of these is his extremely resilient will to win, the second his unshakeable faith in the provenly effective institution and policy, the third the amount of emphasis he places upon frankness and personal integrity. It is equally important to accept that he is basically a very shy and sensitive man though one who takes such a tremendous delight in gagging, even when most absorbed, that this luxury frequently creates an entirely false impression of himself. His main sensitivity is concerned with the misapprehensions which he believes are harboured concerning his father, Robert Clyde Packer, but he can also be deeply hurt by what he considers misunderstanding and misjudgement of himself.'

By the time Kerry was in his mid-thirties arguments between his father and his brother had become regular events. In the early seventies Clyde and his father had a final row. Clyde went to Los Angeles, where he became an extremely successful impresario. Kerry bought his brother's interests in the family business, and when his father died in 1974 assumed control.

When Kerry first worked in his father's business, however, he made little impact, as he was still very much the younger son. His duties were not always the most orthodox ones. During the time Frank Packer and Rupert Murdoch were fighting a newspaper battle in the Sydney suburbs, Packer heard that a Methodist newspaper, which owned a valuable printing press, was closing down. He instructed his younger son to collect a dozen or so men of about the same size from the organization and to take possession of the building housing the press and to hold it against all comers. When Kerry and his troops arrived they found Murdoch's men already in possession, and after a tussle were unable to remove them.

Yet before Clyde and his father parted company it had been the two brothers who had been principally concerned in the sale of the Sydney *Daily Telegraph* to Rupert Murdoch, of whom Kerry Packer had always been a great admirer.

Others among Kerry Packer's heroes are possibly more surprising. Of Genghis Khan he has said, 'He wasn't very lovable, but he was bloody efficient.' But then he has, it seems, always identified with men of action. The three people he has admired most in his lifetime are a curious mixture – his father, Sir Robert Menzies and Gunboat Smith, an apprentice glassblower who became managing director of Australian Consolidated Industries: a trade union leader who became a millionaire capitalist. Unlike his father Packer is not interested in politics – unless they can serve his purpose.

Kerry Packer has admitted that he does not think that he could ever have built the business empire he inherited from his father. He rightly says that no pilot would be capable of building the Boeing 747 he flies, and that he sees himself as the pilot of the aeroplane his father built. The Packers have a sporting tradition. Sir Frank Packer promoted, financed and took part in two Australian challenges for the Americas Cup with *Gretel I* and *Gretel II*, both named after his first wife, Clyde and Kerry's mother, who had died from a heart attack in August 1960. Besides being heavyweight champion of New South Wales his father later owned many racehorses and a famous stud. He supported Davis Cup tennis, polo and Rugby Football and had a reputation for working with the authorities and not against them. One of his few intrusions into the world of cricket came when he had dinner with E. W. Swanton during Mike Smith's England tour of Australia in 1966/67. Sir Frank stated with some vigour that cricket was a dying game in Australia – persuaded maybe by his younger son. He disputed Swanton's figures, which showed that cricket had never been more popular in Australia and they had a ten-pound bet. Jim Swanton later sent Packer a letter from the Australian Board authenticating the figures, and he duly paid up. A heavyweight contest, indeed!

Kerry Packer himself has always been a keen participant in sport. Nowadays he skis, plays golf off a single-figure handicap, surfs and enjoys boats, but probably sport's main attraction for him is as a means to make money for his business empire. When asked in the High Court if it was true that he had come into cricket for this reason he admitted quite frankly, 'I have never said anything else.' Three years before his adventures with cricket began he was told that the sponsors for the Australian Golf Championship had pulled out and that someone was needed who would underwrite the organizers for a hundred thousand dollars. Packer agreed to do so, and then decided to turn the Australian Open into one of the great championships of the world so that it would rank with the British Open, the American Open, the Masters and the PGA. With Jack Nicklaus as designer, he rebuilt the course of his own club, the Australian Golf Club at Kensington in Sydney. He has sold each of the eighteen holes to individual sponsors, and took his cameras to cover each hole. The Australian Golf Union gave him a three-year contract for the Australian Open in return for a guaranteed one million pounds in prize money. The event produced excellent television and must have made money for Channel Nine, but during July 1978 Packer announced that after the 1978 competition towards the end of the year, he would no longer participate. If Packer's interest had continued the Open would have remained at the same course while there were many people involved in Australian golf who wanted to see it continue to circulate round the country.

Channel Nine also bought one season's coverage of the Rugby League World Series, and in 1977 for two million pounds bought the sole Australian rights for the French, Wimbledon and American Tennis Championships for three years. In 1977, Packer also bought the exclusive Australian rights for the Ashes series in England, this time for £150,000. His channel also tried to buy the Moscow Olympics for 1980, but were outbid by another commercial company. It is easy to see how cricket came into his scheme of thinking.

I have only met Kerry Packer a handful of times, and to judge from our last encounter at a press conference in Georgetown – held on 30 March 1978, after he had flown in from Miami, just before the start of the third Test Match between Australia and the West Indies – our meetings in the future will be brief and probably acrimonious. He does not like opponents, and I unquestionably come into that category. On the occasions I have met him I have gained the impression that he loves having famous sportsmen around him, not only for the reflected glory but also because he does not regard them as an intellectual threat. He has said, 'The ultimate purgatory for me would be to go to the Opera House and hear Joan Sutherland sing; ugh!'

Kerry Packer is not an easy man for journalists to talk to or get to know. It is as though their presence, despite his upbringing, gives him a feeling of inadequacy. He is for ever laying down conditions about interviews, and during them often becomes irritated to the point of petulance. When asked perfectly legitimate questions he can suddenly turn on his questioner or else reply testily that he has already answered the question and is not going to do so again. Naturally, the world's press put him under considerable personal pressure while the first season of World Series Cricket was in progress, and he seemed to resent it. At conferences, whenever an awkward question came along, he demonstrably lost patience and suggested that the journalist concerned and the rest of us too would be better off writing about cricket. There were occasions when I could not help but feel that if a journalist who worked for Kerry Packer did his job as badly as he was continually exhorting us to do ours he would be sacked by nightfall. Through that first season he was never entirely happy with the media unless things were going his way. Yet he was a curious mixture, and at times was both plausible and charming.

Packer gave his own views of the press to Michael Davie in an interview for the Melbourne *Age*. Davie is not primarily a sports journalist. Now in his fifties, he was for a number of years the Washington correspondent of the *Observer*, before being seconded to Australia to help bolster up the *Age*. His interview is the more interesting for his having no particular axe to grind. 'Did you realize you would encounter as much hostility as you evidently feel you have encountered?' he asked Packer.

Packer: From where? I always expected it from the press. I'm not being critical in these remarks because what most people don't really appreciate is the tremendous – I'm trying to find the right word – intensity of competition within the press in this country; and to be able to turn on one of their own is a joy irresistible. I always expected that. What I am disappointed about in some sections of the press – some sections have been fair and some haven't – is that they have painted themselves into corners. I think your paper has been guilty of that also and to justify their position have been monumentally dishonest and have written from a painted-in position, rather than a true summary. If you've got criticisms and they are valid I've no objection; but the fabrication has been quite frightening in places.

Davie: Can you give some examples?

Packer: You have your leading cricket writer saying in his column, 'Of course I'm biased' – a reporter who's not interested in reporting facts but only in airing his own view. My secretary keeps a cutting book which I don't look at but which is *that* high. I can give you examples. I can give you hundreds and having been always a very devout defender of the press I find myself querying the standards of the writers employed. I find that pretty shattering. I've had a fair go out of the News Limited group. [Rupert Murdoch's group: after a meeting between the two men, held two weeks after the WFC matches had begun, Murdoch agreed to report Packer's cricket in greater measure in his papers.] But as for the Melbourne Herald group [as favourably disposed to the Australian Cricket Board as Murdoch is to Packer] I believe their blatant censorship, which could only come about by monopoly, and the dishonesty of their reporting, have been revolting. I can no longer regard that group as moral.

Davie: Do you think there are too few groups in Australia?

Packer: Well, there's more than most places.

Davie: There's quite a concentration of power, isn't there . . . of television and newspapers together?

Packer: You talk about power as though it belongs to those that run it.

Davie: Yes, I do.

Packer: Well, it doesn't. It belongs to those that write it.

Davie: You reckon?

Packer: Of course. You go off to report a story; the management doesn't know if your report of the story is accurate or inaccurate. Therefore it is virtually incapable of publishing anything except what is written. The power of newspapers lies in the writers, not in the ownership. I don't even think it lies in the editor. Time works against editors. They don't have sufficient time to check. Tremendous liberty is given to young and relatively inexperienced men – far more than they would have in any other profession – and I don't know that they've always learned the responsibility that goes with it. But if you've got to produce something new every twenty-four hours it's the only way you can do it, and that's why the integrity of the people who do the job is so important. If you take the English cricket columnists, they've all been made members of the MCC.

1. Frank Packer and his sons Clyde (left) and Kerry at Gleneagles, Scotland in 1959.

2. Happier times. England captain Tony Greig is greeted by Australian Cricket Board treasurer Ray Steele (left) and chairman Bob Parish (centre) before the Centenary Test in Melbourne.

3. The summer's cricket produced many ironies. Kerry Packer and Alan Shiell, the man who first broke the story of the Circus's formation, found themselves on the same side during the journalists' match at Harrogate.

Davie: You've acquired incredible celebrity.

Packer: I could have done without that. We've been up against a tremendous anti-marketing campaign. Take Bill O'Reilly, who said that Toohey – and I'm not trying to belittle him – was the finest strokeplayer in the world. Well, it's farcical, it's stupid; the credibility of those people just wears down. But it takes time. I mean, how do you say that? How do you compare him with Richards or Greg Chappell?

Davie: How do you account for the hostility of a great player like Bill O'Reilly?

Packer: He is part of the cricket establishment. He is a writer who earns his living from writing. His public acceptance, if he continues to make those sort of statements, will diminish.

Packer has also openly referred to journalists and broadcasters who oppose him as 'the enemy', and seems unable to accept that people are entitled to have different opinions about the rights and wrongs of his plans. Somehow he seems to have developed into a man who is prepared to take on anything or anybody. He admits there is one man who works in his organization, brought in by his father, who is able to make him change his mind, but otherwise once he has decided on a course of action he is difficult to stop. He seems to like adventure and is not afraid of danger. I heard the story that a few years ago when there was fighting in Timor one of the men in charge of his television channel wanted to send a ship up there with a camera crew on board. Obviously this was going to cost a good deal of money, so he rang Kerry Packer for permission to go ahead. When Kerry heard of the venture he said that the money could certainly be spent – as long as he could go with them.

Packer's appearance is against him. He is a huge man, and he looks, as Michael Davie once described him in the *Observer*, 'like the man in the stocking mask'. When Packer's first season of WSC matches had been in progress for some time Michael Davie, writing this time in the Melbourne *Age*, further described Packer as talking very quietly and 'occasionaly giving one of his meat-mangling smiles'. It was no surprise to hear that Packer had a reputation for being tough with his contemporaries at school.

Packer himself enjoys the image of the tough, rough business-man who has all the qualities of his American counterpart. The story about the difference between the British and the American worker is always on the tip of his tongue. 'If a British guy saw someone at the wheel of a Rolls-Royce he'd say, "Come the revolution and we'll take that away from you, mate." The American would say, "One day I'll have one of those; when I have worked hard enough".' But his father taught him never to underestimate the qualities of English businessmen.

With his great affection for the American way of life and his dislike of the English it is ironic that Packer should confess to a consuming passion for the most English of all games – cricket. I have seen him watching his own WSC players in action on four or five occasions, and I also played against him at Harrogate in 1977, when he turned out for the Australian press against the English press. He continually declares that he loves cricket, and in his High Court judgement Mr Justice Slade made a point of accepting Packer's love of the game. In the circumstances in which Kerry Packer finds himself it would be extraordinary if he expressed any other sentiment, especially as he is trying to convince many doubters that he has the interests of the game at heart. But during the first few days at the VFL Park, Packer's ground in Melbourne, I am bound to say that I got the impression that he was 'watching and enjoying' his cricket rather too ostentatiously. And then again at Perth during the 'Super-Test' at the end of January when he sat up on the television scaffolding on the platform with one of his camera crews I also felt there that he was too 'unrelaxed' about it all, as one by one his Rest of the World players came and paid court to him. For all that, it was clear from the time we played cricket together at Harrogate that he had played the game before.

Whereas Sir Frank Packer restricted his gambling instincts to business his son, who shares the same instincts, revels in his fortune – the difference, most probably, between inherited and self-made wealth. On his visits to London during the formation of the World Series Cricket, Packer was reputed to have gambled heavily at gaming-clubs in London's West End. Nothing but the best seems good enough for him, whether it is hiring a private aeroplane when the timetables for the scheduled flights are inconvenient, staying in 'eight-star' hotels, eating well or hiring a Daimler for a two-mile journey. A penthouse suite at the Dorchester is always available when he comes to London. Of course, his father lived at a level commensurate with his wealth and Kerry undoubtedly acquired some of his tastes. When I met the matron of his house when he was at Geelong Grammar School I asked her if it had been obvious when he was a boy that he had plenty of money. She said that it was not, but then added as an after-thought, 'but he always knew that he had the key to the main suite in the Hotel Australia [then Melbourne's leading hotel] in his pocket.' When he visited the West Indies in April 1978, there was no scheduled service, so he flew with his aides from Miami to Georgetown in a private jet. After twenty-four hours there he flew on in the same aeroplane to Barbados, where he had booked twenty-three suites at the Sandy Lane Hotel, the most expensive in the island, and where he then entertained his eighteen West Indian cricketers, their wives or girl-friends, and his other sup-porters in the island like Sir Garfield Sobers and Wes Hall, his jet commuting between islands to pick up his various guests.

In some ways Packer is a paradox. I had instinctively imagined him as a hard-living, hard-drinking man to go with his gambling image, but this is far from the truth. He is addicted to milkshakes and, as his figure suggests, he has a liking for ice-cream and pud-dings and anything sweet. He does not touch alcohol and never has, although he smokes about seventy cigarettes a day. He lives in an exclusive villa on Bellevue Hill overlooking Sydney Harbour with his wife, Roz, and his two children, whom he adores. He denies that he is interested in power. 'Power is the most over-rated thing in life. I have been in a position to see it wielded. It doesn't keep you warm at nights.' From what I have seen of Packer and his actions I do not believe this. He gets obvious en-joyment from the power of money. He likes to buy what he wants, expects to be able to buy what he wants and when he finds that he is thwarted, especially by something as crusty and as quin-tessentially British as the world's cricket authorities, he can become unreasonably irritated.

When, finally, I ask myself how Kerry Packer sees the revolution he has brought about the motives behind it seem surprisingly simple. He found himself in a dispute because he wanted to make money out of cricket. He tried to buy the exclusive rights to televise Test matches in Australia and was turned away by the Australian Cricket Board of Control. As a result he bought the services of all the best players he could lay his hands on and decided to stage his own matches. His own anger or pique may have given him the motivation to go ahead on his own, but the profit motive was behind it all.

With his family background his business acumen, like his size, is hardly surprising. But Kerry Packer does not seem content to be another in the line of the Packers, but rather seems determined to prove himself in his own right. I see this ambition running throughout the development of World Series Cricket to the point where the cricket has become a personal virility symbol. Packer is not prepared to countenance anything but complete success: less than that would be construed by him as failure. And success means victory. This can be a dangerous approach, because it can over-rule logic. There is another and opposite side to him, which is that he inspires feelings of great loyalty in those who work for him, and not only in his cricketers, whose loyalty might arguably be de-scribed as a form of cupboard love. In all his dealings within his organization it is roundly accepted that his word is his bond, something he has inherited from his father, who also produced feelings of great loyalty in those who worked for him. His father was tough in terms of hire and fire but generous to a fault when he felt people with a deserving cause needed personal help. But one of the main differences between father and son, put to me soon after I arrived in Melbourne, was that if Sir Frank Packer had decided to take on cricket's establishment in the same way as his son he would have made sure that he left himself an escape route. Kerry has not done so. It may be because he and his sup-porters have had to go so far out on a limb with no seeming means of retreat that total victory has come to seem the only acceptable answer.

But that, perhaps, is to move ahead of the story. At the end of the third week in May Kerry Packer was still to most cricketers just the name of an Australian TV magnate. At this stage the brunt of public interest inevitably fell on the people whom they knew, and who were already in England.

CHAPTER 3

◆

The Dropping of
the Captain

'There is a little bit of the whore in all of us, gentlemen: what is your price?'
Kerry Packer at a meeting with a sub-committee of the Australian Board of Control, June 1976.

THAT PACKER'S INTENTIONS were by and large so unfavourably received in Britain was due more to the way in which they were made known than the nature of the plans themselves. And almost entirely they were explained and justified through the announcements of Tony Greig – someone who was soon regarded as having gone against some of the deepest principles of British sportsmanship.

Here his performance as captain in India is important, for it established the position from which he decided to take on the cricket authorities the following summer. I saw Greig play his first game for Sussex, when he made 156 against Lancashire at Hove in 1966, and I have always admired him enormously as a player. We also became friends. Yet from time to time he had made it impossible for one to give him unflinching support. Two performances – in Madras on Tony Lewis's tour, when he thought he had caught Wadekar at first slip and Wadekar was given not out, and at Port of Spain when he ran out Alvin Kallicharran after the last ball of the day had been bowled – were indefensible, if partly explainable by reference to his impulsive character. Then, early in 1976, having seen Australia beat the West Indies with some ease, he said that when Clive Lloyd's side arrived in England they would be made to 'grovel'. It was anyway an unfortunate word to choose, especially by someone with strong South African connections, and it haunted him for the rest of that summer. Greig may not have been specifically involved but he was captain of the side.

Ever since Greig came to England in 1965 it has been known that he has suffered from epilepsy. There has been an unwritten agreement by the media not to mention this. The time has now come that it cannot be ignored any longer; not that his epilepsy has been directly applicable to the incidents I have mentioned or any other specific occurrences in his life. In any attempt to analyse a man who has lived in such a distinctive fashion the fact of this illness must be taken into account. Because of the wonders of modern drugs he seldom suffers from a bout of epilepsy, but it may help to explain some of his more irrational acts. He is a complex character and although this is not something upon which one wants to dwell, it is as much a part of him as his all round ability as a cricketer.

Controversy, be it of his own making or not, has followed Greig closely, and he has always answered any criticism with an articulate form of self-confidence. He argues well, he is plausible, and it is never long before he has managed to justify his rasher actions to others as well as to himself. While Greig's record for England shows unarguably that he has been a very great asset as a player his impulsive nature has always made him a potential liability. If he had been able to control himself more successfully he would probably have become captain of England sooner. As it was, he captained England at home against Australia and the West Indies in successive summers, and did not have an impressive record. The Indian tour was therefore a great personal challenge for him; and no one was more aware of that than Greig himself.

I was surprised how capably he handled the side and himself in India. Greig likes to do things his own way, and this was, in every sense, 'Greig's tour'. At times his tactical approach on the field was, to say the least, unorthodox, but England won the first three Test Matches convincingly, his own performances making a significant contribution. Off the field he hardly made a mistake. He was diplomatic with the Indians while being kind and thoughtful towards his own players, and always prepared to stand up for them. When, early in the tour, the Indian airline refused to carry the team's supply of bottled drinking water, Greig's answer was simple: 'If the water doesn't go we don't go either.' His players respected him, and his handling of the press was masterly. Greig's press conferences were different from those of other captains because he seldom answered the questions put to him, but rather told the questioner what he should write about that particular subject.

During the Third Test in Madras Greig had to cope with strident accusations that a member of the English side was openly cheating. Lever had come out after lunch on the third day with a strip of gauze stuck to each of his eyebrows to stop the sweat running into his eyes. The gauze was impregnated with Vaseline, and Umpire Reuben thought he was using the Vaseline to help him shine the ball. The Indians seized on this as an excuse for their bad batting in the series, and it became a major issue. On the rest day the Indian journalists wanted to talk to Ken Barrington, the manager, and to Greig; a conference was arranged in Barrington's room. Barrington began to answer the questions but became annoyed by the obvious assumption by the Indians that England had been cheating. In the middle of one question Greig took over and within five minutes was telling the Indian journalists that they should not be writing about such nonsense and suggested instead that they should write encouragingly about the future of Indian cricket, and use their papers to make sure that the public maintained its interest in the remainder of the series. He spoke so persuasively that the following morning several of the journalists had written as he suggested.

On the field Greig played up to the crowds, as he does all over the world, and he was popular wherever he went. But already one was able to glimpse another, less attractive side to his character. He has always been money-conscious, and now he made no attempt to stop his players from selling miniature cricket bats which they had brought with them from England, duly autographed, to children in the Members' Stand for substantial sums of money. In Calcutta, one of the poorest cities in the world, this was not well received by the press nor many of the public. Photographers, working for their papers or magazines, were often asked for money; and when at a party over Christmas Ken Barrington dressed up as Father Christmas and a photographer travelling with the side wanted to take a

photograph Greig stepped forward and told him that there was
a fee for doing so. In Calcutta a local notable, who had been
exceptionally kind to Tony Lewis's side four years earlier, giving
parties for them and even having some of the players to stay
when they had a match off, had two house guests; she asked if it
would be possible to have two complimentary tickets for the next
Test Match. The touring party is given a number of free tickets for
each day of the month. The answer came back that it would be
perfectly possible, but they would cost her money. The money
was paid, but the person concerned pointedly did not watch MCC
play again for the rest of the tour. As captain of the side, Greig
should have ensured that such things did not take place.

In a sense, Greig's involvement with Packer came as no great
surprise to those who knew him. Many first-class cricketers in
England adopted the attitude, 'What do you expect from Greig?'
No one felt this more strongly than the Yorkshire batsman John
Hampshire, who had let it be known after playing for England
against Australia at Headingley in 1975 that he did not want to
play for England again under the captaincy of one whom he considered to be a South African.

The reaction of the public was different: one of anger rather than
resignation. The element of blackmail in Packer's plans and the
threat to Test cricket was immediately evident. That Greig, who
had captained England so successfully in India and Australia
where, in both countries, he had spoken of the future in the most
optimistic terms, should so soon afterwards have surrendered his
loyalties to England was bad enough. That he should now appear
as Packer's most avid disciple and agent, losing no chance of
criticizing the established game which had given him his opportunity and had made him what he was; of castigating its
administrators, with most of whom he had been friends; and that
he had secretly persuaded some of his own team-mates of less than
a month before to join him with Packer, even if it meant forsaking
the England side for ever: all this was intolerable, and offended
deeply against the English concept of fair play. It was not surprising, therefore, that during that first week in England attention was
focused on Greig rather than an unknown Australian millionaire.

For the next few days the media besieged the ground at Hove, as
journalists and radio and television reporters vied with one another
for the first exclusive interview with Greig, who, when seen,

smiled benignly, talked about the weather, and shrugged if anything else was mentioned. The presence of the Australian players
lent Greig some moral support, but they were unable to help him
to any great degree. As far as the English media were concerned
their first reaction was to deal with the story as it would affect
England. The Australians were endlessly cross-examined by their
own journalists who were covering the tour, but at this stage the
journalists from the two countries were each exploiting their own
angle, even though the stories had a common source and involvement.

The Australians left a wet Hove on the Tuesday evening for
Southampton and their match with Hampshire, their place being
taken by the Lancashire side who were starting their game against
Sussex the following day. Greig had meanwhile announced that he
would give a press conference at the ground after the close of play
on the Wednesday. On the Tuesday evening he drove to London
and was interviewed for BBC television. By then the *Bulletin* had
appeared in Australia giving Packer's version of the story and fore-
telling its desirable consequences. At the time it still seemed all
very unreal; as if a fuse had been lit and we were all waiting to see
whether there would in fact be any explosion.

I had planned to leave Hove at the same time as the Australians,
but in view of Greig's press conference the next day the *Guardian*
asked me to stay on and cover the Lancashire match and the conference as well. The Sussex secretary had arranged for the meeting
to be held a quarter of an hour after the close of play in the up-
stairs dining-room of the pub by the main gate at Hove. As it
happened it rained so hard that it was clear by lunchtime that there
would be no play that day, although the umpires did not officially
confirm this until the middle of the afternoon. Soon after this
announcement came the news that Greig's conference would begin
in half an hour. It was not long before we were all crammed into
the room, clutching our notebooks and pens, cramped and ex-
pectant. Everyone realized that this was the moment for the confirmation of Packer's revolutionary proposals, and there was considerable tension under the cigarette smoke as we waited. The
television people played around with lights and cameras and there
must have been half a dozen potential interviewers with microphones in their hands and tape recorders slung over their shoulders, as well as photographers galore. I sat at a table in the corner

next to Rex Alston, the former BBC cricket correspondent who
was working for the *Daily Telegraph*.

Greig kept us waiting for five minutes, then strode in wearing a
new check jacket with a dark blue pullover. He was smoking, and
his smile and general manner was more self-conscious than usual,
as if he was trying hard within himself to play down the importance
of the moment. He sat down, greeted a few people personally,
then waited while one or two arc-lights were arranged. Soon he
began.

His theme was that the 55 days' cricket which Packer had
planned would disrupt future official Test series only if the
world's cricket authorities were not prepared to compromise. He
said that the structure of cricket throughout the world would
escape alteration only if the various authorities were prepared to
talk with Packer. If they decided to ignore him, temporary change
and damage to the game was inevitable. He also warned that
Packer was not a man who often failed in his plans.

He constantly repeated that the way out Packer had offered the
authorities was compromise – although he made it sound more
like a threat. 'The Packer organization,' he said, 'and the thirty-five
players do not want to see the Test Match situation as we know it
broken down. We know that Test Match cricket is what the game
is all about. There must be a compromise. I have spoken to Donald
Carr at Lord's and I've told him that it is urgent he should see
Packer as soon as possible.

'I'm frightened that at Lord's and in Australia and the rest of
the world the authorities will make hasty decisions. Obviously the
players are in danger of being taken out of the game. If there is no
compromise from them we will go ahead with our plans and Test
cricket will be threatened. Kerry Packer would be prepared to
compromise to a huge extent. We could, for example, play only
three Tests in Australia this winter, and this way they would not
clash with the Indian tour of Australia or MCC's tour of Pakistan
and New Zealand.

'Every tour which has been planned can go on. The only way I
am not available to tour Pakistan and New Zealand myself this
winter is if Lord's say so. This summer is in the hands of Lord's.
In the winter it is in the hands of a possible compromise between
Lord's and Packer. I will myself do anything possible to get them
talking. And Packer told me on the phone last night and again this

morning, "Keep telling them that I'm ready to talk to them. England is only a plane flight away".'

He again stressed Packer's business record. 'He is well prepared if the answer is no. He has the grounds for us to play on and of course had to make sure of getting them before the plans were announced. No one is going to want to see Australia's second eleven playing India at the Melbourne Cricket Ground while the Rest of the World are playing the Australian first eleven just down the road.' Greig was insistent that his reason for joining Packer was primarily in order to better the lot of cricketers, particularly those in England. 'I could have said, "Okay, I'm captain of England, I'm all right." That would have been selfish. I have laid my captaincy on the table as a sacrifice. If it's taken away from me I will then live with my decision.

'The plight of the modern cricketer is certainly not the best [sic]. Many who've been playing eight years or more are living on the breadline. In the winter they go abroad coaching, leaving their families behind. Test cricketers are also not paid what they are worth. As a result of this action cricket may in five or ten years come into line with tennis and golf. Then, if a young man is faced with the decision of which game to play, he can choose cricket with confidence. People who give up their lives to a game should be rewarded accordingly.'

Greig admitted that when he was first approached by Packer in Melbourne he wondered whether he should talk to Lord's about it. 'If I did that I felt that Lord's could only advise against it. Colleagues of mine were involved, and I was certain it would be good for cricket. For this to succeed we had to take on authority head on, and it was the top cricketers who had to do it because of their position in the game. And if the best players are seen to be paid very well there is more for the rest to aim at.' He also said he had acted as an agent for Packer in persuading many of the Rest of the World players to sign.

There were two moments during the conference, which lasted for seventy-five minutes, when Greig looked uneasy and his eyes narrowed. The first came when he was asked how the plans he had outlined could in any way affect the payment of the ordinary English county professional who was never going to play for England and yet without whom county cricket would not exist. He was later asked how much he was motivated by idealism and how much by self-interest. 'The whole basis of all this is an ideal, but nobody is going to do it for peanuts,' he replied.

On the whole Greig handled himself well. However, having seen him deal with the press and the media generally on many occasions on tour I detected a strong element of unease. I have no doubt that Greig had underestimated the strength of the opposition he would meet with, and that this opposition brought home to him the full extent of what he had done. He had betrayed the trust which those in authority had put in him when they made him England's captain, and in an unprecedented way. For all that, during this difficult week at Hove there was always his disarmingly relaxed smile and a few words of greeting as he drove his white Jaguar into the captain's parking place, the relaxed, slightly angular walk, the flamboyant sports coat, the well-creased trousers whose colours changed daily: Greig made a magnificent storybook hero.

After that conference events moved quickly. Greig went up to London to be interviewed on BBC television. While there he saw Donald Carr, the secretary of the Test and County Cricket Board. His conversation with Carr was private, but Carr's previous friendship with Greig must have left him both pained and disappointed. He had managed Greig in India and Pakistan with Tony Lewis's side, and again in the West Indies under Mike Denness. He had seen some of Greig's worst excesses on the field, but he had remained loyal to him after both the Wadekar incident in India and the Kallicharran run-out in Trinidad. Before Greig was appointed to the England captaincy Carr's views would have been sought and it would have been surprising if he had not felt let down by Greig. It cannot have been an easy meeting.

Greig's conversation with Carr was held early in the morning after his BBC interview, for he had to be back in Hove for Sussex's match against Lancashire at eleven o'clock. In the meantime an emergency meeting of the Executive of the Cricket Council – who have the ultimate responsibility for appointing the England captain – had been called at Lord's for the following day – which, by a strange irony, was Friday the 13th. Besides discussing Greig's position they also wanted to consider the position of the other English players who had signed for Packer: Knott, Underwood and Snow.

For my part I continued to wait around along with many others in the hope that something would turn up or someone would emerge and be prepared to speak. Still more newspapermen appeared on the Friday, for they had come to hear Greig's reaction if he lost the England captaincy during the day. One was Ted Dexter, who had himself captained Sussex and England and had also been something of a rebel. We were talking in the press box when we heard that Greig had made a decision: he would not hold a press conference when the news, whatever it was, came through from Lord's, but would simply issue a statement. Dexter suggested that the two of us should go up to the captain's room at the top of the pavilion and try to see Greig. We found him in his room, as always drinking copious cups of tea and endlessly smoking cigarettes.

He seemed pleased to see us, so we sat down and talked about his situation. At first he and Dexter did most of the talking. Greig was even more tense that morning, and I could see why. For nearly a week he had talked heroically of losing the England captaincy and even of sacrificing it, calmly and with deliberate intent. Now, within a few hours, he was going to know. With his elbows on his thighs and the muscles tight across his face, he leant across to Dexter and said, 'What do you think will happen?'

Dexter paused before answering. 'I think you'll lose the captaincy,' he said, 'but I expect they'll let you go on playing.'

Greig watched Dexter carefully as he spoke, and when he had finished he straightened up and shrugged his shoulders.

'Well, I knew that might happen when I went into all this,' he said.

At that moment I am convinced that Greig had doubts about what he had done. He would never have admitted it, and part of Greig's armour is the impression he likes to create of controlled certainty. But when Dexter had spoken the doubts were written on Greig's face. How easy was it going to be for him to watch someone else captain England, after all that the job had given him? I am quite sure those feelings went strongly through him that morning at Hove. Greig never likes to let anyone think that a situation has caught him unawares, but he partly admitted that he was surprised at the tremendous hostility with which he had met after the original story broke. As the three of us went on talking he tried to rationalize the decision he had made, repeating constantly that it was for the good of the game and for the benefit of all English first-class cricketers. Dexter was by no means unsympathetic, for it was the lack of money in cricket which brought about his own early retirement.

By this time dressing rooms and press boxes all over the country were rife with rumours. One heard that this player or that player had signed for Packer, then that an umpire had been signed up, and even that television commentators and statisticians were under contract. Such rumours were to go on for the rest of the summer, and as each individual story had many different versions it was impossible to know who to believe. Old friends began to find it difficult to look each other in the eye, reliable informants could no longer be relied upon, and I even heard of lifelong friends becoming enemies overnight because of the views they held about Packer. The most glaring example of this came later when Richie Benaud arrived in Adelaide with World Series Cricket before Christmas and rang his old friend and mentor Sir Donald Bradman. Hardly a sentence had been spoken when Bradman said that he did not wish to speak to Benaud, and put down the telephone.

While Dexter and I were talking to Greig he told us an intriguing story about Geoffrey Boycott, the first player to turn Packer down. Boycott had refused to sign the contract which was offered to him in Australia when he was playing for Waverley in Sydney. There are various versions about what happened. Some say that Boycott objected to playing under Greig and either wanted the captaincy himself or would have settled for Ray Illingworth. Boycott has said that when he read through the contract he realized that it might prevent him from playing for Yorkshire during the English summer, and as a result he had refused to sign. Packer himself said that when he went to America after arranging for the contracts to be drawn up he expected them to be signed by the time he returned, and it was then that he discovered that Boycott had not signed. Boycott's version is on page 99.

Greig's story was that when the game finished that Sunday at Hove the players changed and Greig went down to his car. As he was about to drive off he saw Boycott come out of the pavilion and they talked about the game for a few minutes. Greig suggested Boycott join him for a drink at the pub by the main gate. Boycott declined, saying that he had to return to Chesterfield where Yorkshire were playing the next day and that he had two of their young players with him. As Boycott was about to go to his own car, Greig spoke again.

'By the way, Fiery [Boycott's nickname], have a look at the papers in the morning. There'll be something there which will interest you.'

Greig explained that the Packer story was going to break.

'You don't mean you signed?' Boycott asked him in some astonishment.

'Yes, and thirty-four others,' Greig answered, and again asked Boycott to come to the pub and have a drink and he would tell him the story. Boycott again refused.

Greig went down to the pub himself and stayed for about forty-five minutes before driving home. When he reached his house he was surprised to see Boycott's car parked outside, with the two young players sitting inside. The Yorkshire captain was talking to Greig's wife inside the house, and when Greig appeared Boycott implored him to ring up Packer in the hope that he would give him another chance. Greig refused. The gist of this unlikely tale appeared in *Private Eye* ten days later and went on to suggest that Greig gave Boycott an opportunity to ring Packer himself in order to plead on his own behalf. This he did, but Mr Packer was not impressed. Boycott himself vehemently denied this story when it appeared, and the afternoon following his reported conversation with Greig, the Yorkshire captain appeared on local television in the north of England, saying that he had refused Packer's offer as soon as he realized that it might prevent him from playing for Yorkshire. He said he had gone to Greig's house to see Donna and to thank her for being so kind to him when he had been in Sydney playing for Waverley the previous winter, and that the two players with him, Lumb and Athey, had also come into the house and heard what was said. If the story was as Greig told it it is surprising that it did not come out in the High Court hearing when Boycott gave evidence on behalf of the authorities – it would have been in Packer's interests to discredit him. If it was not true Greig can claim no credit for trying to dishonour Boycott in this way.

After we had seen Greig I drove Dexter to London for the press conference which was to be held at Lord's after the meeting of the Cricket Council. Dexter was sure that Greig would lose the captaincy, but it was nonetheless with something of the feeling of a new batsman walking down the pavilion steps that I went into the

Lord's pavilion. A dozen correspondents gathered in the Long Room, and we talked, as that august room dictates, in hushed whispers befitting those about to witness an execution. We all asked each other what we thought would happen, although I am sure that each of us knew the answer.

We sat at the far end of the Long Room, away from the Committee Room, and yet through the glass door at the other end, across the passage and through the glass panes of the Committee Room door, one could see the large figure of Freddie Brown, the Chairman of the Cricket Council, sitting at the head of the table. There was a cloud of pipe smoke, and from time to time he turned his head to look at a new speaker. The Cricket Council is made up of representatives of the bodies controlling cricket at all levels in the United Kingdom. Such formidable characters as Gubby Allen, for a long time Treasurer of MCC, a former President and the *eminence grise* of English cricket, Doug Insole, Chairman of the Test and County Cricket Board, Tadge Webster, President of the Cricket Council and the MCC, George Mann, former captain of England and Middlesex, successful brewer and administrator of cricket for many years, Jack Davies, present Treasurer of MCC and a Governor of the Bank of England, Cedric Rhoades, Chairman of Lancashire, Mike Turner, Secretary of Leicestershire and others sat with Brown. Looked at through two glass doors Greig's chances did not seem good. Twice while we waited Peter Lush, in charge of public relations at Lord's, walked the full length of the Long Room to tell us that it would be at least another hour before the meeting was over.

The members of the Committee began to leave the meeting at about half past five, coming out of the door in twos and threes, heads down and deep in conversation. Lush called us into the Committee Room. He sat where moments before Freddie Brown had been sitting with a sheet of paper in his hand. We sat round him, glancing first at him and then at each other – even at this meeting there was tension. Finally Lush said he would read the statement:

The Cricket Council's emergency executive committee met at Lord's today to consider the involvement of England players in the proposed series of matches between Australia and the Rest of the World during the coming winter.

The Council have today received a communication from the Inter-

4. The third Test at Trent Bridge. Knott and Brearley congratulate Underwood
after the dismissal of fellow Packer signee Richie Robinson. Behind them Tony
Greig looks thoughtful.

The High Court hearing

5.   Kerry Packer and Tony Greig leave the courts at the end of the first day's hearing.

6.   The establishment out in force: Donald Carr, Doug Insole and Jack Bailey, respectively Secretary of the TCCB, Chairman of the TCCB and Secretary of the ICC.

capacity his firm had worked for the Australian Board of Control. He has been great friends with cricket administrators around the world and on occasions he has advised them, particularly in Australia, in an unofficial capacity. Whatever reason motivated Benaud to join Packer there is no doubt that he was regarded by many people in the same light as Greig, as being a traitor to the game he had apparently supported for so long.

On Wednesday 27 July 1977, the *Australian* published an interview which Benaud gave in England to John Phillips of their London bureau. In the first question, as it appears in the paper, Phillips asked Benaud, 'What is your role in the Packer organization for the Super-Test series?' Benaud answered in the following words:

'We [his company, D. E. Benaud & Associates] are sports consultants and freelance media representatives. On 5 April Kerry Packer telephoned our office and asked if we would be interested in considering a consultancy job for a project he had in mind. Later that day, at a meeting, he outlined the idea of the Super-Tests on the basis that, accepting the retainer or otherwise, the matter would remain confidential as far as our firm was concerned.

'As I had heard nothing of the project up to that time it's not too difficult to understand that my first reaction was one of disbelief that the matter had remained confidential for the previous six weeks. We considered all aspects of the offer, the effect on cricket, the players, the administration and our own business, and twenty-four hours later stated that we would accept a position as sports consultants to the project. That is what we are, and will continue to be for the duration of the five years.'

The following February the Melbourne *Age* Insight team published a series of four articles about World Series Cricket. In the third of these, entitled 'How cricket was turned upside down', the *Age* printed the following:

A key figure in the battle strategy has been former Australian Test captain, Richie Benaud, now a consultant for WSC. 'One of the most challenging . . . eras of my cricketing life began on 5 April 1977, when I was informed of the intention to stage a Super-Test series of cricket matches in Australia over at least the next five years,' Benaud wrote in a WSC magazine in August.

Benaud must have worked quickly, because only one day later he presented Mr Packer with a nine-page 'battle strategy' seen by Insight

– covering the best way to deal with the opposition from the official
cricket authorities. The Benaud memo, dated 6 April 1977, warned Mr
Packer: 'It would be unwise to write off the Board simply because you
have the players signed up on contract . . . Bob Parish as chairman is a
tireless worker, Sir Donald Bradman a brilliant administrator and
business man and chairman of several boards, Ray Steele, solicitor and
one of the best administrators in the world . . . their reaction in the
first instance will be to contact one or two players, sound them out to
find out what is going on, and then their second reaction will be one of
disbelief.'

Benaud advised Packer: 'It is important from the public relations
point of view that you contact the ACB [Australian Cricket Board]
before making an official announcement, so they cannot say they and
the game have been snubbed.' Benaud then suggested that Mr
Packer call a press conference to announce the WSC coaching scheme –
'so that the NSW Cricket Association is in the position of offering its
thanks for something being done at grass roots level.'

He also included a draft of a letter he suggested that Mr Packer send
to ACB chairman, Bob Parish, informing him of the WSC plans –
which Packer duly sent off word for word a month later. Benaud then
suggested that Mr Packer could advise the ACB he was telling them all
the details 'to be of assistance' when the board began TV rights negotiations for 1977/78 . . . 'That, from the PR point of view, would be the
grand gesture,' Benaud wrote.

The Melbourne *Age* also published an extract of the Benaud
memo to Packer.

Benaud's involvement saddened many people. This was perhaps
best summed up by Gerry Gomez, the former Trinidad and West
Indian all-rounder and captain whom I saw in Trinidad during
the Fourth Test Match against Australia in April 1978. Gomez
had managed the West Indies side in Australia in 1960/61, the
series which saw the celebrated Tied Test at Brisbane. Gomez
said that he thought Frank Worrell, who captained the West Indies
on that tour, would be turning in his grave at what had happened.
He was himself astonished at Benaud's involvement because he
had been one of the two captains who had between them produced
the greatest-ever Test series – 'the ultimate in Test cricket' was
how Gomez described it – and he could hardly believe that
he had become one of Packer's main lieutenants in promoting a
form of cricket which was set up in direct opposition to Test
cricket.

Packer and his supporters have frequently expressed surprise that they have met with this type of opposition; but surely in view of the way WSC was set up it was inevitable.

◆

CHAPTER 4

The International Set

'In affectionate remembrance of English cricket which died at the Oval on 29th August 1882. Deeply lamented by a large circle of sorrowing friends and acquaintances. R.I.P. N.B. – The body will be cremated and the Ashes taken to Australia.'

Notice in *The Times* following English defeat by Australia in 1882.

'In affectionate remembrance of International Cricket which died at Hove, 9th May 1977. Deeply lamented by a large circle of friends and acquaintances. R.I.P. N.B. – The body will be cremated and the Ashes taken to Australia and scattered around the studio of TCN9 in Sydney. NTJCBM.'

Notice in *The Times*, May 1977, inserted by three journalists touring with the Australian side.

THE ASHES SERIES between England and Australia has always been the centrepiece of international cricket, but despite the threat posed by Packer the idea that Anglo-Australian Test cricket was already dying because of what he had done was far-fetched in the extreme. But then in the early days of the story many exaggerated claims were made by both sides. Greig had announced, like some modern-day crusader, that he was leading the ranks of professional cricketers out of the bondage in which the wicked Dickensian authorities had trapped them for decades. The other side too had their share of hysterical reaction, making it appear that with the words barely out of Greig's mouth Test cricket was grinding to a halt, the game facing bankruptcy and sponsors departing in droves. On the whole there was little for anyone to be proud of in those opening skirmishes.

For the ten days after Greig's press conference at Hove a phoney war really existed in England, both sides taking up their positions and waiting for each other to fire the first shot. Vague rumblings came from Australia where Packer was to be found, but, after the publication of the *Bulletin*, there was no more hard news. In England Len Maddocks, the manager of the touring Australians and also a member of the Australian Board of Control, made clear his and the Board's total opposition to Packer, so that there quickly grew up two distinct camps within the touring party, with neither trusting the other. Four of the Australians had not been invited to join the circus – Serjeant, Hughes, Cosier and Dymock. Whatever their feelings later on they understandably felt ostracized, good-humouredly referring to themselves as the 'second eleven'. But from the moment Packer's plans were revealed Maddocks and Norman McMahon, his assistant from Brisbane, were in conflict with the leading players, who from then on were fighting as much to uphold Packer as they were to win a Tcst series for Australia. The tour selectors were all Packer players, and they were accused by the press of ignoring the claims of the non-Packer players when they picked sides for the Test Matches. In the case of Serjeant, who made 81 in the First Test at Lord's and was dropped for the Third at Trent Bridge, their decision was difficult to justify. From 9 May they were a divided and unhappy party, and it was no surprise that they should lose the Ashes by three matches to nil.

With the exception of Greig, the English players who had joined Packer refused to comment on the situation, although they were aggressively indignant if anyone doubted their wisdom or questioned their loyalty. Greig, on the other hand, adopted an uncompromising and self-justifying attitude. Meanwhile, from Swansea, where the Australians were playing Glamorgan the following week-end, one heard that some of the younger members of the Australian party were having serious misgivings about joining Packer. At the time of signing they had their doubts allayed by the confidence of some of the senior players, and the conspiratorial way in which it was all done must also have been appealing. The outrage the news produced surprised them, and they were also worried at the prospect of being banned from Test and first-class cricket for ever; this was already being mooted as a likely counter-attack by the authorities.

What had led the players to make their revolutionary decision? It is easy to see the point of view of the older men like Snow, Redpath, Ross Edwards and Ian Chappell. When they signed their Test careers were over, and Packer cricket came as a welcome and unexpected bonus. One can understand, too, those senior players still involved in Test cricket but nearing the end of their careers – Knott, Underwood, Greg Chappell, Lillee, Asif Iqbal and Mushtaq. As for the South Africans involved, they had no chance of Test cricket, and now found themselves presented with an opportunity to play against the best players in the world; one can only have a certain amount of sympathy for the likes of Procter, Barry Richards and Barlow.

Nonetheless, all the Packer players were, except for the South Africans, being asked to choose between Packer's new commercial brand of cricket and the form of cricket which had made them who they were. At the time several may not have realized that their loyalty to their countries and their counties was being called into question. They had been assured that they would be able to continue playing Test and county cricket, and they did not fully appreciate the likely consequences of their actions. By the time one or two of the players realized how far out on a limb they had gone it was too late to do anything about it.

The English players – Greig, Knott, Underwood and Snow – later to be joined by Amiss and Woolmer – had the most difficult decision to make. England is the only country in the world where professional cricket is played; there is more first-class cricket in Britain than elsewhere; and county cricket has become a part of an Englishman's heritage, a closely-knit system of friendships and traditional rivalries. The players have been ill-paid, but towards the end of their careers capped county players are awarded a tax-free Benefit which nowadays runs to a great deal of money (although counties like Kent and Leicestershire are always likely to produce larger Benefits than the smaller, less prosperous counties such as Northamptonshire and Glamorgan). In the three years before the arrival of Packer both Knott and Underwood had received large Benefits from Kent, and both had declared more than £25,000. Snow had had a Benefit with Sussex; Greig was about to be awarded one.

The counties could reasonably have expected the players to have shown some loyalty, maybe only to the extent of discussing with the committee what they were thinking of doing before going off and signing for a private promoter. Packer himself must have realized that some were bound to feel the double pull, that of loyalty to their former bosses and the allurement of his money. He did his best to ensure that his money had the greater appeal, offering amounts which were far in excess of anything players had seen before, and guaranteeing them employment for three years, whereas in the past their futures extended no further than the end of a five-month contract with their counties or the end of an official tour. In financial terms alone it would have been strongly against their interests not to accept. Yet the stark fact remained for the establishment to digest that a system which had reared players over a number of years and had turned them into international figures was unable to produce feelings of loyalty.

To a British audience the 'defection' of some of their most cherished cricketing idols was painful and difficult to accept. Should it be any clearer now, over a year later? It would be hard to imagine a more fastidious man than Alan Knott, for instance – someone most people would never expect to make a hasty decision. His public image is of a brilliant wicket-keeper and a fine batsman, but he is also a man who spends all his time on the cricket field when not actually involved in the game doing physical exercises. He is always bending, stretching, trying to keep his muscles loose. Physical fitness is a fixation with him. Even his food has to be prepared in certain ways, and there are many foods he will not eat. He can never be separated from a pot of honey; every tea leaf has to be removed from a cup of tea before he will drink it; he will not eat meat and potatoes together, so mixing carbohydrates and proteins; he will eat only wheatgerm bread. He is also meticulously clean. These are peculiarities that can easily be catered for in England and Australia but which become a problem in countries like India and Pakistan where his demands can become irritating. But Knott feels that this helps to keep him fit and to make him the player he is and he has the results to justify it. He is also extremely home-loving, and hates to be separated from his wife Jan and his young son. He is at his happiest on tour when joined by his wife, and, as came out in the High Court hearing, almost refused to tour India, Sri Lanka and Australia in 1976/77 because of the restriction on the amount of time wives were allowed to spend on tour with their husbands. One of the attractions of Packer's proposals was that wives and children were allowed to accompany their husbands. Knott always reckons that he plays his best cricket when his wife is with him.

Thus for all Knott's brilliance as a player he has always found it difficult to accept the lot of the first-class cricketer, and although his complaints remained muted while there was no viable alternative I was not surprised that he reacted as he did when Greig first approached him. Knott has always been close to Greig, and he had seen from Greig's winter in Australia in 1975/76 that it was possible for internationally well-known players to sell themselves more dearly and to make money from commercial ventures on a scale which hitherto had been unthought of. Like Greig, Knott is more conscious of money than some, and needs a fair amount to pay his telephone bills; he is a compulsive talker to friends all round the world.

Derek Underwood had a greater internal battle in deciding to sign for Packer. The financial advantages and the job security of Packer's contract were obvious. His loyalty to Kent and England cricket, the warm response to his Benefit from Kent supporters and his own nature, which is not in the least combative, plus the fact that with 265 Test wickets he needed 44 more to become the highest wicket-taker in the history of Test cricket – all must have made joining Packer an extremely difficult decision.

In the end family pressure may have been the deciding influence. If Underwood had realized at the time of signing what the reaction of the authorities would be I do not think he would have signed. Once he had done so he became a militant supporter of Packer – often a way of covering up doubts. For all that, there is no more amiable cricketer than Derek Underwood, and not many less materialistic. In a sense Underwood was as much a victim as a beneficiary of the Packer revolution.

With Tony Greig's influence so strongly upon Packer it was no surprise that Snow was signed – although, now in his mid-thirties, his career as a genuine fast bowler is virtually over. Snow himself, the author of an autobiography aptly entitled *Cricket Rebel*, has frequently been at loggerheads with the authorities, and has on a number of occasions chosen to embarrass them. I have always enjoyed being with Snow when on his own, finding him intelligent and amusing. When attention is focused upon him, however, he feels he has to play a part. The private Snow is immensely more attractive than the public one.

These three and Greig are all intelligent people, and they should have been able to appreciate the risk they were taking in deciding to play a strictly uncompetitive brand of cricket. From the moment of the first announcement it seemed that the one serious drawback to Packer's plans would be his end-product – the actual cricket – which was designed to appeal to mass television audiences in Australia. The Australians are by nature extremely competitive, and this is never more apparent than when watching Test cricket in Australia. They love to win, and they love even more to beat England. When Denness's side was being comprehensively beaten by Lillee and Thomson in 1974/75 in Australia the crowds came in their hundreds of thousands to watch long after it was clear that England had no hope of preventing huge defeats. It was an impressive illustration of the strength of the cricket rivalry between the two countries.

Not that the Australians are alone in their love of victory; it is just that they are marginally more open about it than some. In England in 1977 huge crowds packed into Old Trafford, Trent Bridge and Headingley long after the Test Matches there had ceased to be interesting games of cricket. The spectators came to see Australia beaten. This strong element of national competition which enables spectators in England, Australia and elsewhere to identify with the players on the field was to be absent in the Packer Super-Tests. The players must have wondered about this; but Packer's leading protagonists, Greig, the Chappells, Lillee, Marsh and Asif Iqbal did all they could to dispel these doubts.

The pressure applied by Packer's main supporters was too great for any of the doubting younger players, yet soon after Packer's plans were revealed there were constant rumours that as many as five of the younger Australians were doubting the wisdom of what they had done. David Hookes's name was continually mentioned, and he was indeed unhappy. By the end of the tour he had played six Test Matches for Australia and was unlikely to play again. If Packer's cricket was not a success his career might now be over at a very early age.

On Hookes's return to Australia I was told by one of his friends that he had taken a solicitor and gone to see Packer in an attempt to withdraw from his contract. Packer agreed he could do so, but then reminded him that the World Series Cricket organization had spent well over £100,000 advertising a product with his name attached to it, and that Hookes would himself be sued for the return of a proportion of that money. Hookes had no option but to stay, and he was given a five-year contract. When in late January 1978 the official Australian party to tour the West Indies was announced Hookes intimated in Adelaide at the time of the Fifth Test between Australia and India that he was extremely sad not to be accompanying his erstwhile colleagues.

Packer's involvement with cricket began with his attempt to buy exclusive television rights in Australia, his cricket was to be played in Australia and at first there were more Australian players on his books than from any other country. The Australians had been approached and signed first, and in the High Court hearing Packer said that the alacrity with which they had joined him had been frightening. Over the years the Australian Board have been strongly attacked for their unwillingness to better the lot of their players and have several times been guilty of doing too little too late. But their present Board were aware of the situation and of the discontent among the players. In the season 1976/77 they formed a committee consisting of the State captains and members of the Board to look into the general question of sponsorship, and at once the captains expressed themselves satisfied with the way the Board was handling affairs on the players' behalf. Within weeks of this committee being formed four of the six State captains (Tasmania had been included) had signed for Packer, yet they continued to take part in these discussions.

When the Australian tour of England in 1977 had finished Bob Parish, Chairman of the Australian Board, issued a statement in order that the Board's position should be made clear. A section of the statement reads:

The Board resolved in 1974 that it would pay to the players the maximum it could afford, taking into consideration its overall responsibility to Australian cricket at all other levels. The principle was unanimously accepted by the State captains, Greg Chappell, Doug Walters, Richie Robinson, Ashley Woodcock and Rod Marsh at the inaugural meeting of the Board Cricket Sub-Committee on 22 December 1976.

The Board is of the opinion that it is honouring this undertaking and that Australian players are well paid. The Board's opinion is confirmed by Greg Chappell in his recently published book, *The 100th Summer* published by Gary Sparks, Melbourne. He says,

'Cricketers' rewards have increased dramatically in a comparatively short time. In a matter of just two seasons the base Test payment doubled from $200 to $400. Sizeable bonuses have been handed out at the end of the past two series, provident fund money has been increased, cash endorsements are flowing as never before, and the Test team is now sponsored for three years. It's hardly surprising that Australia leads the way in providing a far better deal for the cricketers.'

Each player who participated in the tour of New Zealand received for that 35-day tour A$2430.

Each player who participated in the Centenary Test received from the Board A$2277.

For the tour of England of 134 days each of the seventeen players will receive from the Board A$10,890.

If a player played in two Pakistan Tests, for which he received A$2481, toured New Zealand, played in the Centenary Test, toured the UK and was selected to play in the first two Tests against India, for which he would receive at least A$3704, he would receive from the Board in the calendar year 1977 nearly A$22,000. This, in addition to match fees, prize money and sponsoring in Sheffield Shield and Gillette cup matches and all expenses. With rare exceptions most of the Australian players are not full-time professionals and have other jobs.

At this time Australia were far ahead of the other Test-playing countries as far as the payment of players was concerned. The England players were still receiving £210 for a Test Match in England, and the previous winter they had each been paid just £3000 for the tour of India, Sri Lanka and Australia – a tour which lasted almost four months. The authorities at Lord's were aware that the pay was poor, but perhaps did not appreciate the urgency for improvement. There was no sign of industrial action by the players, who had grudgingly come to accept their low levels of pay as inevitable, and there was no precedent of a private promoter taking things into his own hands as Packer was to do. The English authorities were more guilty of caution than meanness, for they were still all too aware of the extremely lean period that cricket went through in the 1960s. There was also a wage-limit policy in England which could not be broken. However, there was also an understanding that the terms of payment would be improved when the sponsorship for home Test series, then under offer, had been completed. There were other general promises of money to come, but Packer got in first and used his cheque book to back up his words.

As events developed England, Pakistan and the West Indies all increased significantly the payment for Test cricketers, and county players in England received appreciably more for their services in 1978. This is one of the benefits from the Packer revolution, but it may have an unhappy side effect. The new terms the counties have offered to their players mean that they are wholly bound to sponsorship, and when the contracts for 1979 are reviewed it may be that players who would normally expect to be retained and who should be able to earn a living from cricket have to be sacked so that the counties can afford to pay their best players. Internationally Pakistan and the West Indies have not been able to match the amount of money Packer is offering his players, and because of the weak financial positions of both Boards these two countries are likely to remain his main recruiting centres; he is fortunate that they both have such an array of talented players. But again this is going ahead of the story.

♦

CHAPTER 5

Kerry Packer
in England

'In business you don't tell your opponents what you are going to do;
you do it and let them get on with it.'
Kerry Packer, in an interview he gave me in the pavilion at Hove on
Sunday 22 May 1977.

THE PACKER AFFAIR had its origins in Australia, but the main battleground was Lord's. The authorities there, along with their
Australian counterparts in Melbourne and Sydney, were extremely indignant. An operation had been planned with military
precision and with a secrecy designed to put them under the
greatest possible pressure. They had been informed that a Mr
Packer had bought the exclusive services of thirty-five of the game's
main assets, and that if they were not prepared immediately to sit
down with the Australian entrepreneur and work out a satisfactory
compromise established cricket would suffer. These may have
been admirable big business tactics, but they were strange and
immensely distasteful to those who ran the game of cricket.

Yet suddenly the English authorities were faced with the
realization that their captain had not only signed for a man who
was setting up in direct opposition to the established game, but
also that he was being paid to act as his main recruiting agent. It
was a confrontation which the game's rulers were totally unpre-
pared for, and from which they must have thought they would be
immune. Who were these people whom Packer had decided to take
on, and why did they feel that divine right was on their side?
Were they, in fact, as so many now claimed, out of touch with
reality?

In England and Australia cricket has always been administered in an honorary capacity by men who have a deep love for cricket and a heavy involvement with the game. Mostly they have been businessmen of considerable stature who have been prepared to give a great part of their lives to conducting the affairs of the game in the way that they felt best looked after the interests of those concerned with cricket at all levels. It is a paradox that certain administrators who are veritable tigers in their company's board room should, as soon as they appear in another role at Lord's or Sydney, be labelled as fusty old reactionaries who are out of touch with the modern world. But that certainly is the case.

It is largely explained by the mysticism of cricket. From its earliest beginnings the game has been about standards: of play, of behaviour, of spectatorship. It has been a game which has combined and held on to what are now considered to be old-fashioned virtues. It has never moved with the times, although it has inevitably reflected the tenor of society when it changes, for this is reflected by those who play it. The administrators are not only therefore looking after and running a business; they are also protecting a heritage. There is a reasonable analogy between the administrators of cricket and the committee of a London club. They have to strike a balance between a commercial approach which aims at profits and the traditional approach which is to remember that their prime function is to look after the needs of the members. The two often run in opposite directions.

'It isn't cricket' is not a phrase which has crept into English usage by chance, and cricket's administrators still have a certain responsibility to that phrase. The stately Victorian atmosphere of the Committee Rooms at Lord's and the Melbourne Cricket Ground are hardly conducive to radical change. The reaction of the authorities to Packer was predictable, and Packer was surely right when he said that his tight secrecy was necessary because if the authorities heard about his plans in advance they would try to block him. But Packer was always set on a course of confrontation; he could have acted in a different way and have been completely open from the start, trying to work with the authorities from the moment the idea first gelled. But that was not his way.

In the High Court Mr Justice Slade said how impressed he had been by the integrity of those who administered the game. To laymen it is incredible that men like Gubby Allen, for years a highly successful stockbroker, David Clark, a hard-working farmer, George Mann, a brewer of great distinction, Doug Insole, now in the building industry, Edmond King, a chartered accountant, and the other figures at Lord's who are equally well qualified in business terms should have stood so ponderously, and obviously, on their dignity. But then cricket had never been challenged before.

The Australians were themselves fighting a more personal battle. When Packer found he had been thwarted in his attempts to win exclusive television rights he spoke about the Board in the most disparaging terms. After listening to this abuse Ray Steele, a hard-working solicitor, Bob Parish, who works in the timber trade, Tim Caldwell, a retired banker, Sir Donald Bradman, a retired stockbroker, and other able and influential members of the Board were unlikely to be prepared to sit down at the same table as Packer, let alone talk terms to him. Packer chose a battle because he wanted one; he also chose his battleground, presumably because he felt it was the terrain on which he would win. He never doubted that the authorities would fight; he may have underestimated the strength of the tradition represented by those authorities.

Packer arrived in England on 21 May. With him came John Cornell and Austin Robertson. From Heathrow they drove to Hove where all three stayed with the Greigs. The following day, Sunday, 22 May, I went to watch Sussex play Gloucestershire at Hove in the Sunday League. Surprisingly there was no one else from Fleet Street in the press box. John Vinicombe of the Brighton *Evening Argus* and Jack Arlidge, whose presence in the press box at Hove has for years been one of the pleasures of watching Sussex at home, were the only others there. A piece of simple espionage enabled us to discover that the large, balding man who had arrived in a chauffeur-driven Daimler was Kerry Packer. Even seen through the car windows it seemed surprising that he was only forty. It was important to get an interview with him, but not easy to organize. We discovered from the Sussex dressing room that Packer and his colleagues were closeted with Greig in the captain's room. Rather than barge in hopefully I suggested that we should ask Stanley Allen to arrange an interview for us. He agreed to try.

When he came back to the press box he said he did not think that Packer would be prepared to see all of us and that, if he was prepared only to talk to one of us, would I come? He went away and about half an hour later he came quietly round the corner of the door and beckoned to me. I followed him through the back of the pavilion, up the stairs and into Greig's room. As we entered conversation stopped, and for a moment there was an awkward silence, broken by Greig saying, 'Ah, Blowers.' He introduced me to Packer, Cornell and Robertson and we all shook hands; Packer rather limply. I had seen many photographs of him, but even so I was not prepared for quite such an enormous man. At first we were all uncertain how to begin, and settled for the usual banal exchange about the journey and the weather.

Every time I have met Packer he has surprised me. On this first occasion, although I never saw him so again, he appeared to be nervous. He gave me the impression of finding himself in a situation to which he had not yet grown accustomed. At times he appeared to be searching for his answers, and his later self-assurance had not yet developed. Although he said very little, Cornell was the one who appeared in control at that meeting. It was Cornell who had had the original idea, and I suspect that his mind is the most nimble of the three.

In appearance, Packer might have been a prize-fighter or a film producer's idea of an Australian sheep farmer from the outback, and yet in his movements and gestures that day it was as if he found his body uncomfortably large.

'What are you doing here?' was my first question. He answered in a gentle voice, 'Watching cricket, which I love. And I don't know many people with these facilities – the captain's room, I mean!' He laughed, as did Greig.

I then asked him if he had come over to see the authorities at Lord's.

'I am prepared to see the relevant cricket authorities at any time they wish to see me, but they have not shown any indication of doing so yet. I have not come across as a pressure tactic, though,' he assured me.

As the excuse for his appearance in London he said he had been rung up by the organizers of the new David Frost BBC programme and asked to come to London to put across his point of view. Packer and Frost were friends, and Frost had appeared on Packer's Channel Nine in Sydney. He was also planning to meet the press. 'I haven't got anything to be ashamed of. I wouldn't be here if I had.'

He looked out of the open window. 'I'm very excited about cricket, and I've never seen Procter play before. I'm hoping to see him bat today.' Packer was smoking all the time, and admitted to getting through seventy cigarettes a day.

I asked him if he had been surprised at the hostile reaction to his plans in England. 'They have been mixed in the press, more hostile than favourable, but reaction in Australia is important too. The Australian journalists who are not here with the side have given it a good go. And it is undoubtedly an enormous success with the public.'

I did not know whether I would be allowed ten minutes or fifty with him, and I asked questions fast to keep him talking. Cornell was sitting behind Packer and occasionally when he felt that Packer had not made something clear he enlarged on the answer in quiet, well-modulated tones. Austin Robertson, large with curly black hair, was perched on the window sill, with Greig by the wall on the far side of the window, smiling and looking alternately at Packer and out of the window at the cricket.

I suggested that a constantly recurring series between Australia and a Rest of the World Eleven would have a limited public appeal. Packer agreed, and said that it had never been suggested that it would go on for ever.

'There may be other sides we can bring to Australia, and then we would have Test Matches between two countries. One thing I want to make clear is that there is no chance of us going away, just disappearing off the scene. We are here to stay, I can assure you of that. I know this will be good for cricket in both the short and the long term. In Australia the public are not getting the top-class cricket they want. Australia are playing India this year. Lillee and Thomson versus India will be a débâcle. Then there is the series against England next year which will produce good cricket. The following year Australia are in India and Pakistan, and there are no Tests at home. Australia is the best place to play cricket, for crowds and money. And yet only one successful tour is planned in three years.'

He said this on 22 May and by 23 June the full West Indies side had been signed. In retrospect I think Cornell was restraining Packer from explaining his intentions in full, and that the premature breaking of the story had probably come just before the plans had been completed.

'Cricket is short of money, and the organization of the game is denying the best players in the world opportunities to earn what they deserve. This is not a panacea that will solve cricketers' financial problems overnight. It is, though, the biggest step taken by cricketers to try to find that solution. Where the benefit will come is that it will lift the payment for ordinary cricketers above what they are getting now.'

I asked him how, and said that Greig had been unable to answer this satisfactorily at his press conference. Packer said quickly that he did not want Greig to answer any questions and that one of the reasons he had come to England was to take the pressure off him. I repeated my question, and Packer said that he would come back to it. He never did in any but the most general terms.

'To go on with what I was saying. When top players start to do much better, as happens in any successful business, it gives the player at a lower level the incentive to work harder. He knows there are real financial rewards for him if he can succeed. We've just had the Centenary Test Match. It's taken the cricket authorities a hundred years to recognize the plight of cricketers; don't expect me to solve it all in twelve months. But this is a big step towards it, and to making cricketers work harder and therefore to making cricket more attractive.'

By now he was speaking more fluently, as if he was moving into a well-rehearsed routine. He became more belligerent when we talked about the authorities. He stressed that it would not make the slightest difference to him if they refused to talk, for he had planned everything in considerable detail. 'How can they find out if we are going to benefit cricket if they are not prepared to talk to us? I think there is a suggestion in people's minds that we are trying to take over cricket. The reason I would like to have talks is to find a solution where we do *not* have to take over cricket. We don't want to. We would like to see it administered by the traditional authorities. That's why I would like to talk – not to have more influence, but to have less.'

Was he really surprised by the attitude of the authorities, considering the strong element of bullying and blackmail in his approach? Why had he not gone to the authorities with the thirty-five signed contracts in his hand and said, 'Look, I'm intending to do this, but I want you to know about it before I make it public, and perhaps we can work something out together so that our respective plans do not clash'? With the thirty-five contracts already signed they would have been unable to stop him.

'In business you don't tell your opponents what you are going to do; you do it and let them get on with it,' was his uncompromising reply. 'Whether you like it or not I have influence given to me by the top players in the game who thought they were getting a raw deal. If the authorities want a fight you would have thought they would have talked to me – if only to see how I fight.'

Just how Packer could fight did not emerge all at once. He first met the press at the Television Centre in Shepherd's Bush on Tuesday, 31 May, but nothing fresh emerged from what he had told me at Hove. Two days later he made his appearance on the Frost programme. Frost had invited Robin Marlar, the *Sunday Times* correspondent, and Jim Laker to oppose Packer, and had collected together a largely teenage studio audience. Marlar so nearly lost his temper that he became almost inarticulate, whereas Packer dealt coolly and capably with the flustered opposition and was never asked any really awkward questions. During the programme Marlar said that he had rung Packer in Sydney when the story broke and Packer had told him something in the strictest confidence. Marlar now asked to be released from that confidence; Packer quite reasonably replied that Marlar might have asked him before the programme began, and in the circumstances he would not release him. By the end of these exchanges the young studio audience was strongly on Packer's side, and so, I am sure, were many people watching this television battle who had approached the issue with an open mind.

Laker, who had had his own fight with the authorities at Lord's over his autobiography – a fact which would certainly not have been lost on Packer – followed Marlar, and asked one question which deserved a fuller answer. Laker was talking about the way Greig had betrayed the trust put in him as England's captain, and asked Packer how he would feel if his managing director suddenly defected to the enemy and had tried to persuade some of his senior colleagues to go with him. Packer sidestepped neatly, saying that he was his own managing director, and Frost never brought him back to the question. Laker later turned down an offer to commentate for Packer in Australia.

When Packer was later asked in an interview with the *Sunday*

Times if he thought there were any ethical problems appearing on this programme with one of his best friends acting as the mediator, he answered, 'Well, I think that's the reason he didn't interview me. That's the reason he got people from the other side to interview me. For exactly that reason.'

Frost's company, Paradine Patterson, is involved in taking pop stars and other show business personalities out to Australia, where they appear on Packer's Channel Nine. Packer pointed out that the stars of other promoters also appeared on his channel. Frost himself had worked for Channel Nine but Packer said that there was no conflict at the time of the interview, for apparently Frost was not working for Packer's company then. When asked if he was saying that Frost had not appeared on his channel until after the interview in London, Packer answered, 'I don't think he had appeared – I don't know. You see, for years David was tied up with Channel Seven and then over a period of time there was a disenchantment by David with Channel Seven, or vice versa. Whichever way it was, I gradually said we had better work together in some areas. Now that was probably twelve months ago, I don't know, but at that point in time I don't think David had appeared on Channel Nine. But I think the agreement to appear there had been about six to eight months old. Something like that.'

The final effect was to leave the issue clouded; and if those who read the *Sunday Times* interview carefully came to the conclusion that Packer had masterminded his television appearance from start to finish they were very much in the minority. To most people in Britain Packer's appearance had for the first time put his circus into a sympathetic light.

Packer spent just a week in England, but by the time he left Heathrow for New York the authorities at Lord's should have realized from his public pronouncements that they were dealing with a formidable opponent. He had made his position abundantly clear in several interviews. He was giving the formation of JP Sports Ltd, later to become World Series Cricket Pty, as much if not more attention as he would have given any other new business interest. There was no room for sentiment or emotion. He had taken some of the pressure off Greig and the other players simply by being there, and by being the focal point of interest. He had above all stressed that his brand of cricket was here to stay.

◆

CHAPTER 6

Hostilities Continue

'I will take no steps at all to help anybody. From now on it is every man for himself and let the devil take the hindmost.'
Kerry Packer, speaking to the waiting press when he emerged in a fury from the Lord's pavilion on 23 June.

THAT FIRST WEEK in England revealed Packer as a man in complete control of what he was doing. Although he said that he had not come to England to put pressure on the authorities, I am sure one of the reasons he came was in the hope that the English authorities would take the opportunity to talk to him once they knew he was in the country. He would have backed himself to have convinced them of the good of what he was doing, and have relished the chance to talk to them without any of the Australians present: Packer's previous dealings with the Australian Board must have made him realize that he had no hope of making headway in that direction. The English authorities, on the other hand, by taking no action over the players who signed for Packer – as we have seen, the captaincy was a separate issue – had tacitly admitted that it was not for one country to act alone in this. From the outset it was central to Packer's thinking that he should try to divide his opponents, and he must have felt that he could engineer a difference of opinion between the English and Australian Boards. Later he was to try to isolate the Pakistan and West Indies Boards.

When Packer left England it was with obvious annoyance that the authorities had not been prepared to speak to him. Strangely, he decided to leave on the same day as the hastily convened meet-

ing of the ICC at Lord's. The earliest he could have expected to
receive an invitation to meet the ICC was that evening, yet when
the invitation came he was on his way to New York, and complained that the ICC had known for some time the date of his
departure. It was all part of the war of nerves which he was conducting. After spending four days in America he returned to
London amid great publicity, giving the impression that he was
going to Lord's as the hero who had been wronged, but who was
doing everything he could not to disrupt cricket and to find a
solution. Just before his return it was announced that Dennis
Amiss, Alvin Kallicharran and Collis King had signed for him, and
this news was released at a highly sensitive time when it would
cause the greatest shock: it did nothing to help Packer's cause with
the ICC but it was a reminder to the authorities of what he could
and probably would do with his money if they did not come to
terms with him. With such threats in the air it was hardly the
atmosphere for genuine compromise.

Packer arrived at Lord's smiling benignly, an air of injured
innocence about him. He was not alone, for Lynton Taylor, an
executive from his television network in Sydney, and David
McNicholl, a protégé of his father's and an influential figure in
Australian Consolidated Press, had flown with him from Sydney.
Richie Benaud, looking decidedly uneasy, also attended the
meeting.

The descriptions of events in the Lord's Committee Room that
afternoon have important differences. Packer's own version of the
meeting comes from the interview he gave to the *Sunday Times* on
7 August. He said first that the telegram he received from the ICC
asking him to come to Lord's was an ultimatum telling him that
the ICC was the sole governing body of cricket; he considered the
meeting to be a PR set-up, he said. After he arrived and introductions had been made he was told that the ICC had five points for
him to consider, whereupon he told them what he understood by
the word compromise which was a willingness by both sides to give
a little. The five points were read out and with each he felt there
was a negotiable area, and he spoke about the necessity of setting
up a working party to decide the details. They were:

1.   The programme and the venues are acceptable to the home
     authority and the length of the programme be six weeks unless

otherwise agreed. The matches would be under the control of the home authority and played in accordance with the Laws of Cricket.

2. No player to participate in these games without the permission of the home authority; this permission would not be withheld unreasonably.

3. No teams taking part in these matches could be represented as national teams. (It would have to be an Australian XI and not Australia.)

4. Players contracted to Mr Packer to be available for first-class fixtures and other matches sponsored by the home authority where there was no clash.

5. The home authority must be able to honour all contracted commitments to existing sponsors and advertisers.

After the first two ultimatums (his word) he had repeated what he had said earlier about compromise, and when the fourth point had been read out he did so again. He was then asked what exactly he was looking for, which, according to Packer, was the first time the ICC had ever accepted that he might want anything. He said that, first, he wanted a guarantee that his players would not be victimized, and then that he wanted the exclusive television rights for Test series in Australia when the present contract with the ABC came to an end in 1979. He told them that he wanted to buy the rights, and that this should be another area for the working party. The fifth point was read to him, and Packer suggested that it would be helpful to the ICC if he and his team withdrew to give them a chance to discuss the proposals and he asked if he might go out and look at the wicket.

Packer said that he had not asked for a firm commitment on the exclusive television rights, and that he had put them in the same category as the five points the ICC had brought up. When Packer's party left the Committee Room they felt everything was going to end satisfactorily. Just before they went out Packer assured the two West Indian delegates that their players would be back in the West Indies in time to play in the series against Australia in March and April. When they returned they had hardly sat down before the chairman said to Packer that it was the unanimous decision of the ICC that they would be unable to grant exclusive television rights in advance which was the property of the Australian Board. Packer replied that if they were having trouble in wording the granting of the television rights it was something for the working committee to decide. But if they were saying that they would not give him a commitment there was indeed a problem. They told him, 'No, that is unacceptable.' Packer himself completes the story:

'I said, "Well, what do we do?"

'They said, "Well, the meeting's over."

'I said, "Thank you very much indeed for your time," and walked out.'

As for the official version a verbal précis was given to me a day or two after the meeting. After the initial introductions Packer appeared to be happy with the idea of a compromise. The ICC produced their five points, to each of which he agreed in principle, and he spoke of the necessity of setting up a working party to discuss the details. Packer insisted that his players would not be victimized, and that he must be guaranteed exclusive television rights in Australia when the 1978/79 season ended. He then suggested that he and his colleagues should withdraw for the delegates to discuss the situation among themselves. Before they went one of the Australian representatives asked Packer if his co-operation depended upon his being able to stage his matches in the peak periods of December and January. Packer replied that he would be mad not to want to play his games then, for it was the most popular period, but that he felt this was an area for discussion. The second question was whether his co-operation depended on his being guaranteed exclusive television rights after the 1978/79 season. 'That, gentlemen,' Packer replied, 'is non-negotiable. I must have that guarantee.'

While he was out of the room the delegates agreed unanimously that he could not be guaranteed exclusive rights for the future, and that exclusive rights in Australia were besides not theirs to grant. But the two Australians said that they would give an undertaking to recommend to their Board that the principle of exclusivity be seriously considered when the present contract expired. Packer then returned, and this was explained to him. He could put in his company's bid along with any others who were interested, it was added. Packer asked if that meant that he would have to stand in the queue and wait his turn with the others. When told that it did he said that he saw no point in continuing the meeting, and left.

The differences in the two accounts come partly from the different emphasis each side put upon the issues. When Packer himself was interviewed he would have made every effort to have appeared reasonable. The important question at the end of it all is whether either side ever had any real intention to compromise except on their own terms. Both had taken up deeply entrenched positions. During his *Sunday Times* interview Packer claimed that if the ICC had agreed to his two points of compromise the Super-Tests would have been played over a six-week period in Sydney for three or four years, and all the players taking part would also have been available to play in official Test cricket. Packer calculated that by reducing his tour in this way he was making a concession of about a million dollars.

For all that, it is important to remember that his compromise course would have been possible only if he had signed the original thirty-five players. Yet already, six weeks after his original plans had been made public, they had been greatly enlarged. He went through the meeting at Lord's without giving any intimation that this was so, however. Only after he left the meeting and angrily addressed the waiting press did he reveal that he did not have just thirty-five players but had signed an entire West Indies side too. This meant that at the time of the meeting he had fifty-one players. It is difficult to accept, therefore, that six weeks' cricket in Sydney would have been enough for him to have fitted in all the cricket he wanted. As he never told the ICC about the West Indian players the sincerity of his stated desire to compromise must be in doubt.

Soon after Packer's dramatic exit from Lord's an Australian businessman commented, 'He has staked so much on this, his reputation included, that I have no doubt he will come out on top. Quite what happens to cricket is another matter, of course.' It was a salutary warning.

It is arguable that pride distorted Packer's judgement while he was in the Lord's Committee Room. He knew that he could not buy the exclusive television rights in Australia for another two years. If he had accepted all that the ICC had given him – and whatever Packer or his supporters say the authorities who had at first refused even to see him had given him more in the five points than he had any right to expect – he would have been granted respectability; his matches would have been played on established grounds; they would have been first-class; and the authorities would have run them for him. If at the end of two years, when the television rights had again come up for auction, the Australian Board had again turned down his offer and he would have been forced to organize his own matches, he would have been in a far better position to judge the mood of the public. For two years he would have been able to watch what was happening while his circus became an accepted part of cricket in Australia, and to alter the format as he felt it was necessary. Above all, if he had accepted the ICC's offer and not pressed for exclusive rights he would have had a foot in the door, and with the money he had at his disposal he would have been in a position of great strength. When Packer was asked why he was so insistent on the guarantee of exclusive television rights on the day after his meeting at Lord's he replied uncompromisingly, 'That was the reason that we got into it from the beginning.'

Shortly afterwards Packer returned to Australia, and his pronouncements at a distance of twelve thousand miles continued the war of nerves he was fighting with Lord's. On 1 July he said, 'My attitude will be much harder if the Boards start victimizing my players. If any action of that sort is taken then there will be an all-out scrap.' He added that retaliatory action could include taking his cricketers to England as well as holding Super-Tests later in the year at the same time and in the same cities as the official Test Matches between Australia and India. A short while after this he threatened to take legal action if his players were banned by the ICC. 'We will claim restraint of trade. I am a man of my word and will stick by my players.' In the same interview he was asked if he had any regrets. 'Yes, I have one: that we could not work out a compromise. I have said all along I wanted to co-operate.'

The annual meeting of the International Cricket Conference was to be held at Lord's on 26 and 27 July, and it was then that the world's cricket authorities would decide what corporate action to take against the players who had signed for Packer. By now the English players who had signed had made it abundantly clear that they would not be available for the England tour of Pakistan and New Zealand in the coming winter, and the others had all reaffirmed their support of Packer and their determination to play for him. This meant that the Packer-signed Pakistanis were unavailable to play against England, and that the Australian signees would not be available for the official series against India.

The ICC had to protect the game that they controlled to prevent
Packer or another similarly-minded tycoon from poaching the best
players from the traditional system. It was likely that the ICC
would propose a ban on the Packer players from Test cricket. The
only country which was unlikely to support this was the West
Indies. As has been seen, they were not immediately affected, and
as Packer had signed their entire side the West Indian population
regarded the team which was to play for Packer in Australia as
fully representative of the West Indies. The West Indian temperament tends to live in emotional extremes on a day-to-day basis,
and there was a considerable public outcry that the heroes who
had made the West Indies the best side in the world might no
longer be allowed to play in Tests. A small island like Antigua has
produced both Andy Roberts and Viv Richards, and the population there are rightly proud of their achievements. It is not surprising that legislation passed at Lord's banning these players
from their rightful place in West Indian cricket should be deeply
resented.

Throughout July forecasts of a ban being imposed grew more
confident, and Packer's threats to take legal action if his players
were banned became stronger. Events in the Packer saga now
moved at such a pace that the only satisfactory way of recording
them is in diary form. In these few days rumour and truth were to
intermingle inseparably, indeed as they had done since Sunday
8 May.

Saturday 23 July: In Sydney Packer launched another tirade
against the Australian Board for refusing to listen to his offer for
exclusive television rights. He said that if he had got the exclusive
rights he would not have been interested in starting his Super-
Tests. 'The Boards are saying how could one man do this? What
one man? I can't do anything. I can't bat and I can't bowl. The
players want it. They are the ones. They are the reason it will be
successful.' He added that he had no idea whether the dates of his
matches would clash with the Australia versus India series. 'But I
don't want to upset them, and I am not doing this out of spite. I
don't want to disrupt Test cricket, but I don't think the present
Board represents the good of cricket. The next Board might, and
I will be right behind them.'

Tuesday 26 July: Jim Laker announced that he had turned down
a five-figure offer from Packer to commentate on his series of

Super-Tests in Australia. 'The time has arrived for everyone to decide which side they are on. I assessed my own loyalties and opted to stay put.' He also said that he did not blame the players for accepting Packer's offers; something like this had been bound to happen sooner or later.

In the evening of the same day Jack Bailey, the *ex officio* secretary of the ICC, issued a statement after the ICC meeting had considered the question of the Packer players. The players were to be banned from playing Test cricket unilaterally.

The ICC had decided to ban from Test cricket the fifty-one players who had signed for Packer and anyone else who made himself available to play in a match disapproved by the conference after 1 October. Any match arranged by JP Sports Ltd, Mr Kerry Packer, Mr Richie Benaud or associated companies or persons to take place in Australia or elsewhere between 1 October 1977 and 31 March 1979 would be disapproved of. 'The conference also strongly recommended that each member country should pursue at first-class level and other domestic cricket activities the implementation of decisions made with regard to Test Matches.'

This was the fateful decision which was to lead the two sides to the High Court and was to end with a bill of about £250,000 for the cricket authorities and an overwhelming victory for Packer. In the light of what was to follow, it is extraordinary that no one accurately foresaw the outcome of the restraint of trade issue, especially as legal advice was taken throughout.

Immediately after the meeting Jack Bailey stressed that the decision had been taken unanimously which makes it appear that the West Indies delegates had not objected to the ban. After lengthy discussions Jeff Stollmeyer, a Trinidadian and Chairman of the West Indies Board, and Allan Rae, a solicitor from Jamaica who opened the batting for the West Indies with Stollmeyer after the war, had agreed to follow the other countries, although they were far from happy with the decision. Neither man felt passionately about Packer, and both were prepared to play a waiting game. They also realized that public opinion in the West Indies would be unable to accept a decision which prevented them from seeing their heroes in Test cricket.

In the morning session the two men had said that while they appreciated the sentiments of the other member countries they would regretfully have to vote against the resolution. Efforts were made to make them change their minds, and eventually it was decided that they would vote again on the resolution after lunch. The strong man on the ICC was Walter Hadlee, chairman of the New Zealand Cricket Council, and he and Tim Caldwell of Australia talked the two West Indians round during lunch. When the vote was retaken the West Indies, for the sake of unanimity, voted with the other countries, although Rae insisted that their reservations be registered in the minutes.

Packer had always said that any form of compromise had to include a promise by the authorities not to victimize his players, and his organization now duly announced that they would be examining the legal implications of the ban. His players for their part immediately reaffirmed their loyalty to Packer; but the ICC announcement made those who were having doubts about the wisdom of joining him even more uncertain.

Wednesday 27 July: In the late evening, the day before the Third Test Match started at Trent Bridge, it was announced in Nottingham that Jeff Thomson had decided to pull out of Packer's circus and that Alvin Kallicharran and Viv Richards were thinking of following suit.

All three players were managed by the Australian journalist David Lord, a former Grade cricketer in Sydney in his early forties. He had run a cricket magazine and had ghosted a book for Tony Greig, and was now trying to make his mark in the agency business. He was a dedicated opponent of Packer, and during the night of 27 July when after frantic activity in the Albany Hotel in Nottingham where the Australians were staying it was announced that Thomson had decided to leave Packer, he said, 'This will be the beginning of the exodus from the Packer circus. I will now be putting the same pressure on my other players as I have been putting on Thommo – because frankly I have been waiting for the moment to break Packer. The players themselves have just followed each other like sheep without thinking about it, but suddenly they have had an attack of brains.'

A year and a half before this Thomson had, with Lord's help, signed a ten-year contract with Radio 4IP in Brisbane which was worth A$630,000 and included a clause which said that he must be available to play for Queensland. The ICC decision to outlaw the Packer players would have prevented Thomson from doing this, and during the Wednesday evening he met Frank Gardiner, an

Australian solicitor who was representing the radio station. Thomson himself said afterwards, 'I realized maybe I was doing the wrong thing. I just went along with the boys. I will now be available for Australia and Queensland for the next three years.' Thomson was in doubt for the tour of England almost up to the day the party left, for he had suffered a serious injury in a Test Match against Pakistan in Adelaide the previous December and this had caused him to have his shoulder pinned. The possible effects of this injury had also put Packer off initially, and Thomson only signed for World Series Cricket just before leaving Australia for England. When later it was decided in the High Court that the ban was illegal Thomson could not have rejoined Packer, because all the Australian State cricketers who would automatically benefit from the large Benson and Hedges sponsorship had to sign a contract promising that they would work for no other promoter at the same time; thus no Packer player could have done this. As it was, by signing for Packer, Thomson was breaking his contract with Radio 4IP and, although Packer threatened to sue Thomson, he took no action, almost certainly on legal advice. In the light of this it was surprising to read of unconfirmed reports in August 1978, even though Thomson's radio station was now owned by a company in Sydney, that he was about to rejoin Packer and World Series Cricket.

Thomson had been a maligned figure, for his public image of the fast bowler who hates batsmen and loves to hurt them with his bouncers is very wide of the mark. Yet his reputation had been won even before he began to play regular Test cricket against England in 1974/75, for as a teenager he had struck a football referee and had been banned from the game for life in Australia, a ban which has only recently been lifted. At first he was much more of an innocent than an agitator, but Ian Chappell was happy to perpetuate his image, telling him who he should talk to and who he should not bother with. Of course, he matured and the true Thomson was seen in the West Indies when he was Bobby Simpson's vice-captain.

While the Packer organization refused to comment about Thomson or the other possible defections, the *Australian Financial Review*, a newspaper widely read and respected by the business community and similar to the British *Financial Times*, foretold of the legal problems which would come from the decision to ban the players from Test cricket. The *Review* argued that Packer and his players would be entitled to take the Australian Board to court for breaking Australian trade practices legislation. The threat of the ban might easily prove to be illegal and in restraint of trade. This was the first warning of the legal battles which were to follow.

Thursday 28 July: It was widely rumoured that Len Pascoe, Thomson's partner with the new ball and one of his best friends, was also contemplating breaking his contract with Packer. Pascoe's real name is Durtanovich, for he came to Australia with his parents from Poland and was the first New Australian to play Test cricket. His agent had come to England and held discussions with his client. Meanwhile Lord confirmed that he had followed up his threat and had advised Kallicharran and Richards, who were also contracted to Australian radio companies, to follow Thomson's example – although the players themselves now denied that they were likely to withdraw.

On the same day, in Australia, Packer's legal advisers were carefully examining the contracts which his players had signed with JP Sports Ltd in case there were loopholes; Packer was not going to let his players desert if he could avoid it. There were reports circulating round the press boxes and the committee rooms in England that some players had signed under considerable pressure, and in one instance before a player could consult his manager or legal advisers. Packer himself decided to return immediately to England in order to forestall any further defections.

It was reported also in Australia that Packer was now likely to be allowed to use the Sydney Cricket Ground. The ground is controlled by a Trust, who had originally turned Packer away; the Labour Government of New South Wales had then sacked the members of the Trust. Those appointed to succeed them were expected to favour Packer.

Sunday 31 July: Before leaving Australia Packer rang up Kallicharran to tell him that he could not break his contract and that he would be sued if he tried to return his £400 signing-on fee. A lawyer representing Packer set out to see Kallicharran. The West Indian had meanwhile been advised by Lord and his Warwickshire captain, David Brown, who did not want pressure put on one of his leading players, not to attend the meeting. It did not take place.

Monday 1 August: Rumours from Australia said that Packer

was coming to England in order to remove his contracted Australian players from the current series. When he arrived he went immediately to his suite at the Dorchester Hotel from which he did not emerge all day. Instead he consulted with his lawyers, for there were still doubts about the legality of his own contracts. That morning he had found himself confronted by another opponent, for an English businessman, Mr David Evans, the head of an office cleaning company, had come forward with a plan costing half a million pounds to 'beat Packer and save English cricket'.

Mr Evans had for a long time been a cricket supporter, and he was also a friend of Mike Brearley, who had been privy to Mr Evans's intended offer although he was later surprised that there should have been so many conditions attached to it. Evans's plan was to buy back the contracts of the five English players who had signed for Packer, to pay each England player £1000 for every Test Match, and to pay a retainer of £1000 a year to fifty top English cricketers as long as they guaranteed their availability for England. But it was not quite as straightforward as it sounded. Evans said that he was doing this first for his company and second for cricket, and that the money would be forthcoming only so long as other companies and organizations agreed to place three-million-pounds-worth of cleaning business with his company. He would then come forward with the £500,000 needed to finance his plan. It was hardly a reliable scheme and was never in itself taken seriously, but Evans was later to play an important part in raising the Test fee for England players to £1000 a match. He also met Packer together with Brearley during the Leeds Test Match.

Tuesday 2 August: Packer announced that he was going to start proceedings before a High Court judge to prevent the ICC and the TCCB from banning his players from Test and county cricket. He also said that some of his players would be seeking damages from and bringing injunctions against the two authorities; Greig, Snow and Procter were the three chosen at random to do this. Rather ambiguously, he then stated that 'if need be' he would take legal action against Thomson and Kallicharran. He also began proceedings against David Lord on the grounds that Lord had wrongfully induced Thomson and Kallicharran to break their contracts with JP Sports Ltd. Actions against the authorities were beginning in Australia.

As usual Packer tried to obtain the maximum publicity from

his actions. 'I believe the restrictions by the ICC and the TCCB to be unlawful,' he said. 'I'm doing this from the goodness of my own heart, not at the request of any of the players. I am acting more in the role of a benevolent uncle. I am convinced what I am doing is for the benefit of international cricket.' He also said that most of his players had been given personal guarantees from his television empire for the amounts due to them over the next three years within the terms of their contracts.

Almost incidentally, and against this background of intensive legal activity, England won the Third Test Match at Trent Bridge by seven wickets to give them a 2–0 lead in the series. On his return to Test cricket after a self-imposed exile of three years Boycott made 107 and 80 not out, Knott made a brilliant 135 and Botham, in his first Test Match, took five wickets in Australia's first innings.

Wednesday 3 August: Trans-World International, the television sporting group in London, acquired the British rights for Packer's Super-Tests. Head of the group is Mark McCormack, the American who manages most of the leading international golf and tennis players, and who once was Geoff Boycott's agent. It was an indication that Packer was already looking to the American television market as an outlet for some of his cricket, probably the one-day games.

In the High Court, Mr Justice Slynn reserved his decision for twenty-four hours on the injunctions being sought by the Packer organization and by Greig, Snow and Procter. Similar actions began in Australia, in the Supreme Court in Sydney and the Federal Court in Melbourne. It was also reported in Australia that Greig's contract with Waverley for whom he plays Grade cricket in Sydney was worth more than £45,000, and that Kerry Packer was among residents of New South Wales who had been awarded the Queen's Jubilee Medal. Back in London Packer arranged a meeting of all his players at the Dorchester Hotel, even flying Pollock and Hobson over from South Africa for the purpose. Both Packer and his players reaffirmed their loyalty to one another, while the players were reminded of the legal consequences should they break their contracts.

Thursday 4 August: Mr Justice Slynn refused to grant two injunctions sought against the ICC and the TCCB, but only after the two bodies had undertaken not to implement any ban on players contracted to Packer until after a full hearing. This was in effect a victory for Packer, for the ban had been put off until it could be judged. The injunction against Lord was granted, and although Lord said he would appeal nothing came of it.

On BBC television that evening Packer spoke about his contracts. 'I make no apologies for the fact that the contract is tough. I told every player, "This is a tough contract and you'll do as you're damn well told." I mean, this was never meant to be a garden party, and it was always intended that they had to behave. They were becoming full-time professional sportsmen. They were going to be paid a great deal more money than they had ever been paid before in their lives, and they were expected to behave in a fashion befitting people who were full-time, properly-paid professional sportsmen. There will be no mucking around. You're starting something which is completely new and, like Caesar's wife, you must be beyond reproach. I mean, you've just got to behave on and off the field. There will be no nonsense.'

When asked about the hostile reaction his plans had received, he said, 'I have stepped into an area which the cricket writers of the world feel is their own domain, and I think they look upon me as some form of threat. The hysteria which has come from these people has helped whip it up among people who don't quite understand what has been happening. Of course, among many of the players I am far from Enemy Number One, and a great many of those players are very happy with the arrangements which have been made.'

Tuesday 9 August: Mike Brearley, England's captain, was promised a cheque of £9000 before the start of the Fourth Test Match the following day as part of a fund set up by three businessmen and arranged by David Evans to defeat Packer. It was suggested that the money should be given to the nine players not contracted to Packer, but Brearley replied that he would be unhappy for the money to be divided in that way, for no one as yet had been banned from anything. In the event, the whole side shared the money.

Wednesday 10 August: Subject to the ruling in the High Court – then expected in September – the Test and County Cricket Board announced that they intended to ban from English county cricket all those players who appeared for Packer in his proposed series of matches in Australia the coming winter, or in any other matches disapproved of by the International Cricket Conference. The ban, if allowed to stand by the High Court, was to last for two years from the last day of the last disapproved match in which a player had taken part or for which he had been available for selection.

By mid-August the main issues were in the hands of the lawyers and the pace of events slackened. Packer's presence in London kept all those involved on the alert as they tried to anticipate his next move, but the shadow of the High Court hearing hung like a pall of black smoke over the rest of the summer. During the last two weeks in August both Chris Old and Bob Willis were approached by Greig and invited to join Packer. At some point Derek Randall was also approached. None of these three accepted, but towards the end of the summer Bob Woolmer was also approached and he signed gleefully.

Stories kept filtering through from Australia where Packer's pitches were being grown in greenhouses and general preparations were going ahead. England won the Fourth Test at Headingley by an innings and 85 runs and regained the Ashes. Boycott scored his hundredth hundred in front of his home crowd and the Australian side was again shown to be extremely weak: the Australians, all of whom except for Thomson were Packer men, were not a good advertisement for their new boss. It was while the Fourth Test was in progress that I had another fascinating meeting with Packer, one which threw an interesting light on the man himself and his relationship with his players.

On the rest day of the Fourth Test a match had been arranged between the English press and the Australian press on the county ground at Harrogate and no less a person than Kerry Packer was going to turn out for the Australians at the suggestion of Ian Chappell, who was commentating on the Test series for BBC TV. I had been selected for the English side, and drove up to Harrogate with two friends, Joanna Briffa and Morag Brownlow, who had come up to watch the cricket on the Saturday. The afternoon was given an ironical twist by the presence of David Lord in the Australian side and also two journalists whom Packer was suing for libel (the cases were later dropped), while the English side included Peter Lush, Public Relations Officer for the Test and County Cricket Board.

One had to admire Packer for taking on his opponents in so open a fashion. About half an hour before the start he drove up with Ian Chappell. He was very cheerful, although he was at once submerged by journalists on the ground floor of the pavilion. Politely, he attended to their needs, and then asked to be allowed to enjoy himself in peace. 'Look,' he said, 'we're all here for a civilized afternoon. Cricket is a very civilized game.' It was his first game of cricket for eight years. He changed into immaculate kit, which he had bought at Harrods some days before and had then brought up with him in his private aeroplane. The Australians batted first and there was just time for Packer to come in at the end of the innings. He faced seven balls and scored two not out, but his greatest moment of the afternoon came later on when he was fielding in the slips.

Peter Lush of the TCCB, the only English batsman to make the Australian total of over 200 look in any danger, had reached fifty and was facing the seam bowling of David Lord. Lush played a cut and the ball flew off the edge to first slip where Packer held a sharp chance up by his chest. Only cricket could have produced such an absurd situation. In the end the Australians won comfortably and afterwards we filled the bar, where Packer was extremely relaxed. After a time he turned to Joanna and Morag who were talking in the same group and suggested that they might like to have dinner with his party. I interrupted and said that if he was going to give them dinner he was going to have to give me dinner as well. Packer smiled.

We drove back to Leeds and had dinner at the Dragonara Hotel, where the England side and Packer himself were staying. While we were having a drink Tony Greig, who had borrowed Packer's aeroplane to fly up to a benefit match during the day in Durham, joined us. Also present were Ian Chappell and King Watson, the editor of Sir Frank Packer's Sydney *Daily Telegraph* from 1953 to 1970 and now in charge of Packer's Consolidated Press Holdings in London.

When we sat down Greig gave an account of his day and then the conversation turned to cricket. It was fascinating to see the way in which Packer seemed to hang on Greig's every word. Packer's answer would be that Greig is an expert about cricket, while he is not. Greig is a definite enough character but so too is Packer, and yet he hardly queried anything which Greig said. Packer may not be an academic but he is an astute businessman with little to fear from anyone. When I was in Australia I saw a photograph of him and Jack Nicklaus on the golf course at Kensington. Nicklaus was pointing at something while Packer sat smirking in the latest of the mechanized golf buggies. Packer likes to be seen with the top performers in whatever sport it is – another reason possibly why he has found it so easy to fight the battles of so many of the world's leading cricketers.

It was during dinner that night that I learned that Packer never touched alcohol. 'I've got to have some vices to enjoy in my old age,' he said, smiling. 'I don't do it through any sense of conviction, though. When I was twelve my father bribed me not to drink before I was twenty-one. He said he would give me a big new car if I didn't. When I got to twenty-one I thought I held all the cards, but I was out-negotiated. All I got was a second-hand Triumph.'

When we had started to eat Chappell asked Packer if he had signed Ashley 'Rowdy' Mallett yet. Packer looked at him and said good-humouredly, 'You know I don't think he can bowl.'

Chappell was mildly indignant and reminded Packer of a bet they had made. Packer had said that Mallett would never get him out, and Chappell had replied that he would back the South Australian off-spinner to bowl Packer in about ten balls. Packer was not impressed, and it looked as if Mallett would never have the chance. Then Greig spoke on Mallett's behalf and from different parts of the room Alan Knott and Derek Underwood were called over. They were asked their opinions of Mallett, and both said he was a fine bowler. Knott went so far as to describe him as the best off-spinner he had ever faced. Packer took all this in, and when Knott and Underwood had returned to their tables he said, 'Well, we'll see.' It was not long before Mallett had signed a contract.

Conversation then turned to umpiring, and Greig said he thought David Constant was the best of the English umpires now that he had the confidence to give a few people out. Packer was interested, and remarked that he had always thought that Dickie Bird had been considered to be the best. Greig said again that in his opinion Constant was the best, and Packer seemed surprised. Greig then leant across the table and said quietly to Packer, 'Do you want him?'

It was a simple enough question, but it was done with such an air of arch-conspiracy. There was in Greig's voice the implication that if Packer so much as nodded his head in reply he would be able to arrange it in a matter of moments. This was a question which Greig, as Packer's agent in recruiting the Rest of the World side, had presumably put to Packer on many other occasions, and he had probably been used to receiving the answer 'yes'. This time Packer contented himself with another, 'We'll see.' Constant never went to Australia.

For a time after that they talked about the Australian summer when they would all be in Australia. Packer told Greig about some of his plans for October when Nicklaus would be in Australia for the Open. When it was over he was taking him to New Zealand for some fishing. 'Do you want to come too?' he asked Greig.

Greig thought for a moment, 'Yes, I shall be in Sydney then. That'll be fine, I'll come.' It was as if he was doing Packer a favour.

Packer was an extremely good host, and unlike many tee-totallers he saw that the wine kept circulating. The conversation eventually turned to the present situation and his fight with the cricket authorities. He spoke of the attitude of the press, who had been heavily against him. Looking at me, he said that it was strange how on these occasions the press behaved like so many Victorian matrons when at other times they took up endless column inches criticizing the establishment. I said nothing.

'Yes, Blowers,' Greig began beside me in a loud voice, and looking over his left shoulder, 'you were one of those who rubbished me over that Kallicharran thing in the West Indies, weren't you?'

'Greigy,' I said, smiling, 'you were very ill-advised then and you deserved all you got.'

'Did you hear that, Kerry?' Greig asked across the table. 'Go on, Blowers, tell Kerry what you said to me just then.'

I repeated what I had said, and when I had finished Greig laughed loudly and said to Packer, 'There, you see what I mean about the press.' Packer smiled.

Not long after this exchange Packer said to me, 'Of course, there will be free trips arranged so that you'll be able to come out and watch us in Australia.' It was the last I ever heard of this, but I did say at the time, 'As long as that is not intended to affect what I write.'

The cricketers left soon after that and for half an hour before the girls had to catch the sleeper to London, Packer talked at great length about baseball and golf and tennis in America. He had studied all three games with a view to televising them and he knew a good deal about the American approach to sport. It was fascinating.

During dinner Packer had said that he was going back to London on the same train, the sleeper, which Joanna and Morag were catching. I left the table with the two girls at about eleven o'clock to buy tickets at the station which was three minutes' walk away and Packer gave me his ticket in order that I could reserve a sleeper for him. He said he would meet us on the platform. We made the reservations and waited until midnight when the train left, but he did not turn up.

The events of the second half of that evening are related in detail in Mike Brearley's *Return of the Ashes*. Mike had left the table to go to bed at about half past ten. Half an hour later Tony Greig came into his room and asked him to go and talk privately with Kerry Packer in his bedroom. Greig and Ian Chappell were there, and for a time they talked about Packer's overall plans.

He (Packer) said, 'Let's come to the point. What do you think of the idea of me signing up the whole England team? As you know I've got the West Indians and the Australian team, and what I would like to see is if the full England team could take on the full Australian team with the Chappells and Lillee. What a tremendous bill!'

I hedged. 'From what point of view, what do I think of the idea?' It struck me as odd if he thought I could answer for players other than myself. It also struck me that without the captain there could be no 'whole' England team. Was this an academic question?

'Come on,' he said. 'Would you do it?'

'No,' I replied. I had of course like other Test players considered the possibility of being invited. I had decided that I did not want to join, let alone recruit.

After that the conversation became general again and both Brearley and Greig stressed that they did not want a head-on collision between Packer and the TCCB. Brearley also suggested that Packer might talk to the representatives of the Cricketers' Association which he did at the Dorchester the next Thursday. Brearley also knew that David Evans was keen to try and bring about a suitable compromise and before they went to bed it was decided to ask Evans to Leeds the following evening. By then England had won the Fourth Test and the Ashes and at eight o'clock the same four met in Packer's room.

Evans arrived at nine o'clock. Evans and Packer had met before and had liked each other. Evans's suggestion was that Packer should join a consortium of businessmen who were determined to support first-class cricket in England. Packer declared yet again that he had no quarrel with English cricket, yet they were heading for all-out war. If the TCCB saw that Packer was prepared, whether privately or publicly, to help the financing of the Test Matches of 1978, might they not postpone their ban on his players for a year? I was in favour of such a moratorium. I suggested that perhaps, too, Packer would agree not to sign any more England players during this period. Packer did not respond to that; perhaps he had already decided to invite Willis, Woolmer and Randall to join him. He was prepared to offer a financial inducement to have the ban called off. He told Evans that if the TCCB accepted such an offer they would have an extra £50,000 and no expensive law suit. For a year negotiations could go on.

Evans put the proposals to the TCCB, two of whose members, Raman Subba Row and Bernie Coleman, had already met Packer unofficially in Brighton – they felt the two sides should somehow accommodate each other – and they were turned down. If they had accepted them Packer would in effect have taken control of the TCCB.

Within a day or two Packer had departed to Australia and once again became just a name in the British newspapers. Each day I read of his plans to convert Australian Rules Football Stadiums into cricket grounds, his intentions if he lost or won in the High Court, the number of lawyers he had working for him, his declarations that he was not going to gain anything himself from the case, which would yet cost him a quarter of a million pounds. Finally there was his belief that fifty cricketers had given themselves to him and he was not going to let them down. Already the High Court case was a massive public relations exercise.

♦

CHAPTER 7

Glamorgan's Number Ten

WHEN PACKER'S PLANS were first announced Greig had told the world that he had agreed to better the lot of the ordinary first-class cricketer, as it were the Glamorgan Number Ten. Neither he nor Packer were ever explicit about how this would happen. What were the views and reactions of the county players in England, the cricketers who formed the base of the pyramid and who made it possible for Greig and others to climb to the top?

At first many first-class cricketers wanted to hear about Packer's plans in more detail before making up their minds, and the immediate reactions I came across in England in early May varied according to the ability and the characters of the players concerned, and their opinion of Tony Greig. Those who were in or around the England side dreamed initially of themselves receiving a cheque from Packer, and felt that, before the full implications had become clear, Packer's concept of cricket should be given a chance. There were others who felt, just as reasonably, that this sudden influx of money should not be turned down out of hand: cricket was too poor to throw away money on this scale. Then there were those in county cricket who were known to dislike or even distrust Greig, and they would not hear of it. Greig was also known to be extremely money-conscious, and many resented the way in which he had exploited himself over the previous two years. Perhaps more importantly, many of the ordinary county players soon became suspicious of Packer, for they saw his plans as a threat to their own livelihoods. County cricket was financially insecure, and depended largely on the distribution of the profits from Test Matches and the increasing amount of sponsorship. More money was coming into county cricket, in particular through the Schweppes sponsorship, and although not enough was as yet reaching the players a start had been made, and it was felt that conditions could only improve.

At Hove during the week the Packer story broke I came across two reactions from the Lancashire side. Jack Simmons's comment was that when asked by Greig what he thought of it all he had told him to bring two contracts into the Lancashire dressing room and see what happened – but that could be taken either way. They would probably have been eagerly signed, but whether Simmons would have been the first to get out his pen is another matter. On another occasion I mentioned to Barry Wood that I thought that the players would have shown more loyalty to established cricket. Wood simply laughed. And Lancashire pay their players more than any other county.

Another interesting reaction at the outset was put to me by John Lever, who had toured India, Sri Lanka and Australia under Greig in the months before Packer appeared. During this tour he formed a high respect for Greig as a captain. He had helped Lever, listening to him and advising him about his bowling and had played a considerable part in turning him into an extremely useful Test cricketer. Lever's opinion was shared by many of the others. When Greig revealed the extent of Packer's plans early in May these same players were naturally unwilling to accept the hostile interpretation of most of the press. They were sure that he had been misjudged or misinterpreted. Greig had inspired such loyalty; but when the players found they had been let down their reaction was correspondingly bitter.

Going round England in the following weeks I came across more opposition than support for Packer and considerable hostility towards Greig. As often happens in similar situations, those supporting Packer were more articulate than those defending the *status quo*. Those who had contracts with Packer would try to persuade their colleagues of the advantages of signing, and here no one did more than Greig. This was understandable, for he had isolated himself from the authorities and needed all the support he could find on the 'shop floor'. Throughout the season there was often tension and suspicion in dressing rooms which contained Packer players. On the county circuit it was almost the sole topic of conversation, and it was not surprising that cricket itself suffered. Thus for most of the 1977 season the principal participants in first-class cricket in England played the game with a large part of their minds elsewhere. For instance, I watched Warwickshire's last game of the season, against Kent, at Edgbaston on 7, 8, 9 September. Kent won, and so became joint county champions. This match was played soon after the Extraordinary General Meeting of the Players' Association, and their vote in favour of the ban on the Packer players from county cricket. John Whitehouse, one of the most articulate of the anti-Packer spokesmen at the meeting, now found himself at the start of the match standing in the slips next to Amiss, who had of course by that time signed for Packer. Even before the first ball had been bowled they had begun to talk and they carried on throughout most of the Kent innings. When they were fielding at mid-off and extra-cover the conversation continued, and twice they were so preoccupied that they had to be reminded to change over for a left-hander.

From the point of view alone of keeping the peace among cricketers, England were extremely lucky to have Brearley to take over from Greig. Neither an establishment nor a non-establishment figure, he appreciated the reasons why the players had joined Packer, and considered the proposed ban from county cricket by the TCCB to be unfair. Again, he had felt for a long time that cricketers were miserably rewarded, and when in 1976 Middlesex won the county championship he had ensured that photographers and interviewers paid for the privilege. However, he did not like the idea of players being allowed to play Test cricket as and when they or Packer said they could, and in the end of course himself turned down the chance to join Packer's circus.

Opposition to Packer was not left to Lord's or the leading individual cricketers, however. The Player's Association, under John Arlott's presidency with David Brown, the Warwickshire and England fast bowler as Chairman, and Jack Bannister as secretary, was worried about the long-term implications of Packer, and cannot have been happy when it looked as if some of their own members would be banned from county cricket. The Executive decided to ask Packer for a meeting, and in time they went along to the Dorchester Hotel. Packer brought Greig with him, a natural move but a pity, for it was Greig rather than Packer who talked the most, and the Executive wanted to hear Packer's plans for the future, not those of England's ex-captain. During the meeting Packer explained how he had offered the TCCB £180,000 for the exclusive coverage in Australia of the next Ashes series in England, and that this offer had not been accepted because the TCCB had agreed that the Australian rights were now the property of the Australian Cricket Board. And the Board, of course, had been less than pleased that Packer had been allowed to buy the exclusive rights for the 1977 tour. This story of Packer's, drawing sympathy from the Executive, was all part of a plan followed throughout his negotiations to turn the players against the authorities – in this instance, the TCCB. For the Executive later discovered that the £180,000 included derisory amounts for the exclusive coverage in Australia of some of the intervening series in England against the other touring sides and the World Cup in 1979, and that the amount specifically put aside for the Australian series in England was therefore much less than £180,000. This discovery almost certainly hardened the Executive against Packer.

The Extraordinary General Meeting of the Association was held at Edgbaston early in September and by a seemingly narrow majority of fourteen the players voted in favour of the ban. Greig hoped that his oratory would be able to sway the meeting, and had organized a coach from Hove for all the contracted Sussex players, confident that he could count on their votes. It was not altogether a dignified exercise, and in the words of one player at the meeting Greig 'had scraped together every member of the groundstaff at Hove.' In spite of this, one of the younger capped Sussex players, John Barclay, asked for a secret ballot. In his actual address to the meeting Greig took the line that here was Packer with an enormous amount of money and that it made sense to milk him for as much as possible, and then try to push his cricket into a small corner of the year, leaving the rest of it free for normal Test and first-class cricket. I wonder how pleased Packer would have been to hear this – unless of course it was a method of approach they had worked out together.

The vote in favour of the ban was 91 for and 77 against, but these figures are misleading. The Somerset and Hampshire sides were involved in the Scarborough Festival and could not be at the meeting, and they asked if their block vote might be accepted. This was refused by the Executive. Hampshire's vote had been fifteen in favour of the ban and one against and one abstention – thus, remarkably, with Barry Richards abstaining, either Andy Roberts or Gordon Greenidge, both Packer men, must have voted in favour of the ban. One of them must have been exceedingly bored with county cricket – probably Roberts who like Richards terminated his contract with Hampshire by mutual agreement during the 1978 season. The majority of the Somerset players were said to be also in favour of the ban, and the votes of these two counties would have swelled considerably the final margin. As it was, about forty of the 77 votes against belonged to the overseas players, and with the Sussex vote on top of that the final figures represent a strong vote in favour of the ban by the English county cricketers. There was another complication at the meeting, for the resolution was worded in such a way that some players were confused and thought they were voting on the continued presence of overseas players in county cricket!

Many of the English cricketers felt that if the Packer players were allowed to continue in county cricket they would regard its matches only as practice for the Packer games. They would not then be as committed as the ordinary county player, and county cricket would be devalued. This meeting also agreed by 120 votes to 55 that the ICC and the TCCB be urged to reopen negotiations with Packer on the condition that he was prepared to alter the dates of his Super-Tests to avoid a clash with the official Test Matches in Australia against India. They voted thus because most appreciated how drastic it would be to ban, and hoped that by talking to Packer something might be worked out. Bannister wrote to Packer telling him of the resolution, but never received a reply.

Greig was visibly annoyed at these proceedings, and as the meeting broke up protested that the wording of the two motions had meant that nothing had been achieved, and it had been a farce. However, the indisputable fact was that English county cricketers had voted in favour of banning their own members from playing in county cricket; and as if to emphasize the strength of their feelings the following January in Karachi, when the England players were on the point of refusing to play a Test Match against Packer players, one of their main complaints was that no attention had hitherto been given to their views.

The players' initial interest and reaction to Packer's proposals were motivated by a mixture of self-interest and curiosity. Many wanted to hear Greig spell out his initial comment when he said that cricketers all down the line would benefit from the action he and others had taken. In one way Greig was fortunate that as the summer progressed the opposition of the establishment and the support it received produced a sudden increase in the amount of money coming into Test cricket; but the Glamorgan Number Ten was still having a job to keep pace with inflation.

Packer's plans and Greig's words had brought the low payment of county cricketers and their hazardous conditions of employment sharply into focus. The greatest drawback to a career in county cricket has long been its uncertainty. Payment has not been good, but the game itself has generated so little money that there has simply been no more to go round. Each year the counties depend for their survival on the hand-out of the season's profits from the Test and County Cricket Board, and this in turn is dependent on the weather, the popularity of the touring side, the closeness of the Test series and the enthusiasm of the various sponsors – all variables from year to year. Just recently more money had come into English cricket, but committees were still mindful of the lean patch in the 1960s, and if enough had still not been coming through to the players it was because the authorities had been trying to build up their assets by making expensive capital improvements in order to stabilize the position should there be another lean period. It is a form of insurance, or good husbandry. The time had come, though, when new sponsors had to ensure that more of the money they put into the game went into the players' pockets. In such a delicate situation goodwill is crucially important.

Packer's arrival on the scene had not only had an immediate effect on the amount of money being paid to the county players, but he also caused the haphazard contractual arrangements to be regularized. In the days before Packer a basic contract was usually sent by the county club to the individual players. Often it was not returned or even signed, and in one or two instances with overseas players at the end of one season they had received a letter from their club thanking them for their services and hoping that they would again be available the following year. This was left as their only guarantee of future employment, yet it is not something even enforceable at law. These contracts were mostly for five months' duration, leaving the player free to take on another job in the winter. This might have suited an independently-minded bachelor, but it did not offer much security to the player married with children and with a sizeable mortgage to pay off. The failure of established cricket in England at Test or county level to contract their players during the winter months, thereby giving the job a greater degree of permanency, was made much of by Mr Justice Slade in his summing up in the High Court judgement. For all that, cricket has always been that sort of game, and haphazard though the system was it had seemed to work – until Packer's formidable challenge showed how ineffectual and inadequate it was.

It must be remembered that before the sudden appearance of Packer the players were not threatening industrial action, and there seemed to be a tacit acceptance of the gradual but hardly adequate improvement which was taking place. In the winter of 1975/76 Greig had successfully turned himself into cricket's first superstar when he went to Australia to play Grade cricket in Sydney, making somewhere between fifty and a hundred thousand dollars – the first indication of what cricketers who appear to the public as 'characters' with a strong personal image might be able to do for themselves. Greig was also captain of England, which gave him an important advantage. The life of the Glamorgan Number Ten consists of five months of cricket, constantly travelling around England driving long distances in the evening or the early morning from one county to the next, from one hotel to another – at times an arduous existence and one which many people would reject in favour of a nine-to-five job behind an office desk. There is still some prestige to be gained from playing county cricket, however, and even if, each year from late July, the winter for some is a time of struggle and anti-climax, the arrival of the New Year and later the first snowdrops revives a spirit of eager anticipation. Then, at the back of the minds of all but the most successful players must be lurking the thought that at the age of forty, if not earlier, all this must end. What then? A thousand first-class runs for ten to fifteen seasons or somewhere between fifty and eighty wickets a year are not ideal qualifications for the next thirty years of life.

In the summer of 1977 the best of the overseas players in county cricket were earning some £6000 a year from their clubs. The senior capped English players earned £3500, the junior capped players around £2500, while some of the youngest players received little over £1000 a year. They were all able to supplement these earnings by appearance money, by cash for winning, and by picking up bonus points in the Championship, but although these were nice extras they did not add up to enough to change a player's lifestyle. In the last few years garages have begun to lend players new cars as a form of advertising, and for the top players there can be opportunities in journalism. There is also some demand for ghosted autobiographies, while a number of players find themselves being used for promotional purposes. In the close season there is the prospect of a coaching job abroad, and occasionally well-known players may be taken temporarily on to the payroll of some big company for publicity reasons. But our Glamorgan Number Ten may often be looking with alarm at the dole queue, his total income still some way below the national average.

No one at present playing county cricket was first lured into the game by the amount of money he was likely to make out of it. In fact, the poor pay for county cricketers must have put off a number of talented young players from ever considering cricket as a career. Anyone who is less than totally dedicated would soon realize the overwhelming financial advantages of many alternative means of employment. It must seem surprising to the uninitiated that so many people remain in county cricket – there are about 250 such cricketers active in England at any one time – for such slender rewards. Yet there is one great inducement. For all its frustrations and irritations county cricket offers a strangely compelling way of life. Only a person who lives on the cricket circuit will probably appreciate this, but friends both new and old, favourite hotels and friendly pubs, plus the constant chatter of cricket which for some never palls, all help to make it such. I have heard many players complain about it, yet when the time comes for them to retire many find it a great wrench to do so.

To cricketers involved in a pay structure of this kind Kerry Packer's offers were obviously attractive. Nonetheless, four of England's cricketers – Boycott, Willis, Old and Randall – turned them down, all for slightly different personal reasons, but with their love of and preference for the traditional form of cricket the strong common denominator.

Boycott was the first player to turn down Packer's offer, made to him at the time of the Centenary Test Match in Melbourne. As we have seen there are various stories about Boycott's failing to be-

come a Packer player. It was said at first that he had refused because he wanted either to captain the Rest of the World himself or
to choose the captain. Boycott told me his version of the story in
the transit lounge at Colombo Airport on his journey from
Karachi to Auckland by way of Singapore as England's captain.

He had been in Australia the previous winter playing Grade
cricket for Waverley – the same club that Greig had joined. At the
same time John Spencer of Sussex was coaching in Sydney, and
Spencer had spent some time with Kerry Packer's son. Packer
was delighted at the boy's improvement, and thus inspired decided
to set up a coaching clinic in Sydney, to which scheme he gave a
great deal of publicity. Spencer wanted Boycott to take part.

'John Spencer approached me through a Waverley guy called
Ian McFarline. Waverley had already said that they wanted me
back the next season, and I had said I would come. It only remained for them to find situations where I could earn enough
money. They had to find me work. This seemed ideal, for then I
could play and coach if the contracts were properly drawn up.
McFarline had told me that Spencer was putting together this
coaching scheme for a six-week period, and that during mid-
February it had been suggested that I should be the named player
to sell it around. I talked to Spencer on the telephone, who told me
that Packer wanted to see me.

'I went to his office the Tuesday before the Centenary Test. We
spoke for five minutes about the coaching scheme and then he
dropped the subject and told me that he was going to tell me something confidential, and that he wanted my assurance that whatever
happened I would keep it confidential. I gave him my word, and
kept it until he accused me in late May of turning down his offer
because I wanted to be captain. Only then did I make a statement
to make my position clear.

'At that meeting he went on to tell me that in the next Australian season he was putting on a series between a World XI and
an Australian XI which would include some of the players who had
just retired like Ian Chappell, Ross Edwards and Ian Redpath.
Australia were only playing India, which would not be of much
interest, and would I be interested in playing for his World
Eleven? I said yes, as I was anyway coming back to play for
Waverley. Packer then began to pick my brains about the best
players in the world. He asked me who I thought were good players

and then he asked about the captaincy. I said, why not consider me? My thoughts were that a lot of people would not be available because of tours. It should be remembered that at this point Boycott had not returned to Test cricket. He asked about Greig and I said he would be with England in Pakistan and New Zealand.

'Next he asked me about Clive Lloyd. The West Indies had no tour, but Clive was not the right man to get a world side together. I told him the track record of the West Indies in Australia was bad. Only Frank Worrell was a good captain, and even he lost. We talked about Eddie Barlow. I told him he hadn't captained an international side although he is very good and I have a lot of respect for him. He then asked me who I suggested. I told him Ray Illingworth. His track record as captain is excellent, and I knew his personal ability. If you want the best side to play well he'll make them play. For some reason he dismissed Illingworth.

'Then Packer said to me, "Well, I'd like you to play." I said I would, for I thought it was a one-off situation. He never talked of the length of time it was going to continue, and he did not tell me that his series would be against official cricket. He roughly mentioned money, and said he would send someone to see me. I asked him about the coaching, and he told me to forget about that. Packer and I shook hands on the deal and when I left I still didn't know who the captain would be.

'Austin Robertson came to see me at the Melbourne Cricket Ground during the Centenary Test Match. He showed me the official contract, but he would not let me take it away and show it to my solicitor. It was renegotiable after a period of three years and he never intimated that by signing I might be unable to play for Yorkshire. He said that secrecy was the reason I could not take away a copy of the contract, but said that he was coming to England soon to sign up players, and was also coming to look for suitable grounds where they could play in the future. I asked him if he meant county grounds and he said, "No, I mean other grounds." This set me thinking, and he said he would come and see me in England when I told him I couldn't sign the contract in this form. Playing in England was the main stumbling block. After that I never heard from him or Packer again.'

I reminded Boycott of a story I had heard during the summer of 1977 that John Spencer had asked Boycott to run his eye over Packer's son in the nets and that Packer had not liked Boycott's attitude. He also told me about this. 'He's a nice boy, and I went up to the net in the garden some time after Christmas and he wasn't a bad little player. His father was there, and he has strong views about his son's cricket – with which I disagreed. Dad thought he knew more about cricket than me. I told him that making money was his job and playing cricket was mine. He was a lovely boy, though, and a nice little cricketer.'

Knowing Boycott, I am sure he was more interested in the captaincy of the Rest of the World than he admits, and if he had appreciated the size of Packer's plans he might have had second thoughts; but I would never doubt a Yorkshireman's loyalty to his county.

Willis and Old were both approached by Greig towards the end of the English season. Both players said that he did not try to put them under any pressure. Greig rang Old at his home in Yorkshire and asked him if he would like to join, but Old quickly told him that he was not interested. He had a Benefit in two years' time, and said that he was not going to jeopardize that. He never considered accepting Packer's offer, he says, since he enjoys playing for Yorkshire and England and he wants to go on playing the game he knows.

Randall nobly tried to keep Packer's approach and his decision not to join him a secret. He was being well paid by Nottinghamshire and preferred, like Old, to play the cricket he knew.

Greig also rang Willis, who was offered a three-year contract at £15,000 a year. It was a great deal of money for a three-month period, but Willis eventually decided that he had no wish to take part in 'exhibition' cricket, which he realized Packer's Super-Tests must be, being suspicious of their inbred nature.

One of the chief attractions of Packer's money was the guarantee that it would be paid regardless of loss of form or injury; and although Willis was likely on recent showing to make a comparable amount of money in English cricket if he played in all Test Matches he could not guarantee either his form or his fitness. Accordingly he set about working out a counter-package for himself so that he could turn Packer down, a particularly important ingredient being an insurance policy to guarantee the amount he would be paid regardless of loss of form or possible injury. Warwickshire duly guaranteed him a salary over the next three years of £3500 a year, while he would receive £5000 from

the TCCB for the 1977/78 tour of Pakistan and New Zealand and
Test fees of £6000 in the summer of 1978 under the Cornhill
scheme. In addition to this he was guaranteed by his agent, Barry
Gill, a minimum of a further £3000 a year for three years for his
promotional activities off the field – a figure which will almost
certainly be higher. This gave Willis potential earnings of around
£20,000 for the twelve months immediately following his refusal
of Packer's offer, compared with a total of £7000 which he would
have collected in the twelve months before that. Having secured
these fees he then arranged insurance to cover him against injury
or loss of form, so that his income was guaranteed. Willis put it all
into true perspective when he said at the time, 'Packer's offer
came in a lump sum, but after I had decided which way I wanted
my career to go it was only a question of assembling lumps from
a number of different sources.' The moral seems to be that if the
best players are determined to stay within the traditional form of
the game roughly comparable earnings can probably be found so
long as the players themselves are prepared to go out and look for
them.

Willis's reaction was in sharp contrast to Woolmer's. Although
Woolmer made a hundred in each of the first two Tests against
Australia in 1977 he was still a marginal choice for Packer, yet he
gave me the impression that he was disappointed not to have been
chosen earlier by the Packer organization, regarding it almost as a
slight on his ability. As soon as the offer came he went to the Kent
committee and asked that his Benefit be brought forward and his
pay increased. Otherwise he would join the circus. No county club
could be expected to submit to such an approach – Willis, for
instance, had kept Warwickshire informed throughout every
development in his own negotiations with Packer – and Kent duly
replied that they were unable to help. Woolmer then carried out
his threat.

It would be nice to think that the players who turned down
Packer have suitably large Benefits when the time comes, a reward
for their loyalty to the system which made their success possible. I
hope that the Glamorgan Number Ten, a figure I chose at random,
will have a good Benefit too. On the day I wrote this Andrew
Mack went in at number ten for Glamorgan against New Zealand.
He was born in Norfolk, went on to the Surrey staff, was not re-
engaged after 1977 and moved to Glamorgan. Just the fringe

county cricketer Greig was apparently sacrificing the England captaincy for. I would have thought that good Test Match receipts would have given Mack more to hope for rather than the fact that Greig and others were earning upwards of £20,000 a year from Packer.

♦

CHAPTER 8

In the Law Courts

A heedless Alexandrine ends the song
That like a wounded snake drags its slow length along.
A couplet by Alexander Pope, quoted by Michael Kempster, QC,
counsel for the defendants, towards the end of the 7-week hearing.
'Alexander' was the name of the plaintiff's counsel.

ONE OF THE more remarkable features of the whole Packer story
has been the confidence with which Kerry Packer has faced every
obstacle which has been put in his way. Apparently nothing
worried him. The possibility of having to pay £250,000 for the
High Court litigation was not the smallest deterrent, and indeed
it was a very small percentage of his total investment. When the
legal battles were at their height Packer said with disarming sim-
plicity, 'I've got more money than they have.' In a sense he was
playing a game of poker with the world's cricket authorities, raising the stakes regardless in the hope that they might be frightened
off and throw in their hand.

His money also enabled him to afford the best possible legal
advice in England and Australia. In England he hired probably
the outstanding advocate of the day in Robert Alexander, QC,
a man who in court was able to exude the same self-confidence
which Packer displayed out of it. He is, incidentally, a member of
MCC, but they were not the defendants. And in any event,
business is business. When Alexander had to leave the case for
another engagement his place was taken by Andrew Morritt, QC,
an extremely attractive advocate who made a long and brilliant
final speech. They had against them Michael Kempster, QC, a

thoroughly able barrister who made what he could of a difficult brief. The legal fraternity in general were certain as the case progressed that Packer and the three players, Greig, Snow and Procter, would win on the restraint of trade issue. There were many others far less sure.

The High Court hearing began in front of Mr Justice Slade, the brother of Julian Slade who wrote *Salad Days*, in Court Number Fifteen at the far end of the Strand on Monday 27 September. The infighting, the verbal scuffling, the attempts by both sides to score debating points off each other, Packer's tireless efforts to embarrass the Establishment and the general air of subterfuge which had continued since 9 May were now formalized by the stiff, unbending tradition of the law.

In the weeks before the court hearing Packer's plans continued apace in Australia, and each day brought reports of new signings or attempted signings, stories about the condition of his pitches and details of the innovations he was planning for World Series Cricket. Packer appeared extremely confident of the legal outcome, and unconcerned that each attempt to undermine the Establishment would alienate some people still further. It was good publicity, and of that he needed all he could get. In those terms alone the case would have been cheap even if the decision had gone against him, for his prospective series in Australia was given daily coverage in the parts of the world that most mattered. Packer could not have been sorry that the authorities had decided to fight him all the way; he may even have felt that it went some way towards guaranteeing him success.

The first-class season ended in England on 9 September, and the next eighteen days went by in limbo as everyone concerned focused their attention on the High Court. On the morning of the 27th many people who would have looked more at home in the confines of the Long Room at Lord's or in committee rooms in other parts of the cricketing world or simply in white flannel trousers hopped out of taxis and buses and cars in front of the law courts. Adversaries greeted each other with tight-lipped smiles and embarrassed glances, and from the start it would have been easy to distinguish the two groups even if they had sat muddled up in court and not on opposite sides. The representatives of the Establishment came to court in respectable dark suits which any stockbroker up the road in the City would have been happy to wear. Their hair was short, their ties sober. The Packer contingent seemed to represent a totally different lifestyle. Packer himself came to court in a series of those round-shouldered, two-piece suits, sometimes dark, sometimes pale-coloured, and as often as not with a brightly coloured tie. Richie Benaud wore light-coloured suits, crocodile shoes and flashing ties. Another supporter was dressed in a splurge of yellow, while from another there was a flash of orange leather. John Snow's unruly hair usually flopped out of a roll-necked sweater. Greig mostly chose a sober, pin-striped dark blue suit, but it looked so new and the MCC touring tie so obvious that he resembled a Hollywood hero dressed to look like an English City gent rather than the genuine article.

In the hall of the building a piece of paper pinned inside a glass case stated, 'Court 15 before Mr Justice Slade. Greig and Ors v Insole and Ors. JP Sports Limited v Same. Action and counter-action.' Inside the court the seats were full to overcrowding, with the judge appearing to be the only person there capable of some kind of detachment. Participants and spectators alike were anxious for the case to get under way, and at half past ten that morning Mr Alexander finally rose to outline Packer's and his players' arguments against the cricket authorities. He spoke for two days, in which he made the life of a top-class cricketer appear similar to that of a Victorian workhouse inmate and invested the authorities with the arrogance of so many medieval barons. He discussed the full extent of the players' poverty, drew attention to the basic insecurity of their jobs, and under his direction an interminable number of documents were produced and examined. The details of a player's contract for the previous winter's MCC tour of India, Sri Lanka and Australia were read out and compared extremely unfavourably with a Packer contract. How could the authorities expect to tie players to them, Alexander asked significantly, when they were not prepared to offer them a contract for the months in question?

When the plaintiffs began to call their witnesses Alexander's assessment of the miserable lot of an English first-class cricketer was scrupulously supported. Greig was the first witness. The Test and County Cricket Board needed a good shake-up, he said; no matter what happened he was sure that he was right to have acted as he did. As his evidence went on he managed to make the most outrageous statements seem plausible. For instance, he told the judge that there was a restriction on the number of nights a member of an MCC tourist party could spend with his wife in the same hotel. The limit was twenty-one. What he did not say – although it came out later in the case – was that he had told the sub-committee at Lord's dealing with the arrangements for the previous winter's tour that he did not think that wives *should* come out until the team had reached Sri Lanka, which was right at the end of the trip. Again, Greig said that the old fee of £210 for playing in a Test Match at home was wholly inadequate, and that the rise to £1000 had come about simply because of Packer. He did not mention that the TCCB already had the sponsorship of Test series in England up for sale, that more than one firm was interested, and that if a little more time had been allowed for negotiations the TCCB might well have been able to come up with an even higher figure. As it was, the TCCB felt that they had to get someone to come in quickly at maybe a lesser figure so that they could be seen to be mounting effective opposition to Packer and his money. Greig also complained that there was no security as England's captain, and that he had accepted Packer's offer because he did not want to be hounded out of the England side, as had happened to some captains in the past. He said that few players had the opportunity to earn much money from advertising and endorsements. 'I think in my case I am a bit of an exception in that I tend to be a bit of a pressman's dream. I have been concerned in one or two things which the press picked up, and I seem to be a pretty flamboyant character.'

Greig said that he had first met Packer at the end of the Centenary Test Match, and that after he had signed he had agreed to talk to players in England and the West Indies on Packer's behalf. He said that if the authorities wanted the best players to remain loyal to them they should pay them something during the winter months when many cricketers are forced to go on the dole. He told the court that he was getting A$30,000 for playing for Packer and another A$10,000 for captaining the Rest of the World and acting as Packer's consultant. When his career ended he had an undertaking from Packer that he would be found a job in his organization, and that Packer would help Greig with an interest-free loan to buy a house in Australia. He also said that when he signed he did not know that the World Series games would clash with Australia's official series against India. He had hoped that the two sides would put cricket first, and that there would not be a clash, and he ended by saying that he had been prepared to sacrifice the England captaincy in the long-term interests of his family and his future.

Greig was followed into the witness box by John Snow. He too complained about the way in which the game was run and about the slender financial rewards for players. Next came Mike Procter, who said that in 1977 he had earned £7500 from Gloucestershire who had had one of the most successful seasons in their history. It was made clear in court that his own contribution to their success had been remarkable, and that in a more perfect world he would have received much more than this. His Packer contract would give him the chance of playing again at the highest level since South Africa was banned from Test cricket. He thought that World Series Cricket would push up the salaries of county cricketers, and added that his contract with Packer was worth A$27,000 for every WSC tour in which he took part.

On Friday 30 September Kerry Packer began to give evidence. He traced the development of the idea which had produced World Series Cricket, and talked about his meeting with the ICC at Lord's. He said that he felt the proposed ban subjected his players to unreasonable and unjust pressure and was a denial of their rights. He admitted that his contracts contained a clause which said that WSC could play in Australia and elsewhere and that if the ban were implemented the facility to come to England was there. If there was no ban there was no intention to come to England. He spoke about the Australian Cricket Board's refusal to accept his offer to buy exclusive television rights, describing the Board as 'grossly incompetent'. He said that the sponsorship of sport was a family tradition, professed a love for cricket, and admitted to being amazed at the speed with which the players had responded to his offer. He had also warned his players that they had been given tough contracts, for he wanted them to be 'like Caesar's wife, beyond reproach'. He told the judge that his company was committed to spending A$12,000,000 on cricket over the next three years, and that his 'goodwill, prestige and believ-ability would be destroyed if the series did not go ahead'. He and his colleagues had decided that a series of Super-Tests would be good for the public, good for television and good for the players, and that they had decided to go ahead on those three decisions. If any of those conditions had not been present he would not have gone into Super-Tests.

When cross-examined by Mr Kempster Packer said that he did not regard his plans as a chance to get even with the Australian Cricket Board. 'I don't go around holding grudges.' Kempster then asked, 'Is it right that you went into the Super-Test business to make money?' It was then that Packer replied, 'Of course, I have never said anything else.' He went on to say that the Australian Cricket Board were in his view self-centred and interested only in their own perpetuation. He also spoke about some of the gimmickry he was intending to introduce into the game for the benefit of his television audiences and which he described as 'progressive innovations'. Finally, he accused the TCCB of not keeping their word when he was negotiating to buy the Australian rights for the 1977 Ashes series in England.

Packer was followed by Ross Edwards, the former Australian batsman, who had been brought out of retirement by WSC. He thought the whole idea would be a great fillip to the game in Australia, and he agreed with the need for the secrecy in the early stages. Next, Alan Knott spoke at length about the loneliness of a touring cricketer's life and the strains it put upon his own marriage. He complained that there was no security in cricket although he admitted to receiving a tax-free Benefit of £27,000 from Kent. Then Derek Underwood entered the box, and said the biggest worry of his life was what he was going to do when he had finished playing, as he had no academic qualifications. He also said that the Cricketers' Association had tried to persuade him to break his three-year contract with Packer.

On the ninth day of the hearing the cricket authorities made a surprise amendment to their defence, claiming that they were an 'employers' association', and as such could not be sued for restraint of trade or inducement to break contract under the terms of the 1974 Trade Union and Labour Relations Act. The question now was, 'Are the ICC and the TCCB employers' associations?' The 1974 Act says that an employers' association is an organization of employers whose principal purposes include the regulation of relations between employers and workers. Could a body which governs a national sport and administers the activities of the sport on behalf of everyone engaged in it be sufficiently partisan in a labour/management situation to qualify? There proved to be little mileage for the authorities in this amendment. As Mr Alexander said at once, if it could be held that the defendants were employers' associations 'it will come as much as a surprise to them as to us.'

Asif Iqbal climbed into the box later that day and 'swore by Allah' before giving evidence. He complained of bad pay, and said that cricket had caused him to miss the best part of his married life and the pleasure of seeing his young family grow up. He, like the others, spoke as if he had been compelled to take up a grotesquely unfair form of life and not that it was something he had chosen of his own free will.

Lynton Taylor from Channel Nine was the last witness for the plaintiffs, and he said that he had been at the meeting at Lord's between Packer and the ICC and that he had thought that it was only a public relations exercise on the part of the authorities, because the ICC were not genuinely seeking a compromise.

At the half-way stage Packer seemed a long way in front. He had created the impression of a businessman trying to do the best for his company, only to find that he had been frustrated by a lot of crusty old Establishment figures who obviously did not know one side of a balance sheet from the other. It appealed to him, too, to be seen as cricket's Messiah. Yet in spite of the ringing words of the cricketers who had come to support Packer about taking the game into a brave new world one was left with the feeling, just as one had been after Greig's press conference at Hove, that they were too embarrassed to admit that Packer's money had been the deciding factor. The players' motives, however, were not on trial.

It was now the turn of the Establishment. They fielded a twelve-man side in the witness box. There was Ray Steele, treasurer of the Australian Board, Peter Short from the West Indies Board, Matthian Chidambaram from the Indian, Walter Hadlee from the New Zealand Cricket Council, Jack Bailey, secretary of MCC and therefore the ICC, Donald Carr, secretary of the TCCB, Doug Insole, chairman of the TCCB, Geoffrey Boycott, who had turned Packer down, Ray Illingworth, the former England captain, Jack Bannister, secretary of the Cricketers' Association, Edmond King, chairman of the finance committee at Lord's, and Mike Vockins, secretary of Worcestershire. It was an impressive list, even if the presence of Sir Donald Bradman might have added more weight, but his wife was not well at the time and he was understandably reluctant to make the journey to London.

Whereas each witness called by the plaintiffs had something different to say and some different story to tell in the attempt to denigrate the Establishment it was not so easy for the Establishment to counter so successfully when their turn came. To start with, several of the witnesses told virtually the same story. The representatives of the overseas Boards of Control were all saying much the same thing, while the same could be said for the three representatives of the home authorities: it did not make for lively listening. It is almost impossible, moreover, to be as articulate or as glamorous when defending the *status quo* as it is when attacking it. At least the defence witnesses did all they could.

Mr Steele was the first into the box, and spoke of Packer's initial approach to the Australian Board and his meeting with the sub-committee in June 1976 when he had made it clear that he was only interested in exclusive television rights. He felt that Packer would make the game too gimmicky, and cited the way in which Packer had commercialized the Australian Open Golf Championship. He thought that Packer had been unwise not to accept the terms which he had been offered at Lord's, although, with hindsight, he felt the authorities had been wrong to have offered him so much: if Packer had accepted it would have meant the establishment helping him along for three years. He said that private promoters could only have a harmful effect on the game, and later under cross-examination that the proposed bans on the the players were 'eminently reasonable'. He went on to say: 'Mr Packer was a competitor, and I was prepared to do everything within my legal power not to help the opposition.' Cricket below Test level in Australia, he explained, was a subsidized game, and he thought the diminution of the Test income would have a serious effect at all levels. There would be divided gates, divided sponsorship and divided television receipts. The previous year the Board had negotiated a contract worth about £70,000 with Channel 0/10, another commercial channel; such a contract would be out of the question in the coming season. At one point when talking about the Packer contracts he said, 'I've heard the only way to get out of a Packer contract is by becoming pregnant.' He felt badly let down by the Australian players because with their complete agreement the Board had negotiated a A$350,000 a year team sponsorship with Benson and Hedges for three years.

Steele was followed by three more overseas administrators, Peter Short, Matthian Chidambaram and Walter Hadlee, all of whom spelt out the harmful ways in which they felt the Packer series would affect cricket in their respective countries. The general feeling was that touring sides without their leading players would be less of an attraction to the public, and that guarantees and gate money would therefore fall. Ultimately tours would have to be cancelled.

Jack Bailey was the next witness, and after setting out the case for the Establishment he proved a lively adversary for Mr Alexander in cross-examination. When asked if county cricketers did not have to search around for further work once the English summer was over, Bailey countered by asking if it was not the same in many other walks of life. He then asked Alexander if he knew what his next brief would be before the present case had finished. Alexander admitted he did not. When a witness was in the middle of replying to his questions Alexander had the habit of seeming to busy himself with other matters. Once Bailey stopped half-way through his reply, saying, 'I thought you had stopped listening to me!' In fact he, Doug Insole and Donald Carr all made valid points as to why for the good of cricket Packer should be opposed, yet they made little headway in persuading the judge that the ban was not in restraint of trade and that the TCCB had not been guilty of using the ban to try and persuade the Packer players to break their contracts.

Insole in particular was plagued by some bad luck. Before the High Court hearing the TCCB and the ICC had been asked to provide the minutes of all the relevant meetings at Lord's. Then, during the hearing, they were asked to provide the actual short-hand notes from which these minutes were written. At the various meetings the secretary of the particular Board in question would take down notes in shorthand – notes which were never intended for publication. Thus strong phrases were recorded which would never normally find their way into the official minutes, a perfectly common procedure. When these shorthand notes of the meetings at Lord's were produced, however, they turned out to be extremely relevant to the case in hand – and damaging to the defendants. (When the Packer organization were asked to produce similar shorthand notes of their meetings it was discovered that they had all been destroyed.)

The extracts which were read out in court included the following:

Rhoades (Chairman of Lancashire): Wants, with Middlesex support, to propose a total ban on Packer players from county cricket.

Insole: Counsel's view is that nobody who signed before the ICC meeting with Packer on 23 June when he made his views known could reasonably be extricated, but after the ICC meeting it would not be so difficult. In the short term the feeling is that we should extract our players as quickly as possible. War situation. We've got to try and see that this does not get off the ground.

Wheatley (Glamorgan): Our duty is to drive in this wedge of uncertainty into the players' minds. It is important that the Cricketers' Association go to a great deal of trouble to explain the situation to the players.

Brown (Gloucestershire): Gloucestershire's point is to protect the playing of the game. We would rather like to see the players kill Packer off.

Insole: Vote. The players contracted to Packer should be banned from first-class cricket, unless they rescind their contracts with him by the end of the 1978 season. [This was later changed to 1 October.]

These notes hardly helped the authorities in their claim that they had not tried to induce the players to break their contracts with Packer, and Insole suffered an unpleasant time under cross-examination.

Donald Carr during his spell in the witness box listed five reasons for the need of the imposition of the TCCB ban:

1. A requirement to support the ICC.
2. A deterrent to other players from leaving the authorized game.
3. Adverse reaction from other county cricketers.
4. Safeguarding places in county cricket on behalf of players who remained available for Test Matches.
5. The disruptive influence of the Packer players who would be aiming to recruit future star players.

Financial questions were raised, and the importance of Test Match receipts to the continuity of county cricket and the real fear that Packer's plans would lessen these receipts. While Insole was giving evidence a letter by Dick Stone, treasurer of the Oxford University Cricket Club and a representative on the TCCB, written to Donald Carr on 12 July 1977, was read out in court.

After apologies for being unable to attend a previous meeting of the Board, Mr Stone continued:

When the Australians came to Oxford recently I had an interesting talk with one of them who had joined up with Packer. His story was that one day in January (or February) he was called to Packer's office and had such a lucrative offer made he could hardly refuse. He was promised a cheque before he left the room for A $30,000 (£18,500) if he signed the contract, but on condition that he didn't tell a soul about the matter without Packer's permission.

He fell for this tempting offer, but, of course, was precluded from seeking advice on the contract or discussing possible repercussions to his long-term career with anyone else. In due course he came to realize that he'd made a very bad mistake, but as he had already spent part of the money, he couldn't withdraw. He now bitterly regrets what he's done and would dearly love to escape his commitment with Packer.

I understand from him that there are several other Australians with a similar story who would now like to withdraw from their contracts, but see no way to do so. Perhaps the TCCB could set up a loan fund and offer advice on the terms of the contract in order to explore the possibilities of terminating it within the letter of the law – bearing in mind that Packer's own behaviour and actions do not merit any undue adherence to the spirit of the law.

The name of the player was not revealed.

There was an entertaining session when Boycott was in the witness box. The plaintiffs heard only on the Friday that he would be giving evidence for the defence immediately after the week-end, and that evening Boycott reported that he had received a telephone call from Greig at his house in Yorkshire. Greig had asked him, 'How the hell have you got involved in this?' and went on to say that he wished Boycott was not going to give evidence because they were going to have to work during the week-end so that they could 'throw some mud at him'. 'I thought that charming,' remarked Boycott. However, the two players did meet on the Sunday, at a sports fair in Birmingham, and Greig made remarks similar to those he had made on the telephone. 'I walked away to the toilet because I did not want to get involved,' said Boycott.

Both these conversations were reported by Boycott to counsel for the defendants and passed on to the judge, who spoke in court to Mr Alexander. 'I have today heard that there has been a conversation last Friday between Mr Boycott and Mr Greig. I have said nothing because the remarks seem to be of a jocular variety, but I would point out that if there were any attempt to influence witnesses on either side I would be bound to take a very serious view. I am sure you will speak to Mr Greig about this.'

In evidence Boycott said that the players who signed for Packer wanted 'the penny and the bun'. He agreed that players had not been paid enough money, but that they could not serve two masters. Players who earned 'cream-money' with the Super-Tests during the English winter could not expect to return to England and resume playing county cricket which depended on income from official Test Matches. In cross-examination Mr Alexander asked him if he had sided with the authorities in order to further his hopes of becoming the England captain. Boycott vigorously denied this. He did not agree that the players should have more security, and said that they should be expected to be selected as their form warranted. Finally, he was asked if he thought that leading players proved a big attraction locally, as for example in the case of Derek Randall at Trent Bridge. Boycott said immediately, 'Randall at Trent Bridge? I thought they were Yorkshiremen come to see me.' This remark was greeted with great laughter. He was reluctant to leave the witness box when his evidence was finished, feeling that he could do more to assist the Establishment. Yet there was in fact considerable worry about Boycott's presence in the witness box, for he had himself for three years refused to play for England, arguably putting his own interests before his country's.

Ray Illingworth was not so impressive as Boycott, but he said that he did not blame any players for signing with Packer. 'If I had been offered a contract I would have considered it very carefully. But if I had accepted it I would have expected to be banned from Test and county matches because I think the two games – Mr Packer's and conventional cricket – will be in direct conflict.' Edmond King, chairman of the finance sub-committee at Lord's, then told the court that the county clubs would share a surplus of more than £900,000 after the 1977 series against Australia. He warned that any diminution of Test income could mean a return to the bad old days with players badly paid and clubs on the breadline. He told the judge that a working party had been set up to provide the counties with guidelines on pay to players within the Government guidelines. Earlier, Jack Bannister, the secretary of the Cricketers' Association, had said that the earnings of rank and file players ranged from £2500 to £4000. He also pointed out that part of the Packer players' fight to retain county status was not so much for the right to come back and earn a living but rather to be able to retain their form and fitness. In this way county cricket would be devalued. Finally, Mike Vockins, the Worcestershire secretary, said that it cost a county club £30,000 to turn a young player into an established county cricketer over a five-year period.

Mr Michael Kempster then began his summing up for the defendants. The plaintiffs, he said, had sought in part to found their case on a detailed denigration of the efficiency and integrity of those responsible for the welfare of cricket in Britain and around the world. He suggested that Mr Justice Slade must be satisfied 'beyond a peradventure' that the various aspersions cast on the administrators during the first weeks of the case were misconceived, if not unwholesome. These early sallies demonstrated the unhappy frame of mind of the real plaintiff in both cases, Mr Packer, following his unpalatable discovery on 22 June 1976 that, for once, money could not buy him what he wanted. Kempster claimed that the Packer contracts were void because they were unduly restrictive and that, if this were so, allegations that the ICC and the TCCB had attempted to induce Packer players to break their contracts had failed. He then listed the obligations which the cricket authorities had to protect the game they ran, but although many cricket supporters may have felt that there was much morally in his favour there was little of legal substance to back up the Establishment case.

Mr Morritt, for the plaintiffs, spoke for twelve hours in his closing address. Altogether it was an impressive speech. He listed the war-like noises which had come from those shorthand minutes of meetings at Lord's which had so pursued Doug Insole in the witness box, and claimed that the authorities had used every weapon at their disposal to try to defeat Packer. He referred to quotations such as 'wars not being won by appeasement' and 'a siege situation'. He said that they had tried to introduce provisions which were dictatorial, penal and an infringement of the liberty of the individual. The authorities wished to bind players to their system without giving them any choice or contract. 'That sort of system can only properly be described as feudal.' He went through a Packer contract and claimed that it left no doubt about

World Series Cricket's commitment. He examined each of the Test-playing countries in turn and their immediate future tours, and decided that Australia was the only one which was likely to be affected by the Packer games. Towards the end of his speech Mr Morritt asked why a professional cricketer of standing should not be able to choose for himself whether he wanted to play for a private promoter, and running the risk if he so chose that his club might not wish to have him back when he was available. The player should be the one to decide whether he was to play for Mr Packer, and his club were the ones to decide whether or not they wanted him at other times. Mr Morritt went on to say that the plaintiffs had always accepted that players might be excluded in the interests of team building, but this was a matter that should be left to selectors or individual counties.

The High Court hearing ended in its seventh week, on its 31st working day and in its 137th hour. The court rose, and Mr Justice Slade retired to his Chambers to sift through the welter of evidence. The case had gone on and on, and undoubtedly a great many people, whatever their loyalties or feelings, were confused by what was relevant to the legal points at issue and what was not. While the judge was deliberating on his judgement Louis Blom-Cooper, QC, wrote an extremely interesting article in the *Guardian* which set out the issues clearly. It can hardly have encouraged the authorities. He wrote:

The Packer team's case is based on two distinct legal bases. The first is that the ban imposed during the summer by the TCCB and the ICC on anyone contracted to Mr Packer to play in his World Test series, that they would no longer be allowed to play in county cricket or be available for selection for the England side, is a tort, a wrongful act for which the law provides a remedy.

The tort alleged is the inducement of breach of contract. Putting aside the player's future unavailability for Test Matches (no player could obtain a right to be chosen to play for England) it is said that the ban means that a Packer player will be allowed to play county cricket only if he reneges on his contract with Mr Packer.

The point was put in a brutally frank way by the Chairman of the TCCB, Mr Douglas Insole, at a meeting on 15 July. The minutes record, in shorthand form, Mr Insole's conclusion: 'Vote, the players contracted should be banned from first-class cricket, unless they rescind their contracts with him by the end of 1978 [subsequently changed to 1 October 1977].' The question that Mr Justice Slade will be asking

himself is: Does that statement along with all the other events leading up
to and including the imposition of the ban constitute in law an action-
able interference with contractual rights?

The ingredients of the tort are clear and simple. Did the cricketing
authorities know of the existence of the Packer contracts? No problem
with that; they clearly did. Did they intend by their action to procure a
breach of the Packer contracts? Mr Insole's statement would seem to
provide an unequivocal affirmative to that question. The third and
crucial point is: did the authorities definitely and unequivocally persuade, induce or procure the cricketers – Messrs Snow, Procter,
Knott et al. – to break their contracts with Mr Packer with the intention
to procure the breach of contract? That is answerable only when one
has heard all the evidence about the events of the summer when the ban
came into existence.

But one thing is certain. If Mr Justice Slade answers that question
affirmatively the welter of words about the public interest involved in
the authorities' action becomes irrelevant. Once there is held to be an
inducement of a breach of contract the inducer can escape liability only
if there is a legal justification for the inducement. It is not enough that
the inducer has acted out of the highest motives, that he is an altruist
who is seeking only the good of others and is acting against self-interest,
performing a public service.

The furthest the courts have gone is in a case fifty years ago where
members of the theatrical Joint Protection Committee were held to be
justified in inducing a theatre manager to break his contract with a man
who paid his chorus-girls such low wages that they were obliged to
resort to prostitution. The justifiable object was to promote the status
of the theatrical profession and to stop the evils resulting from underpayment in it. Whatever fulminations have been directed at Mr Packer,
nobody suggests that underpayment is the evil of his intrusion into the
world of cricket.

As a consequence, if Mr Justice Slade decided the first part of the
claim in favour of the Packer team that really is the end of the affair.
Nothing else matters. But the judge is unlikely to skirt the other issues,
only because, if the case goes on to appeal, the appeal court judge will
want to know the judge's view on the evidence relating to the second
claim.

In these seven paragraphs Blom-Cooper has dealt with the
inducement of breach of contract. In the next two he moved on to
the restraint of trade issue, and once again his thinking is extremely
clear.

Contrariwise, the claim to restraint of trade necessarily involves the heart of the issue that has been fought out these last four weeks. Restraint of trade is a lawyer's term of art. In the context of this case it means briefly: does the ban on county cricket players not contracting with bodies that are not recognized by the established cricketing authorities unreasonably interfere with the liberty of professional players to use their skills in some employment during the winter when they are not employed by their counties?

The law declares that it is contrary to public policy to restrict this liberty unless the restraint is justifiable in the interests of both parties and in the public interest. The burden is on those who justify the restraint to show that everyone involved – the administrators of cricket, the player and the public – is better off if the ban is maintained. We can only sit and wait for Mr Justice Slade's verdict on that.

The court reassembled on Friday 25 November. In the meantime Mr Justice Slade had not been idle. His judgement covered 211 pages of foolscap and took him five and a half hours to deliver. He found overwhelmingly in favour of Mr Packer's World Series Cricket and his three players, Greig, Snow and Procter. He had considered that there were nine principal questions which he had had to answer.

1. Are the contracts between WSC and its players void?
2. Has WSC established that, as at 3 August, and subject to any statutory immunity conferred by the 1974 Act (The Trade Union and Labour Relations Act), it has a good cause of action in tort against the ICC based on inducement of breach of contract?
3. Has WSC established that as at 3 August and subject as aforesaid it had a good cause of action in tort against the TCCB based on the same grounds?
4. Subject to the provisions of the 1974 Act, are the new ICC rules void as being in restraint of trade?
5. Subject to aforesaid, are the proposed new TCCB rules void as being in restraint of trade?
6. Is the ICC an 'employers' association' within the 1974 Act?
7. Is the TCCB an 'employers' association'?
8. If either the ICC or the TCCB or both be 'employers' associations', does this itself bar any cause of action that would otherwise exist?
9. In the light of the answers, what relief (if any) should be given to (i) the individual plaintiffs and (ii) WSC?

Mr Justice Slade found for WSC and the individual players concerned on every point. He said that he had been impressed by the obvious disinterested dedication to and concern for the game

by the top administrators of cricket who had given evidence. He
went on to say that he could see the possible force of criticism
directed against Greig, who, when he signed his contract with
WSC and recruited others to do so, had just completed a tour of
Australia as captain of the England side, was still generally
regarded as its captain and could have looked forward with reasonable confidence to his formal reappointment as such. There was
obviously a case for saying that his responsibilities to the TCCB
were of a rather special nature.

Later in the judgement he said that a professional cricketer
needed to make his living as much as any other professional man.
It was straining the concept of loyalty too far for authorities such
as the defendants to expect him to enter into a self-denying ordin-
ance not to play cricket for a private promoter during the winter
months merely because the matches promoted could detract from
the future profits made by the authorities, who were not themselves willing or in a position to offer him employment over the
winter or guarantee him employment for the future. The players
concerned, with the possible exception of Greig, could not
justifiably be criticized on moral grounds for having entered into
contracts with WSC in conditions of secrecy. The defendants'
subsequent actions made it abundantly clear that, had they been
informed in advance of the WSC project, they would have done
their utmost to prevent it from taking root and thus to prevent the
players involved from enjoying the advantages offered to them by
WSC.

In conclusion, the judge listed the five positive beneficial effects
of WSC which the defence had already acknowledged. It had
offered the promise of much greater rewards for star cricketers.
Indeed it had gone further – it had offered secure, regular, re-
munerative employment in cricket to more than fifty cricketers
in most cases for three English winter seasons at a time when most
of them would otherwise have no guarantee of regular employment in the game. Secondly, it had already stimulated new
sponsors for traditional cricket. Thirdly, it had brought back to the
game in Australia several talented players. Fourthly, it, or the
group of companies of which it formed part, had initiated a useful
coaching scheme for young players in New South Wales. Fifthly, it
had increased public interest in the game.

Judgement was given to the plaintiffs in both actions with costs.

These, which would be shared between the ICC and the TCCB, amounted to about £250,000 – more if the authorities decided to take it on to appeal although, in the New Year, they decided against this, feeling that their case was not strong enough. The TCCB's share of the bill would be paid out of the profit of nearly a million pounds which came from the series against Australia in England in 1977. The seventeen first-class counties had each had £10,000 of the amount owing to them withheld in case the judgement should go against the authorities. It was a huge bill for a game short of money, and there were many only too anxious to blame the authorities for what had happened. Their argument was that when the time came it would have been as easy and as effective for the counties and the Test selectors simply not to have chosen the Packer players without anything so controversial as a formal ban. One wonders whether all of the counties would have been prepared to have gone along with that, especially the one or two who had already prejudged the issue by renewing the contracts of their Packer players after the original announcement and before the High Court case. And would opposition to Packer have been so sharply focused if it had not been for the High Court action?

The judgement was a sickening blow for the game's authorities, just as it was a triumph for WSC. Yet from quite early on in the proceedings the Establishment must have known that they would lose the case, but were carried along on a wave of emotion – in reality the basis of their case all along. In terms of cold law, as Blom-Cooper suggested, the authorities appear to have been disastrously advised – or it may have been that they were advised correctly but felt that morally the force of argument was so much on their side that they must win. With hindsight it seems extraordinary that they should have let themselves in for such a costly piece of legislation when the result was so one-sided and clear-cut.

Looked at in the light of the final judgement the authorities' case and hopes appear based on little more than moral indignation. This is not enough with which to take on the rights of the individual in the law courts; and the fact that the authorities may have felt that it was only showed how unable they were to balance the rough commercialism of Packer with a game which by its very nature demands moral standards. Cricket's administrators behave in a traditional way; thus by a gentlemen's arrangement it has been agreed not to have an open transfer system between the counties. This was shown when Imran Khan went from Worcestershire to Sussex in the summer of 1977. Sussex knew that Imran would improve their side, and it was felt that they had enticed him away – although Sussex said he went of his own accord – and Worcestershire did not want him to go. This seemed to be too near the soccer form of transfer, and the authorities at Lord's tried to hold it up. Sussex appealed, and it was found that in terms of the law governing the individual's right to work Sussex were in the right, and Imran's sentence – he was given a period to wait before playing for Sussex – was considerably shortened. A far-sighted administrator might have seen that as a straw in the wind.

Although lack of money is the basis of this whole saga more money coming into the game recently has meant that in effect gentlemen's agreements are being increasingly ignored. It used to be a crime to run a batsman out for backing up too far without the bowler first warning him. In a Test Match between Australia and the West Indies in January 1968 I saw Redpath run out in Adelaide by Charlie Griffith. In a Test Match at Christchurch in February 1978 Randall was similarly run out by Chatfield. On neither occasion was the batsman warned.

The authorities are in an increasingly difficult situation. They are trying to guard the game's conscience and to preserve its tradition, at the same time as helping it to move into the commercial world of the latter half of the twentieth century. Such a role is not the basis for taking on the law.

Another weakness of the Establishment case was that although they might have been working all the time with the best interests of the game as their objective they seemed to ignore the interests of the players themselves. This was particularly true in their failure to understand the motives of those who had signed for Packer. In the transcripts of the various discussions at Lord's leading up to the decision to ban there were few references to what these players wanted, and it was made to seem almost as if the very immorality of their having dealt with Packer excluded them from any personal consideration. That was another side to the way moral indignation blinded the game's administrators.

All the same, the more one considered the judgement the less clear-cut it all became. The judge had said that the contracts the players had with Packer were valid, that these same players could be considered by Test selectors and that those who still had contracts with county clubs were legally entitled to enforce them. He did not say that the players had to be chosen to play Test or county cricket. If Test selection committees – anywhere in the world – decided that in the interests of team building they were not prepared to select players only available for part of the time no one could prevent them. He said that it would be wrong to impose a ban on those players who had already signed for Packer, although he implied that a ban on anyone who signed in the future might be acceptable. Although Sussex responded to the judgement by reappointing Greig to the county captaincy – a decision which was to have several repercussions – the judge had said nothing about compelling a county to re-engage a Packer player when his contract came to an end. This was an important victory for Packer and his players, coming just as WSC were about to start their matches. But it did not guarantee World Series Cricket ultimate success.

By the time Mr Justice Slade read his judgement I was in Melbourne, having already watched the first two days of World Series Cricket.

CHAPTER 9

◆

The Circus Entertains

'I've been against what you've been trying to do. But I would nonetheless like sincerely to congratulate you on a considerable victory.'

'I can see from your face how sincere you are. I've read some of your stuff. You've never been prepared to give me a chance.'

'I don't know. I think I said that good might come of it.'

'Good might come of evil? I don't think that's much of a compliment.'

Conversation between John Woodcock of *The Times* and Kerry Packer, following news of the WSC victory in the High Court.

As THE DAY of Packer's first match came closer I had grown increasingly curious to see what would happen. The three World Series Cricket sides, Australian, West Indian and Rest of the World elevens, were to take part in two competitions – the International Cup Series and the International Country Championship Cup. In the former there would be two series of Super-Tests of three matches each and a series of one-day matches in the four big cities. In the second series the three sides were to play thirteen two- and three-day games for the cup, in addition to a practice match in Adelaide at the start and a game in Tasmania at the end.

In all six Super-Tests were going to be played on grounds wholly designed for other sports and never used for cricket. Two sets of pitches had been produced artificially in greenhouses, while the other two were prepared on site, but so quickly that their quality could not be guaranteed. Packer's company had evolved new techniques for television coverage and had doubled the number of cameras normally used from four to eight. Other novelties – microphones on the batsmen and bowlers, instant interviews with umpires when they had given decisions – had been talked about but for some reason were discarded and the only alteration to the rules was that fast bowlers were allowed to bowl bouncers at tailenders. However, I felt, even if the end product might be heretical, it would be fascinating to see.

I had originally planned to go to Pakistan and New Zealand with the England side for the *Guardian*, the *Sunday Express* and the BBC, but as October went by it became increasingly clear that the place to be on Thursday 24 November was the VFL Park in Melbourne. I rearranged my plans accordingly and, as if to show how high feelings ran over Packer, several of my friends accused me of being a hypocrite in that I had already declared myself against him and yet here I was going out in support. Apart from the fact that a newspaperman's job is to be where the news is – and Packer's first few days of cricket were bound to be extensively covered by all the English papers – I thought that it was extremely important that as far as possible they should be reported by people who were used to covering Test cricket. I was also anxious not to prejudge WSC cricket, but to see it for what it was.

I arrived at Tullamarine Airport on the evening of Tuesday 22 November, three days before Mr Justice Slade pronounced his judgement in the High Court. The significance of the moment made Melbourne seem unusually tense, much more so than in the days before the Centenary Test Match. Of course this was only a reflection of my own feelings. The city was emptier than it normally would be on the eve of a Test Match, and I was surprised at the indifference that greeted any mention of Kerry Packer. The new Australians, mostly of European origin and with seemingly a monopoly over the taxi business in Melbourne, had no interest in cricket but were prepared 'to give Packer a go'. The Australians more interested in cricket mostly seemed to think that Packer's circus would be short-lived. In the entire fortnight I met no one who said they intended going to watch, and I asked a good many people.

In each of the centres in which he was playing his Super-Tests, Packer had virtually taken over one of the main hotels. It was not long therefore before I was in touch with the Old Melbourne Motor Inn, which was the centre of his operations in Melbourne. I wanted a press ticket, and when I rang up I was put through to the World Series Cricket Office and was soon talking to Chris

Forsyth, Packer's press liaison officer, who proved to be always charming and obliging. I asked if I might have a pass, and a clip-on metal badge was delivered by hand in under an hour together with a brochure: it turned out to be a typical example of the streamlined efficiency of the massive Packer organization.

I drove out the next morning to look at the VFL Park at Waverley, a stadium which was built to house the Australian Rules Victorian Football League – ironically after they had fought with the authorities at the Melbourne Cricket Ground, their former home. Melbourne has always produced the biggest crowds for Test matches in Australia, and Packer's organizers had presumably impressed upon him the need to find a ground with a big capacity. The VFL Park holds 77,000 and is a huge, soulless concrete edifice with acres and acres of open concrete terracing. I soon discovered that just finding it was the first problem.

This was my fifth visit to Australia, and I knew the main cities well, but that first drive out to the VFL Park held the unreality of a journey into the unknown. I sensed then that a strange adventure was beginning, and also that there was no knowing where it would lead. I was given a lift, and we knew that we should leave Melbourne by the Dandenong road, but no one I met that morning seemed to know what to do next. After driving about twenty kilometres we pulled into a petrol station and were told to turn left down Wellington Road in about another three kilometres, and that the Park was on the right three or four kilometres after that – we couldn't miss it.

We turned left into Wellington Road, passing Monash University on the left, and far ahead on the right-hand side of the road I saw the floodlights and concrete shell of a gigantic football stadium. It stood out like some Wembley in the middle of a prairie. We drove into a long dip and suddenly it vanished, only to reappear a moment later, looking even bigger and starker than before. There was a huge area for car-parking all round the stadium and a small group of cars away to the right: we duly drove across to the group on the right. A man in uniform whom I took to be a car-park attendant but turned out to be a security guard asked if he could help. I told him who I was and what I had come for. He directed us farther round to the right, to another gate. A second security guard then came over, and I repeated my request. He seemed to understand, but with a friendly smile told me that he had received strict instructions that the press were not to be admitted. Apparently there had been a special tour round the stadium organized for the press the previous day; today the curator was not to be distracted. The guard got out a pen, wrote down my name and said he would ring up the general manager of World Series Cricket, a Mr Ern Street, and see if anything could be done. He then went back to his small caravan inside the tall wire fence running round the back of the ground.

Mr Street was obviously not easy to find. While I was waiting outside the caravan another car drove up and a man with a grey suit and a slightly self-important swagger got out and walked towards me. I introduced myself, and he told me that his name was Lynch and that he was Packer's representative at the ground. I told him that I had to write a preview of the match for my paper, and that it was important for me to have a look at the ground and the pitch. He listened carefully, and finally said he would allow me to walk through the tunnel and have a look at the stadium. This was the tunnel through which the three pitches had been hauled by huge cranes during the past fortnight, and I duly walked through it and stood on the edge of the outfield. The ground was impressive in its starkness, in the way of all big stadiums. The members' area had five tiers of stands and terracing that stretched far into the sky and backed on to the glass windows of bars and restaurants. This area took up a forty-degree arc. The rest of the ground was surrounded by two tiers of completely empty terracing. Bangs and thumps echoed round as the final touches were applied, and notices indicating bars, restaurants, food stalls and the like were widely displayed. The playing area was huge, if anything rather bigger than the Melbourne Cricket Ground. There was a good deal of activity out in the middle, while immediately in front of me there were two fresh strips of turf, about six yards long. I later learned that these were to repair damage which had been caused by cranes while lugging the pitches to the centre.

On the other side of the ground above the terracing the football scoreboard which had been adapted for cricket was constantly flashing its lights. Moving fast across the middle of the board as if its real home should have been above Piccadilly Circus was a strip of words – 'Testing, testing, testing' – another indication of the newness of everything there. The next day they would carry the full details of the scoreboard, a number of advertisements, periodic news bulletins and any other information it was felt that the public might need. The advertisement hoardings round the boundary fence were covered over, for the spaces had been sold for the football and not for Packer, who was hardly likely to allow any free advertising at his games. Ten boards standing on the grass, five at each end, displayed what limited amount of advertising World Series Cricket had by then produced. Although it had just been announced that Qantas had become one of the main sponsors acquiring advertising revenue was obviously still a problem.

I told Lynch, who had once worked for the Packers and had been asked out of retirement to help out at the VFL Park, that I badly wanted to have a look at the pitch itself, but this he firmly rejected. However, by luck the guard had at last been able to make contact with Ern Street, who had given his permission, and so I made my way to the middle. On my way there I was surprised at the smoothness of the outfield so soon after the football season and also at the even covering of grass. It would be a good ground to field on. The centre of the ground was a mess; the laying of the three pitches had involved the use of massive cranes and other machinery, and scars had been left which the groundstaff were now rushing to put right. The turf between the pitches had only just been relaid, and was about an inch higher than the pitches themselves, which therefore seemed to be in a slight trough. The heavy roller was going up and down the pitch for the next day's game, and the surface was mown and compressed as tightly as a fortnight's heavy rolling allowed – a heavy roller could not be used in the greenhouse. The other two pitches had not yet been cut.

It was easy to tell where the two halves had been joined together, for in the middle of each pitch there was a slight indentation about an inch wide. It was an incredible sight, for while the surrounds looked extremely untidy it seemed astonishing that the pitches should have been carried by crane from the greenhouses about three hundred yards the other side of the entrance tunnel and been dropped into place. Each bore signs of careful and intense cultivation, and when one considers that each trough – and there were two to a pitch – weighed several tons it does seem an extraordinary feat of engineering.

Looking round the ground I did not feel it would be possible for the VFL Park ever to produce the proper atmosphere for cricket. The Melbourne Cricket Ground is also huge, but it is steeped in cricketing traditions – one hundred years of Test cricket on the MCG had been celebrated only the previous March – and therefore seems friendly and far from impersonal. Here the ground was soulless, and for me it was to remain so.

I arrived at the centre of the pitch to be joined by John Maley, Packer's groundsman, and a soil expert who had advised on the preparation of the pitches at the VFL Park and at the football ground in Adelaide. The soil expert explained to me how they had been constructed, and it was a remarkable story. The concrete troughs were made first. They are each twelve feet wide, forty feet long and fifteen inches deep. The pitches were laid early in July, when Packer realized that he would not be able to play on normal Test grounds. A network of drainage pipes was put together at the bottom of the tray and then these pipes were covered by three inches of wash gravel, followed by seven or eight of sand to ensure quick water movement. There then came three inches of loam – carefully graded into the sand – and five inches of black Merri Creek soil, which was graded into the loam. The couch grass was sown into the black soil. The pitches had been growing for just over three months in the greenhouses and, because the normal average of four hours' sunlight a day did not provide enough heat, electric cables had been laid six inches apart and seven inches deep in order that the pitches should be constantly heated to 30° centigrade. In the greenhouses this had been boosted by the use of 56 thousand-watt sodium lamps, each with four-an-a-half foot centres. It was impossible to say how the pitches were going to play, but there was enough moisture in them to prevent them having much pace. Maley for his part was confident they would play well, and said that they would soon be the best in Australia. While I listened to the details of their birth I watched the heavy roller go up and down, and it seemed a miracle that so much could have been done in such a short time.

At each end of the pitches there were solid metal containers on wheels which looked rather like the drinks trolleys which come out with orangeade for the players. They provided the power for the heating, and a wire from each was plugged into the underground apparatus so that the pitches were still being kept nicely warm.

When the Packer circus has run its course it may be that these forced pitches will be an innovation which will stay in top-class cricket – in Australia, at any rate.

The drive back into Melbourne was simpler, and I realized that however much I may deep down have disapproved of what Packer was trying to do I felt awe-inspired after seeing big business in action. Packer had apparently reserved 95 suites at the Old Melbourne for his players and administrators. I only went there twice, and each time it seemed that they were all coralled in this rambling old coaching inn, as if they feared they might be treated as outcasts if they ventured much beyond its boundaries. The Australians had already been subjected to lectures about the way in which truly professional sportsmen should conduct themselves, as well as to anti-Establishment lectures and several 'we-shall-never-give-up' sermons.

The Australians were the first of Packer's cricketers to fore-gather in Melbourne, in the middle of November, and they were subjected to these lectures before being joined by their colleagues from overseas. It was amusing that these talks should have been specially reserved for the home side, for as a nation Australians like to win and the organizers had not lost sight of the need for the Australian eleven to do just that. Ian Chappell, Richie Benaud, John Newcombe, who won the men's singles at Wimbledon three times, and Ron Barassi, arguably the most successful Australian Rules Football coach there has ever been, all spoke to the Australian group. Packer clearly regarded Newcombe and Barassi as the epitome of professionalism. The meetings were held in private, but one of the Packer administrators hid a tape recorder on each occasion and sold the tapes to a journalist who works for the *Australian* in which these speeches first appeared. They proved to be extremely instructive.

The Australians first heard their captain, Ian Chappell, one evening at the Old Melbourne Motor Inn. The players had just arrived and many of them must have been nervous, not knowing what to expect. This was therefore an ideal time for such an address. Chappell's manner is brusque, and as always he came straight to the point.

The future of professional cricket starts here and now and it rests with us. Now we've turned professionals, if that's the word, we've got to work and operate as professionals in every sense. Your contract is your own business and it's clear from the fact that you've signed it that you're happy with it. But if for any reason you decide you're not happy with it then talk to the WSC people or Mr Packer and renegotiate it when the time comes. For Christ's sake don't go blabbing to the press about it. That isn't professional.

I know a lot of us will be working hard to establish our positions in the team; that's how it was in the past, and that's how it will be here. We'll make the Australian first eleven on merit and merit only. But as professionals I think we've also got an added challenge, at least those amongst us who are on the older side and are more experienced.

I mean by that, putting aside our natural competitiveness against the other fellow, the younger player working his way up, so that if one of the experienced men spots a technical weakness or a flaw in one of the up-and-comers then I want – no, I expect that man to help the youngster get his problem ironed out. I believe that to be the professional approach.

I'm sick and tired, I've had a gutful of all the arguing and bickering and animosity that followed our decision to try to earn a living from cricket – which is our God-damned right. Now we've got to show all the knockers what we can do. Personally, I'm looking forward to the challenge. It's up to us now, out there on the field.

Richie Benaud followed Chappell, talking in his quiet, precise, clinical way.

I want you to think what it means to be called a 'disapproved person' by the cricket Establishment ['disapproved' was the word used by the ICC and the TCCB when they announced their intention to ban the Packer players]. Those are the words used by their lawyers, and is how the cricket Establishment sees us, all of us involved with Mr Packer, you and me.

I want you to think what that means to me. I've done as much as most for cricket because I love the game and the people – most of them – who are in it. And yet I can't adequately describe the feeling of despair I felt when I heard myself described in London as a 'disapproved person'. It was – well, hard to take. I don't want to dwell on it, but you think about it. It's important to think what that means. It might help you strengthen your purpose and resolve in what we are going to under-take in the months and years ahead.

The next night they were addressed by John Newcombe.

What is happening in cricket today happened in professional tennis. So I want to tell you we've been down the road you're on and we won all the way, just as I'm sure you'll win in the end if you stick together. You'll find many new and strange things happening now you're professionals. You've got to learn that flamboyancy is a big thing in professional sportsmen.

When I started realizing that people wanted to see me as a human being as well as a tennis player I started developing an image. I started acting on the court like I acted off it. It was hard at first, because I'd been brought up to play tennis by looking only at the other end of the court and the player there. But I did it and people started turning up to see me.

And that's what you're going to have to do. People will turn up to see a bowler like Dennis Lillee because he's got an image as well as ability. And that business of Ian Chappell scratching himself every time a ball is bowled [he ostentatiously adjusts his box before each delivery] will bring women in. Image is important, and so are team-mates. You have to be loyal to be successful. The only way it is going to work for you is if all you fellows are pushing it.

Ron Barassi spoke after lunch one day in the changing rooms of the St Kilda Football Club where the players had been training.

You've got to go back to the fundamentals; attitudes and commitments. It always seems incredible to me – I regard it with great disbelief – at the way naturally gifted sportsmen consider themselves. They think they have something that puts them ahead of others, all because of an accident of the womb. I've seen plenty of naturals who've played a hundred minutes of football and come off thinking they've done a good job and I know, and they damn well know, that they only played to eighty per cent of their ability.

Well, that's no good to me. It's people like that I'm hardest on, getting them to give that extra twenty per cent. I prefer a fellow with less ability who plays a hundred per cent, gives everything he's got. My fellows have beaten teams which had more talent because they gave the lot. That's all I'm interested in. It's all you've got to be interested in.

How can anyone who is not giving a hundred per cent effort and commitment dare ask a man to pay four dollars for a seat to watch him? That fellow out there paying has got a right to criticize you, and he will. That's who you're playing for, that's the man who's going to control your future. You've got to give him everything, total effort, total commitment.

The new concept of professional cricket had come a long way from its gentle beginning when Cornell and Robertson had suggested a series of one-day games involving Australia's top players. Packer admitted in August that his investment over three years amounted to twelve million dollars, and by the time his cricket began the figure could not have been much less than ten million pounds.

The first match was to begin on Thursday 24 November. I had been woken during the night by a telephone call from BBC television. The *Tonight* programme on the Wednesday evening in England was to include an item about Packer, and they wanted to end the piece with a conversation with me from the VFL Park half an hour before the start of the first match, the time difference of ten hours making this possible. However, it also meant getting to the ground early to arrange for a telephone call to come through from London, so I took a taxi. It cost me A$13.90, or £8.70, and I realized that one of the main disadvantages of the ground was that being so far out it was expensive to reach. The cheapest way of making the journey from the city centre was to take a tram to Flinders Street Station and then a train to Glen Waverley where there is a free bus service to the ground. The journey took about an hour. During the match the organizers tried to arrange a bus service from the Melbourne Cricket Ground, but the local authorities objected, feeling that the existing transport was adequate.

When I arrived at the ground there was scarcely a car parked outside, but there was an army of attendants, security men and gate-keepers, as well as a large number of WSC officials inside. I found my way to the right turnstile, and with the help of the ground manager organized my telephone call. The press box was big and extremely well laid out, with a telephone for each correspondent, while the ground looked in good order and the square had been tidied up considerably from my visit of the previous day. At about ten o'clock a series of buses glistening with their new paint and covered with World Series insignia arrived and disgorged the players, all of whom were clutching their brand-new WSC cricket bags. They were all changed, and most wore their new sweaters, with gold, red or light blue borders according to which side they belonged. The general atmosphere was very much 'first day of term'. In the big hall area through the officials' entrance stood a kiosk selling WSC T-shirts, sun hats and badges. All were emblazoned with the WSC insignia of three wide black stumps ending in a hollow arc at the top, with the middle stump shorter than the other two so that a large red cricket ball could perch neatly on top.

By the time I reached the press box I was acutely aware that the cricket was not by itself the reason we came to the VFL Park. The game was being used primarily as a vehicle to make money, and it was in this context that it had to be judged. The entertainment content was therefore of paramount importance, and one came not so much to watch the cricket as to gauge its effects. As we were continually reminded, especially after the crowd figures of 2450 were announced, this was a practice match – a point Bill O'Reilly put into perspective when he wrote the next day: 'If I'd known that before I left Sydney these would have been a bad four days for the fish in Lake Macquarie.'

At five minutes to eleven the players came on to the field. The Rest of the World were wearing caps of glaring light blue which made them seem faintly ridiculous in an *Alice in Wonderland* way, for I was used to them wearing the traditional colours of their countries. The Australian openers followed in caps of screeching gold, and one of the Rest of the World side, Padmore, was wearing a bright red West Indian cap. Procter bowled the first over to McCosker, and I commented through it for the BBC. (Tony Lewis was presenting his Saturday morning programme 'Sport on Four' for Radio 4 from Melbourne, and wanted to start with some recorded commentary from the very first over of Packer cricket.) Then I watched from the press box, and after two hours realized I had been talking continuously to friends and had seen less than half the balls bowled. I had made an effort to concentrate and I had found it difficult. Normally, whether I am watching a Test Match, a county match or any other first-class game, the first two hours are fascinating, the period when the game takes shape. By the lunch interval I have often made far more notes than I shall ever need. Yet here I was watching the first two hours of the first match in a type of cricket that had received more publicity than any other since the game began, and it was an effort to watch. There was nothing preconceived about this: it was how it happened.

About half an hour before lunch Greig brought on Underwood and twenty minutes later the Kent player bowled Greg Chappell, playing no stroke, for sixteen. I never imagined I could as an Englishman have watched that moment with such supreme indifference. It had seemed extraordinary that less than a thousand people should have been in the ground at the start, but gradually one began to realize that those who stayed away might have been good judges after all. To start with, the Australian public needs and tradition demands that a representative Australian side should take the field in baggy dark green caps. It is the people who wear those green caps who bring the Hill at Sydney screaming to its feet. Instead of that the public were being asked to believe that the figures in the shining gold caps represented Australia – and they were anonymous enough to make me look twice when Australia were in the field to see if that really *was* Greg Chappell at second slip. For the Australian spectators there was nothing with which they could identify; while one can hardly identify with the Rest of the World. In England the excitement the West Indies side brings with it is largely produced by a big expatriate population. There is no such thing in Australia. The crowd for the first day was 2450 in a ground which holds 77,000. Ian Chappell hit a hundred and Underwood took four wickets, but I remember much more clearly the moment when Greig, standing at silly point for Underwood, thought he had caught Greg Chappell off bat and pad. He, Knott and Underwood appealed, but Chappell was given not out, whereupon the four players involved grinned at each other. That never happened when the Ashes were at stake.

Packer himself watched the first day from the executive suite in the members' area. He clapped energetically and was as self-conscious while watching the cricket as his troops were playing it. The next day almost a hundred more spectators made the journey to the VFL Park, although Packer was not among them: he had flown to Adelaide where another Rest of the World side was playing the West Indies. The Australian press were content mostly to report the facts, although WSC was at the outset given little space and Peter McFarline was consistently hostile in his reports for the *Age*. In Melbourne the Rest of the World were bowled out for 148 on another wholly unmemorable day's cricket in which the batting was poor. As Greig flailed about, eventually getting out for eighteen, I realized that another danger was that the players, knowing how important it was that they should entertain, would try to play their most exciting strokes and bat at their very best before they were ready to do so, and would therefore get themselves out for low scores. This is not a type of cricket which encourages batsmen to graft away for six or seven hours for 70 or 80 runs on a difficult pitch whilst wickets are falling, innings which often play a crucial part in proper Test Matches.

If one takes, say, the six most exciting Test Matches which have ever been played there have been during the course of each some quiet, almost motionless periods of play even though the participants may have been some of the greatest players of their generation. Yet it would have been fascinating to watch, for although nothing much happened on the scoreboard the play was highly relevant to the potential end-object, the final result. Here there was a time during the afternoon when Walker was bowling to Procter, both fine players, and nothing much was happening. One was acutely conscious of how dead the game seemed. If the result does not matter the means of achieving it does not matter either.

The third day, the Saturday, was highly dramatic not because of the cricket which by contrast seemed of even less significance, although Redpath made 152 in front of an audience of 3500, but because of Mr Justice Slade. I had forgotten when I went to bed that his judgement was to be announced during the night. When I opened the paper in the morning only the first part of the speech had been in time for the late editions. Even so it was clear that the judge had found for Packer and his players. The radio confirmed this. Packer had apparently stayed up all night to hear the result, given him on the telephone by the BBC in London. It was half past four when he received the news, and he rang Greig. Packer is reported to have said, 'I thought you'd like to know – we've stuffed them,' but this was later modified. As for Greig, within hours he had told Tony Lewis firmly that now they could force Packer into a corner and get back to the job of Test cricket; a telling reminder of the similar comment he had made at the meeting of the Cricketers' Association in September.

Packer's Press Relations Officer soon announced that Packer did not want to give a press conference as such, but was prepared to talk to us in groups of threes and fours at the same time as he was watching the cricket. Soon after play began he appeared in front of the executive suite smartly dressed in a pale-coloured suit, smoking and looking even bigger than usual, but surprisingly not especially happy. The representatives of the Australian evening papers talked to him first and they were followed by the dailies. Packer was then interviewed by Trevor McDonald for Independent Television News in London and by a representative of Packer's own station in Melbourne, GTV 9.

Maybe Packer's all-night vigil had taken its toll, but he seemed even more than normally to resent being closely questioned by journalists. It was now that I began to meet the strange, almost paradoxical side of the man I have mentioned in my foreword and in Chapter Two. The television interviewers had decided to use the same questions, and Packer answered easily, if without any great enthusiasm. However, when they had finished the GTV cameraman found that his film had slipped off the spool and the whole interview had thus gone unrecorded. Packer was asked if he would mind running through it again. 'No,' he said firmly. 'That's the luck of the game,' and walked back to his seat. It was his own station, too. They eventually made do with the ITN film.

It was now my turn, and with three others I gathered round him in the special enclosure. 'What are your immediate reactions to the High Court judgement? Do you see your players taking part in the Ashes series in a year's time? Are you still prepared to compromise?' And so on. He had answered all these questions several times before; but then it was he who had refused to give a press conference, and had wanted to meet the press in this fashion. Every few minutes he would complain, 'I want to watch the cricket. I suggest you do the same. That's what we're here for' – a strange comment from a man with a considerable victory to celebrate, tired though he may have been.

When he said that he was delighted by the result there was little enthusiasm in his voice, and he was quick to add that it was the players' victory, not his own. 'At least it has finally decided the basic human rights issue that the players can choose who to work for and for more than one boss if they want.' Someone told him that Jack Bailey had talked of the need to compromise. Packer replied, 'I've heard him use the word "compromise" before. I hope he means it this time. You must remember there's nothing the cricketing authorities can give me now. I have the players, the grounds and the wickets. What can they give me? I'll have the Sydney Cricket Ground next year. The present Act of Parliament which governs the trust is being changed.' After a pause he added, 'I never tried to get the Melbourne Cricket Ground. I'm very happy with the VFL Park which has got better facilities and more flexibility.' I asked him if he thought that his form of cricket would be able to compete with the Ashes series. He had no doubts. 'The Australian public prefer to watch Australia play the West

Indies rather than England. You didn't see the series in 1960/61 with the Tied Test, and that was the best West Indies side ever. Well, the one I've got is almost as good as that. England are not nearly so attractive.'

The four of us were just coming to the end of our questions when John Woodcock of *The Times* and John Thicknesse of the *Evening Standard* joined us, and soon Woodcock interposed a question. In a far from friendly voice Packer asked:

'Will you identify yourself?'

'Woodcock of *The Times*.'

'One of the enemy.'

'It's true,' Johnny Woodcock said slowly. 'I've been against what you have been trying to do. But I would nonetheless like sincerely to congratulate you on a considerable victory.'

'I can see from your face how sincere you are,' came the reply. 'I've read some of your stuff. You've never been prepared to give me a chance.'

'I don't know,' Johnny said, 'I think I said that good might come of it.'

'Good might come of evil? I don't think that's much of a compliment.'

Packer was no friendlier to Thicknesse, and refused to answer any of their questions, walking away angrily to the executive suite at the back of the stand. Earlier Tony Lewis had needed to interview him for his early morning Saturday sports programme which he was presenting that day from Melbourne. He had not met Packer, and Ian Davis, the opening batsman, agreed to take him to the Australian dressing room and introduce him that Friday morning. They went into the huge dressing room where Packer, with a WSC sun hat on his head, was drop-kicking an Australian Rules football across the room to Dennis Lillee. David introduced them and Tony asked if they might talk.

'Yeah, we'll talk,' Packer replied, and went on kicking the football for another twenty minutes without saying a word to Lewis. When he had finished he walked out of the door and Lewis, following, asked him if they could do the interview in the quiet of the dressing room. Packer turned round.

'I know exactly who you are, and you're not a friend of ours. A lot of you fellows are hopping over the fence today, aren't you? I must go and watch some cricket.'

Lewis continued to trail behind him, and after Packer had stopped to talk to several people on the way to the VIP enclosure they arrived at the spot where Packer liked to sit. At this point Lewis again asked if he could do the interview. He explained to Packer that, after himself receiving £120 for playing in a home Test Match for England and £1300 for captaining England in eight Test Matches in India and Pakistan over five months in 1972/73, he was not a complete enemy. After that Packer was both charming and diplomatic, and they talked amicably for several minutes.

Overall, however, Packer took the hostility of the media as a personal insult. Yet in his approach to his own personal public relations he was doing his best to ensure that it would grow worse. He made no attempt to get the media on his side, and preferred to adopt the attitude that his idea was so good and his product would become so popular that in the end the world's press would come begging to him. It was interesting that he never once paid a visit to the press box during the first two games at the VFL Park.

During the practice match in Melbourne a glossy yellow booklet which gave the full itinerary of the World Series Cricket in Australia over the next three months was handed round. It was only when I examined it that I fully appreciated the extent of Packer's undertaking. The names of fifty-three cricketers (Graeme Pollock and Denys Hobson, the two South Africans, were omitted) came first under Australian, World and West Indian headings along with the team managers. There followed lists of the various matches. Twenty-three were to be played in the International Cup Series. There were six five-day Super-Tests, a four-day practice game (the one we had been watching) and fifteen one-day games, all of which were to be played in either Sydney, Melbourne, Perth or Adelaide. Eight pages further on there was a list of the fifteen matches for the International Championship Cup, to be played in towns away from the main centres. In all there were 88 days' cricket on 17 grounds. The rest of the forty-page booklet was in the form of a day-by-day diary with the train arrangements, the addresses of the hotels and of the airline agents in each place to be visited. It was a remarkable document produced for the players, the media and anyone else closely involved and a look through it provided a better idea of the vast amount of money which Packer had invested than the huge figures which from time to time appeared in the papers.

The day after the practice match finished an Australian Eleven and a West Indian Eleven went by bus to Geelong for the first Country Cup match, which was a two-day affair. John Woodcock and I drove the forty miles the next morning and found that heavy overnight rain had waterlogged much of the square, so that a start that day was unlikely. There were a few hundred school-children in the ground, and both sides were busy practising on the outfield. This was in effect a second Australian Eleven, managed by Graham Ferrat, a car dealer from Adelaide whom Johnny and I had known for several years and who was a great friend of Richie Benaud's. He took us out to the middle where a circle with a thirty-metre radius had been drawn round each set of stumps. They were used for the limited-over matches when for the first ten overs of the innings nine fielders including the bowler and the wicket-keeper had to be inside the circle. After ten overs six of the eleven fielders had to remain inside. This is done in one-day cricket in South Africa as a way of increasing scoring oppor-tunities.

Ferrat explained the four competitions in detail. He also told us something about the group coaching which all the Packer players had undertaken in their contracts. They were holding the first session the next morning in Geelong on the practice ground. Seventeen schools were each sending fifteen boys, and they were going to be split up into groups of ten, each of which would be presided over by a player. Richie Benaud was deciding that after-noon the exact form these coaching sessions would take, and they would be synchronized by use of the public address system. These sessions would continue throughout the Australian season, but with only an hour's coaching each time they were little more than a public relations exercise as Benaud had suggested they would be in his notes to Packer on 6 April 1977. We also met John Curtain, who was the WSC manager in charge of the Country Cup.

For two months the success of Packer's plans had seemed to hang on the outcome of the High Court case; yet when it came it left much unresolved. Established cricket now knew that it had to compete in an open market with WSC, who in their turn had had magnificent advertising value out of the High Court. The players were understandably jubilant, feeling they had been handed respectability in the most conclusive fashion. Nonetheless, the success of WSC depended upon the television ratings and to a lesser extent the number of people who paid at the turnstiles. Mr Justice Slade may have made more people aware of the presence of World Series Cricket, but he had done nothing to take it any nearer to solvency. After the first two matches, in Melbourne and Adelaide, and the disinclination of the Australian public to pay to see them, even Packer's staunchest and most loyal supporters must have had doubts about the ultimate success of the venture.

There is no doubt that Packer was extremely unlucky that the official Australian side had such a good series with India. Ironically, it was Packer who had made this possible by claiming the best Australian players. But WSC's decision to hold their Super-Tests on the same dates as the official Test Matches was harmful to their cause, and was another example of their over-confidence.

The new Australian Test side was of great interest to many Australians. Ten years after his retirement from first-class cricket, Bobby Simpson had been brought back to captain the side, a romantic choice which heightened people's interest in the series, while the emergence of a new, young Australian side was refreshing for the many people who disliked the image of the ugly Australian built up by Ian Chappell, Marsh, Lillee and company. The young talent was there, but they had had no exposure at Test level and the experience of Simpson was crucial to their development. Simpson also went out of his way to ensure that his young side conformed to the standards of behaviour and dress and language that were prevalent when he had last played for Australia.

In Melbourne the Packer camp remained delighted with everything and outwardly regarded each day as a new success, although there were occasional signs that they were aware of their shortcomings. The main two complaints during the first match there and in the subsequent games had concerned the inconsequence of the final result and the inability of the public to identify with the teams. The next day the Australians and the West Indians had travelled to Geelong on the same bus, and in their hotel that evening the Australians had held a three-hour meeting. At the end of it they asked that when in future two teams were travelling at the same time they should use different buses, and if they were on the same aircraft they should sit at opposite ends. They felt that this would help team spirit to build up, and this becomes easier if the opposition are regarded as the enemy. The travel arrangements were duly amended.

The second day at Geelong produced another problem for WSC. Towards the end of the West Indian innings Ian Redpath came on to bowl – for him an unusual experience. At once he had Clive Lloyd caught. To celebrate, he leapt high in the air, but landed awkwardly, snapping his Achilles tendon. This injury put him out of cricket for six months, and so WSC found themselves one player short for Rockhampton, where the second Australian eleven were playing the Rest of the World. Accordingly, Graeme Watson, the former Australian Test player, was co-opted for this match, and it was soon reported in the papers that there were a number of players on stand-by to play for Packer in just such an eventuality. Richie Benaud, who was in charge of the cricket, immediately denied that anyone had been approached for this purpose, although he admitted that WSC had certain players in mind if injuries should deplete the numbers. A couple of days later Rick Darling of South Australia admitted that he had been approached by WSC, and that he had agreed to be one of the stand-by players. WSC did not want the names of these players to be known, for it would probably have meant that their State associations would not have selected them and they would not therefore have had any worthwhile practice.

The Super-Test that began on Friday 2 December between an Australian Eleven and a West Indian Eleven was obviously a truer test of public opinion than the practice game. Channel Nine was in operation, whereas for the first match only closed-circuit television had been used around the ground itself. In WSC eyes this was Australia versus the West Indies, the series Packer had forecast the Australian public wanted to see more than any other. When last the two sides had met in a Test Match in Melbourne, two years earlier and with many of the same players involved, more than 85,000 had attended on the first day alone.

It was against expectations, therefore, that I drove into the VFL Park to find even fewer cars than at the first three days of the practice match. In fact when the first ball was bowled there were fewer than 400 people in the ground. On the actual playing area there was now at each end a painted area of grass about twenty yards long and six or seven across, about thirty yards behind the stumps. At first sight they looked as if they might be the take-off pits for a shot-putter or discus-thrower. Closer inspection revealed that the WSC emblem had been painted on to the grass in black and red for the benefit of the television audience. They were not attractive additions.

Packer obviously felt that the more big names from traditional cricket he could involve in his own brand the greater impression it would make with the public. He thus especially brought over Sir Garfield Sobers from the West Indies to spin the coin for the three Super-Tests between the Australians and the West Indians. Sobers also made some personal appearances on Packer's behalf while in Australia, and was later to play an important part in winning the support of the West Indies public, especially in Barbados, for Packer and his cricket. The toss was won by Clive Lloyd, who put the Australians in to bat.

When Andy Roberts ran in to bowl the first ball of the match to Rick McCosker there was scarcely a murmur from the crowd, and when McCosker was caught at third slip by Richards off the second ball the few shouts that there were echoed emptily round the ground.

For three days the cricket was of a high enough standard, the players tried as hard as they could, but it was still the same. The result did not matter, and thus nor did the cricket. The weather was ideal, yet the first day's crowd, which rose through the afternoon to 2847, can only have been a shock to the organizers. Meanwhile, as the WSC Australians were bowled out for 256, the Indians dismissed Bobby Simpson's young Australian side for 166 at Brisbane in the First Test. Some 7,000 people watched the day's play – not a bad crowd for a first day at the Gabba. In Sydney Australia took a 2–0 lead against Italy in the final of the Davis Cup: WSC cricket had some powerful competition.

The crowd, or lack of it, was not the only bad news for WSC. The night before the match began John Curtain, the manager of the Country Cup, resigned from the organization. At the same time he made it known that he was extremely critical of the administration saying that it was in chaos, with insufficient people to do the work; those that there were knew almost nothing about cricket, he added, and were unable to do the job efficiently. He said that it was Richie Benaud and his wife Daphne who kept the organization together. Benaud, he said, was working at least fourteen hours a day.

Benaud immediately refuted this, issuing a statement saying how many rounds of golf he had had time to play in the previous week. It was all publicity WSC could have done without.

The second day of the match, Saturday, produced a crowd of 5088. The West Indians were bowled out for 214, which gave the Australians a lead of 42. Lillee, Walker and Pascoe bowled well, and there was a brilliant innings of 79 from Viv Richards. This innings was an absorbing technical exercise, especially when Richards hooked Lillee for six just in front of square, drove him off the back foot for four and square-cut him for another in the space of a few overs. They were wonderful strokes to watch, in whatever circumstances. Yet one looked at the innings as an object of beauty alone and not as a means whereby the West Indians drew nearer to a first-innings lead.

The Davis Cup did not go so well for Australia on the second day, for the Italians won the doubles, leaving the match at 2–1 and the tie to be decided on the Sunday. At Brisbane India were bowled out for 153 and in reply Australia soon lost three second-innings wickets for seven runs before Simpson and Ogilvie batted out the day. More than 10,000 watched what was developing into a marvellous game of cricket.

On the Saturday morning when Richards was batting Packer himself had given instructions that his innings should be televised live in Melbourne. Normally the Super-Tests were not to be televised live in the cities in which they were played until after the tea interval. As the principal reason for World Series Cricket was to win a television war I decided to return to the centre of Melbourne on the Saturday afternoon and watch the last two hours in colour. There were eight cameras round the ground instead of the usual four, with one at each end so that one could see the batsman face on without being obscured by the wicket-keeper. At the end of every over there was a break for commercials, which accounted for twelve minutes in every hour. Every time a batsman was out an interviewer was waiting for him as he came to the steps leading down to the dressing rooms. 'What happened there? Did you think you hit that one? Bad luck, what happened?' the interviewer would ask. Some batsmen replied in good humour, some answered the questions between clenched teeth, and Ian Chappell who was out to Michael Holding for 34 walked straight past without saying a word. Overall it was an excellent presentation, but marred by the constant overkill from the commentators, Richie Benaud, Fred Trueman, Tony Cozier from the West Indies, Bill Lawry and Keith Stackpole. Admittedly I was watching towards the end of the day, but the way in which they tried to sell the cricket to the public and to persuade people to tune in the next day, or better still, to come along if they lived in Melbourne, was dreadful, appearing both forced and unctuous. Fred Trueman had become a staunch Packer supporter, although when Packer's plans were first announced he had come out strongly against them on the BBC. Of the others, I only ran into Tony Cozier who was much more cautious and was prepared to see faults in the cricket. On television, though, they worked strictly to instructions.

The weather was perfect on the Sunday, but even so, and with the match balanced, there were less than a thousand people there at the start. As the day went on the crowd rose to 5990, but for most of the day the television set in the press box was turned to the Test Match in Brisbane or the Davis Cup in Sydney, where Alexander and Panatta fought a thrilling singles match for four hours before the Australian won. At Brisbane there was another crowd of over 10,000 where Australia reached 327 in their second innings, Simpson making 89 and Toohey his second fifty of the match. Thomson then slogged 41 at the end of the innings – the decisive runs as it proved. Needing 341 to win India had lost one wicket by the close. Back at the VFL Park the Australians were bowled out for 171 in their second innings, which left the West Indians to make 235 to win. They began well, reaching a hundred for the loss of one wicket; then came a collapse before Murray and Roberts added 47 for the eighth wicket and the West Indians won by three wickets. I watched the last few overs from the stand outside the press box, and in a similar situation in a Test Match the tension and excitement is thick all round. Even at the crucial stage in the match there was scarcely any atmosphere, and a number of people made their way out of the ground during the final stand thinking that the game was to end in the normal way at six o'clock. Only near the end was an announcement made saying that play for the day would continue until the match finished. It was an unnecessarily poor piece of public relations.

During the course of the West Indians' second innings the WSC press officer, Chris Forsyth, distributed a typed statement round the press box.

P.A.   K

Two years younger than his employer, Forsyth had been at Geelong Grammar School with Packer and had then gone on to become the leading political journalist in Melbourne. Since the early 70s when he had then given up politics he had been working for Packer's television company in Melbourne. His statement, which he prepared without reference to anyone, read as follows:

We promised the world's best cricket and the people who came to see World Series Cricket's first Super-Test in Melbourne got it. And those who saw it on television have already told us in overwhelming numbers how much they enjoyed it. If anyone doubts what went on at the VFL Park, Melbourne, during the last three days is not the best then let the figures speak for themselves.

Yesterday in the Australian Cricket Board's match in Brisbane the Australian and Indian batsmen managed only seventeen fours between them in a day's cricket. And in the WSC Super-Test Australian and West Indian batsmen hit forty-six. Overall the WSC batsmen knocked out a massive eighty-seven fours and three sixes. This alone is enough to stamp WSC's first Super-Test as memorable and far superior to what went on in Brisbane, superior for cricketers, superior for crowds and superior for television. And that is always how it will be so long as the best are playing the best.

At the bottom of the statement it read, 'Mr Kerry Packer will visit the players' dressing rooms tonight after the play to congratulate them on their combined achievements.'

It was impossible not to laugh, as many people did in the press box, and this statement caused WSC considerable embarrassment. At once one saw what John Curtain had meant when he had said that there were too many people in the organization who knew nothing about cricket. The naïveté of the statement was breathtaking – like saying that one novel was better than another because it had six more chapters, or a symphony because it had more notes. The other slight dampener for the organizers was that the first Super-Test, scheduled for five days, the period for which advertising had been sold, had ended in three. Channel Nine played old films for the next two days, on the second of which (the Monday was the rest day in Brisbane) the ABC was showing one of the most exciting of all Test Matches. This cannot have pleased the advertisers, who suffered again when the second Super-Test between the Australian Eleven and the West Indian Eleven at the Showground in Sydney also ended in three days. The third, in

Adelaide, lasted for four, so that in the series as a whole five days out of fifteen were without cricket.

An aggregate crowd of 13,885 over the three days represented a bad beginning. But it was still the television audience figures that were the most important feature, and these caused something of a mystery. Packer had employed a public relations firm to work out the ratings for the cricket on Channel Nine, but with the Davis Cup and the First Test Match in strong competition it seemed unlikely that these would be very high. On my last day in Melbourne I went round to the Old Melbourne Motor Inn to see Richie Benaud and found the atmosphere far from relaxed. He told me that the first figures which had been produced were so extraordinary that they had been sent back for rechecking. After I had gone to Pakistan I heard that the figure was 44 per cent, which was astonishingly high. I can only guess that a great many people must have switched over to the VFL Park during the day, attracted by the novelty value of what was going on; but I cannot believe that so many stayed with World Series Cricket. I later heard that a public relations organization had asked the same firm to produce similar figures at the request of one of its clients. The figure they were given was nine per cent. There is a colossal difference in the two figures, and they cannot both be right.

While the first Super-Test was being played in Melbourne the second Australian eleven were playing the Rest of the World at Rockhampton, 250 miles north of Brisbane, in great heat. Here just over a thousand people came to watch each day. Two of the participants were Richie Robinson, captain of the Australian second eleven, and Bob Woolmer, playing for the Rest of the World. Even in these early days of World Series Cricket these two players must have wondered what they were doing. Robinson had been captain of Victoria before Packer appeared on the scene. As soon as he heard Packer's plans he must have known that Marsh would have been one of the first to sign. If Robinson had turned Packer down he would have been virtually assured of the wicket-keeper's place for the Australian Test side for the next three or four years. As he could have seen from the figures on pay which Bob Parish has quoted, Robinson would have stood to earn between fifteen and twenty thousand dollars a year from Test cricket alone; he would have remained as captain of Victoria, would have kept his job, and his income would have totalled around A $40,000 a year – with his expenses on top of that. All he was ever going to do now unless Marsh was injured was to travel round Australia to the smaller venues, playing in one-, two- and three-day games for the Country Cup as captain of the Australian second eleven. As for Woolmer, he was highly unlikely to get into the Rest of the World Super-Test side, and apart from the occasional one-day game in the cities, when the best Rest of the World side was not always chosen, he too would only be playing in the Country Cup matches. It must be soul-destroying to play continually in front of crowds of between one and two thousand. If Woolmer had backed himself to play for England over the next two or three years and had done his sums again he would probably have decided that he too had made a bad decision. He could have been in Pakistan in early December with three Test Matches there to look forward to, and another three in New Zealand and then three more against each of these two sides in England in 1978 . . .

By the end of the Super-Test Packer himself was saying in public how pleased he was by all that had happened, but John Cornell and Austin Robertson, who long since had seen the idea taken out of their control, were both worried. The day after the match finished the WSC committee met at the Old Melbourne Motor Inn, and among other things they considered whether they should bring down the price of admission tickets. The price was four dollars. They met to the background of a newspaper report which quoted Chris Forsyth as saying that the tickets were too expensive, and that the organizers had miscalculated, thinking that millions would come through the gates. They decided to hold the prices, but it must have been a difficult decision. The tickets were overpriced, and they must have been aware of it; but to have brought them down would have implied a downgrading by WSC of their own product.

On Tuesday 6 December, Johnny Woodcock and I flew from Melbourne to Singapore, on to Karachi and then up to Peshawar on the North-West Frontier to join the England cricketers. At Tullamarine Airport we watched the fourth day at Brisbane on television. There was another good crowd, and the first-class steward brought us the final result from the flight deck when we were two hours out of Melbourne. Australia had won by sixteen runs. The Australian Cricket Board had been the overwhelming victors in the first of the battles between the two types of cricket.

◆

CHAPTER 10

Plot and Counter-Plot

THE AEROPLANE LANDED at Colombo, and in the airport lounge I bought a copy of the local paper, the *Sun*. There on the back page was a long article headed 'Packer Wins Round One'. At five o'clock the next morning in Karachi a customs official talked for a quarter of an hour about Packer, in his enthusiasm over-looking my ample ration of whisky. Later that day in Peshawar the England players were equally anxious to hear about World Series Cricket. Mr Packer was clearly going to be a constant travelling companion for the next five months, even if the logic of that Colombo headline was hard to follow.

The moment I stepped off the aeroplane I was in a completely different world – and not only geographically. At once I found myself in the midst of dramas caused by Packer, and made worse and at times incomprehensible by local intrigue. For eight weeks I was in a constant atmosphere of plot and counter-plot without ever being wholly sure who was on what side. The contrast between the attractive old army ground in Peshawar and the VFL Park in Melbourne could hardly have been more extreme. The ground in Peshawar was ringed by elderly pipal trees, their rich green foliage contrasting pleasantly with the bright shamianas and the ladies in their colourful clothes, grouped together as is the custom in their own enclosure.

The cricket itself was far more personal than I had found in Melbourne, and I found myself, too, much more involved in what was going on. Even small details contributed to this. The TCCB had decided in 1977 that when England toured overseas they would no longer be called MCC except when they played Test Matches. They would still wear the traditional MCC touring colours, however, and the touring cap of St George and the Dragon. It made a pleasantly familiar contrast with the Reds, Golds and Blues of Melbourne.

England had made a reasonable start to the tour on a rain-affected pitch at Rawalpindi and then at Faisalabad where Boycott, Rose and Roope had made hundreds in a drawn match. (The ground at Faisalabad was in April 1978 to gain international fame when it was used for the public flogging of four Pakistanis who had been convicted of rape. This latter fixture was played to a full house; Boycott and company were thought locally to make less compelling watching.)

I had only been in Peshawar for twenty-four hours when rumours began to circulate that the Pakistan Board were about to invite their Packer players back from Australia to play in the three Test Matches against England. The Board of Control for Cricket in Pakistan, the BCCP, was unpopular with the public, who felt that it was the Board who had driven the players to Packer in the first place. The reason for this belief was a row between the Board and the players the year before, during the New Zealand side's tour of Pakistan. Six of the Pakistan side had threatened not to play in the Second Test Match against New Zealand in Hyderabad. The night before the match Asif Iqbal, probably the focal point of the dissent, Mushtaq, the captain, and who would not have been far behind, Sadiq Mohammed, Imran Khan, Majid Khan and Wasim Bari said they would not play unless paid more. During the First Test in Lahore Asif had been asked by the Board to see that the professionals in the side, those who played county cricket, signed contracts saying that they were happy with the terms they had been offered by the Board. The contracts had been signed, with the connivance of Asif, who had significantly not returned them to the Board. Instead he and the others were joined by Wasim Bari, who was to be their captain against England, and together they decided they should try to extract more money out of the Board. With the contracts still in the players' possession there was little the Board could do.

On the morning of the Second Test against New Zealand the six players were seen in their hotel by Hafeez Kardar, the Board's Chairman. He tried to speak with each player in turn, but they

refused, saying that he should see all six together. The outcome
was that Kardar said that he would do all that he could during the
Third Test in Karachi to see that their demands were met. The
six duly played in Hyderabad, and Pakistan beat New Zealand by
ten wickets. Then, during the Karachi Test, Kardar made it
known that if the six did not accept the terms which had been
offered to them by the Board in the contracts they had signed but
not returned they would be thrown out of the team. He would
also suggest to their employers that they should be sacked from
their jobs. It was further leaked to the press that the players
involved were 'unpatriotic' and their behaviour 'that of mer-
cenaries'.

Abdul Hafeez Kardar had for long been the controlling influence
behind cricket in Pakistan. He won a Blue at Oxford for three
years, 1947–9, and he played for Warwickshire in the county
championship. He toured England with India in 1946 under the
Nawab of Pataudi's captaincy, and after Partition represented
Pakistan. He was their first Test captain from 1952 when they
played their first Test series against England, and remained
captain up to his retirement in 1958. Since then he has run the
administrative side of Pakistan cricket. Long an opponent of the
English cricket Establishment, he at one point tried to have Sri
Lanka made a full member of the ICC in the hope that their vote
combined with that from the West Indies, Pakistan and India,
would outvote that of England, Australia and New Zealand, and
enable him to move the headquarters of the ICC away from Lord's.
He is feared by many of the present generation of Pakistani
cricketers, and has never been an easy man with whom to deal.

After winning the series against New Zealand Mushtaq was
sacked from the captaincy, and Intikhab Alam and Zaheer Abbas
were named as captain and vice-captain respectively for the tour
of Australia and the West Indies. As soon as the Third Test had
ended Mushtaq returned to England to organize his Benefit with
Northamptonshire. The five other players who had rebelled in
Hyderabad remained in Pakistan and telephoned Mushtaq after
the touring side had been announced. Soon afterwards they said
that they would not go to Australia unless Mushtaq was reappointed captain. There was much hostility to Kardar's decisions,
and eventually, on the orders of the Prime Minister, Mr Bhutto,
the President of the Pakistan Sports Control Board who was the

Minister of Education intervened and disbanded the selection committee who, under Imtiaz Ahmed, the former Pakistan wicket-keeper and batsman, had chosen the touring side. The President of the Pakistan Sports Control Board also said that the touring party would be re-selected. A new selection committee was chosen, headed by Hanif Mohammad, with two other selectors. The party was chosen again, Mushtaq was reappointed as captain, and only one change was made from the original selection. The man left out was Aamer Hameed, whom it was felt by some had been originally selected because his and Kardar's family were close friends and his father was a business associate of Chaudri Mohammad Husain, who was to succeed Kardar as President of the Board. While all this was going on the Board of Control remained in existence as a body, but was powerless to act.

The tours of both countries were reasonably successful, for Pakistan drew in Australia and lost 2–1 in the West Indies. When the players returned to Pakistan the original selectors were surprisingly reinstated. It was now that Kardar resigned, although relinquishing his position in name only, for Chaudri Mohammad Husain now took over as President of the Board. They immediately took the decision to abolish professionalism in Pakistan cricket, and this was seen as another move inspired by Kardar and aimed at the rebels who, with the exception of Majid who had resigned from Glamorgan and Wasim Bari, were playing English county cricket and were professionals whatever the Board pronounced. This produced little reaction from the players, for by the time he left Australia for the West Indies Asif knew about Packer's plans and had announced his intention to retire from Test cricket, while the others were soon to join Packer. By then Greig had flown out to the West Indies on Packer's behalf and had removed any lingering doubts which Asif had not been able to dispel from the minds of the other Pakistanis.

Through all these toings and froings Pakistan cricket was not shown in the kindest of lights. The Board, through Kardar, had said one thing and done another, and had in no way helped their future relationship with the players. Asif's part in it all probably does not bear too close an examination, but he and his fellow rebels were at least single-minded – they were simply after more money – so that when Packer appeared he solved two problems. First, he produced the necessary money and, second, he enabled these players to snub their own Board. When the first news of the Packer circus broke it was presented in such a way in Pakistan that the Board was held responsible for the defection of their players, so that throughout later events a number of people were busy justifying their position. At every turn the story becomes more confusing, but it is all relevant to the dramatic events in Karachi before the start of the Third Test in January 1978.

When the Board announced that they were trying to bring the Packer players back for the series against England it was thought by many people to be nothing more than an exercise in public relations. It was known that they were all under strict contract to Packer, and there did not seem the slightest chance that he would release them to play in a form of cricket against which he had set up in direct opposition. Like all Boards of Control, the Pakistan Board did not recognize Packer, and was not prepared to deal directly with him. The Secretary of the Board, Colonel Zafar, had been in touch with the Pakistan Ambassador in Canberra in order that he should locate Mushtaq. By the time Colonel Zafar spoke to Mushtaq himself a day or two before the start of the First Test in Lahore he must have known what it was about, and would have been told by the Packer camp and also the Ambassador. When they heard of the Pakistan Board's intentions Packer's associates realized that they had been given a marvellous opportunity to reintroduce some of their players back into Test cricket, and in so doing gain recognition by an official Board of Control – in short, to split their opponents in the cricket world still further. Both Greig and Benaud know Pakistan, and would have been well aware of the situation there and how easily the Board's authority could be disrupted. While this was going on England beat the Governor's XI at Peshawar by 212 runs, only the second victory by England or MCC in Pakistan in three tours, so lifeless are the pitches there. Thus England came to Lahore for the First Test with every confidence, but without any idea who their opponents would be.

When Colonel Zafar rang up Mushtaq and asked him if he and the others were available to play in the series against England he was told that they were indeed available, but that to ensure their release from WSC cricket the Board must get permission from Kerry Packer himself. The Board refused to do this, because they still did not recognize Packer. Meanwhile the Pakistani papers were saying confidently that the four players would be back in time for the First Test in Lahore. The papers in Pakistan had been manipulated skilfully by the opponents of the Board, and throughout the whole episode tried to embarrass the official body. The day before the match I talked at the Gaddafi Stadium to Imtiaz Ahmed, the chairman of the selectors, and he said he did not know if Mushtaq and company would return; I felt sure, however, that he was waiting on instructions from above. We went to the ground on the first morning of the match half expecting to see Mushtaq, Majid, Imran and Zaheer, but they were not there. In the light of what happened later it is highly probable that Omar Kureishi, the sporting director of PIA and a one-time friend of Kardar, now made contact with the Pakistanis under contract to Packer and through them with the Packer organization itself. Omar Kureishi had managed the Pakistani side in England in 1974, and his friendship with Kardar came to an abrupt end during the Lord's Test Match. Kardar liked to watch the game from the balcony in the players' dressing room. The presence of the Chairman of the Board made the players uneasy, and when they told Kureishi this he spoke to Kardar and asked him if he would mind watching from elsewhere. Kardar took this as a personal attack on him by Kureishi and they ceased to be friends.

The situation simmered on during the First Test in Lahore, but by the time the match ended it was in danger of being overtaken by yet another controversy. Before the Test Match the three English county professionals in the side, Sarfraz, Nawaz Sadiq and Javed Miandad, had a meeting and decided not to play in the match if the Board of Control did not refund them the price of their air fares back to Pakistan. With the 'abolition' of professionalism it was in theory up to the players to pay their own expenses, but the whole idea of professionalism having ended was absurd. The main banks and PIA employ good cricketers simply to play cricket – professionalism pure and simple – and the leading cricketers are anxious to be employed. Imtiaz Ahmed saw the three players, and on behalf of the Board promised that their fares would be paid. However, by the time the match was over the money had not been forthcoming.

The match ended on 19 December. The following day I was standing in the foyer of the Intercontinental Hotel in Lahore where both teams were staying, and Sarfraz came into the hotel looking extremely discontented. He came over and told me that as a protest he was leaving Lahore that night for London. He said he was fed-up because the money had not yet been paid to him, and that as vice-captain he had not once been consulted by his captain throughout the Test Match. This was strange, for one of those who had come into the hotel with him was Wasim Bari, his captain, and they did not appear to be enemies. Another was Aftab Gul, Sarfraz's lawyer, who had toured England in 1969. Sarfraz said he would be available for the Second Test in Hyderabad if the Board recalled him and paid his fare. He left for Karachi that evening, reaching London the following day.

When Sarfraz had originally come back to Pakistan from England after the county season he had gone first of all to Ahmedabad in India to play in Dilip Sardesai's Benefit match. Presumably the organizers there had paid his fare, but Sarfraz was adamant that the Pakistan Board should also pay him his air fare in full. In Pakistan Sarfraz is employed by the United Bank, who had also agreed to pay his fare from England. It began to look as if Sarfraz was being used as the front man for another group who wanted to embarrass the Board and to try to extract more money from them. Sadiq and Miandad were originally involved with him, while Wasim Bari was one of the six a year earlier. It was an impossible situation to unravel.

The Board reacted sharply to his return to London and said that he had let his country down and would therefore not be considered for either of the last two Test Matches against England. In the meantime Sarfraz was issuing statements thick and fast in London, and Aftab Gul was issuing more in Lahore. First Sarfraz said that he would return if the Board recalled him and paid his fare. When told of the Board's hostile reaction he then said that because of his loyalty to his country he would pay his own fare back and if necessary would pay for his lunch and tea on each day of the Test Match. It was all rather absurd; but presumably Sarfraz felt he had made his point.

Immediately after Christmas the fast bowler was momentarily forgotten when David Clark, President of MCC and of the International Cricket Conference, and Jack Bailey arrived in Lahore to talk to the Pakistan Board on their first stop on a journey round the world. They were to meet the Boards of all the Test-playing countries in order to discuss the Packer situation and to see what the feelings were about an appeal being made against the High Court judgement. Clark and Bailey were hoping to find a common purpose and a common method of approach with which to deal with Packer. The two men had a highly satisfactory meeting with the Pakistan Board, and found that their objectives were indeed the same. After two nights in Lahore they flew on to Bangalore, then Melbourne, Christchurch and Port of Spain.

England played one-day internationals at Sahiwal and Sialkot on either side of Christmas, and were on their way to Hyderabad for the Second Test when General Zia-ul-Haq, the Chief Martial Law Administrator, who was principally responsible for the overthrow of Bhutto, decided to call representatives of the Board and other important administrators of the game to Rawalpindi on the rest day of the Test Match. They were to discuss the state of cricket in Pakistan. He had been persuaded to try to sort out the infighting and intrigue which was once again bedevilling Pakistan cricket. Among those who went up to Rawalpindi were Colonel Zafar, the secretary of the Board, Mahmood Hussain, member of the Board and manager of the tour to England in 1978, Imtiaz Ahmed, the chairman of selectors, Fazal Mahmood, the former Pakistan fast bowler who with Mahmood Hussain did so much to help Pakistan beat England at The Oval in 1954, and now a journalist and broadcaster, Hafeez Kardar, who in addition to everything else was a confidant of General Zia-ul-Haq, Hanif Mohammad, the famous opening batsman and committed opponent of the Board, and Omar Kureishi, another committed opponent. It was a meeting which was to have dramatic consequences, and what actually happened in Pindi is of the greatest importance to all that follows, culminating as it did in the decision by the Pakistan Board not to include the three Packer players in the Third Test in Karachi at the end of the month.

Those going to the meeting watched the third day's play dressed conspicuously in suits, then surreptitiously left. When they returned the story was told in whispers and of course as a matter of utmost secrecy. The Pakistanis love to make a mystery out of anything. For all that, I heard two accounts of the events in Pindi. The first was Hanif's version of the story, although it was not told me by Hanif himself. Omar Kureishi and Hanif were the only two opponents of the Board at the meeting, and as the story only emerged after the Packer players had been told that they would not be selected for the Third Test in Karachi one may have to allow for a certain poetic licence. In any event, it is a tale conspicuous for its gaps.

According to my informant Hanif was asked to the meeting later than Kureishi, although it is not certain whether this meant that he arrived after it had begun or merely that he did not have time to do his homework. When the meeting broke up Hanif asked the General's secretary if he might have a word with the General on his own. This was arranged, and the General assured him he was going to look into the whole situation. He wanted to know from Hanif why the Packer players did not go to Lahore for the First Test, and conversation inevitably turned to Packer. The General told Hanif that Kureishi had asked if he could contact the players in Australia, for he had said that he was on good terms with them and that he might well be able to get them to come back. It is perhaps significant that the General is not reported by Hanif as instructing Kureishi to go ahead in his mission.

I get the impression from this account by Hanif of a secondary meeting that the General was anxious to be as fully informed as possible and was unwilling at this stage to commit himself over the Packer players – or anything else. This account also says nothing of what Hanif himself wanted to see the General about in private, or whether Omar Kureishi inspired Hanif to seek such an audience. The same source which produced this story then went on to relate the sequence of events which ended in Karachi during the Third Test. It is told with sympathy towards both Hanif and Omar Kureishi. There are gaps in both stories, although they are worth telling to give some indication of the total confusion at the time. One must not forget that the outcome was of considerable importance to Packer, even if for the moment he seems only a background figure.

After the meeting in Pindi Kureishi contacted Packer, who told him that he was prepared to release his players only in return for a surety that they would be selected. A week after the Second Test had finished Packer himself flew to Singapore with Zaheer, Imran and Mushtaq – although they had an eventful time leaving Australia because Mushtaq lost his passport. Kureishi met them and told Packer that his authority had come from the Chief

Martial Law Administrator, and he gave a guarantee that the three Packer cricketers would indeed play. Packer was evidently satisfied with this, for he allowed the three cricketers to continue their journey to Karachi.

Of the three players themselves, Mushtaq, one of the famous Mohammad brothers (Wazir, Hanif and Sadiq being the others), was their spokesman. His life was based in England where he had lived for more than ten years and he had played for and recently captained Northamptonshire, who announced in the autumn of 1977 that they were to dispense with his services. He is an excitable character with the temperament of a rubber ball. Zaheer, on the other hand, is quieter and more studious as his bespectacled appearance suggests. He would have needed more persuading to join Packer than Mushtaq, and in any case was not included in the first batch of signings. A Gloucestershire player, he is a wonderful batsman with a less mercurial style than some Pakistanis. Imran, a cousin of Majid, is similarly something of an enigma. He comes from an upper-class background in Pakistan and spent three years in the Oxford side from 1973 to 1975. He played county cricket for Worcestershire – who had helped him with his education – and then decided to move to Sussex. He is another who is aware of the value of money, and would have needed no prompting to join Packer.

As the three journeyed from Singapore to Karachi stories of their impending return were everywhere. Hafeez Kardar, who still had the ear of the General, was summoned to see him in Pindi. In this version of the story he is said to have explained all the implications and consequences of including the Packer players in the Pakistan side. He reminded the General that the visit of the British Prime Minister which had just taken place had been a great success, and that if Pakistan now decided to play their Packer players to obtain a quick and slightly dubious advantage Callaghan would almost be bound to take a dim view of it. It was at this point that the General realized he had made a bad mistake – which implies that the selectors had been told to include the Packer trio in the Third Test side – and had not appreciated the circumstances of their return. But it was too late to avert a controversy. The three players were by now practising with the rest of the Pakistan squad, and the selectors announced three days before the match that they would be considered.

Late in the afternoon of 17 January, just two days before the game was due to begin, the General arrived in Karachi and summoned the President of the Pakistani Board, the selectors and Hafeez Kardar to the State Guest House where he was staying. They briefed him on the situation and he was informed, presumably by Kardar, that the inclusion of the Packer players would give Pakistan a bad name and would generally lead to bad publicity. If they were selected, he was told, it was unlikely that there would be a Test Match. It was now that the General changed his mind and turned against the Packer players. They were asked to make a public apology, to acknowledge the overall authority of the Board and to agree not to sign contracts with outside bodies without first obtaining the Board's permission. Inevitably they refused to do this, and they were told they would not now be selected. There was another meeting with the General as a result of which a long statement was drawn up and issued by the President of the Board at a hastily-called press conference at 10.15 that evening in his hotel room.

This is the sequence of events which was related to me by one whose sympathies then and the year before had been with the players. Obviously the cricketers themselves were hostile to Kardar, who had been the focal point of their distrust a year earlier, and it would have annoyed this faction that Kardar was close to the General. They would also have been keen to discredit him still further, and maybe by implication the General too, and it will have suited those putting round this story to depict Kardar as the villain of the piece. It is of course true that after his experience of the previous year Kardar would have been highly unlikely to have offered the same rebel players much hope of comfort.

The Board's version of the story is more brief. When they met the General in Pindi they first discussed Sarfraz, and it was agreed that if he came back to Pakistan of his own accord he would be considered for Test selection – provided that he made a public apology. The discussion moved on logically from Sarfraz to the Packer players, and it was again agreed that if they returned voluntarily they would be available for selection. Nothing was apparently said about a public apology, although the implication was that if they were brought back they would have to make an apology if they wanted to play for Pakistan. It was at this point that Kureishi told the General that he thought he would be able to get them back. According to this informant the General made a non-committal reply and presumably thought that Kureishi had meant that he could help in their voluntary return. At no time did the General authorize Kureishi to approach Packer or the players on his behalf, and he was never instructed to proceed over the heads of the Board, as Kureishi himself later claimed.

Kureishi therefore helped to bring the players back and wheeled and dealed with Packer in order to do so. By no stretch of the imagination could it be called a voluntary return, and the day before the match the Board saw the players and demanded a public apology. The three players again refused to give this, but Imran asked if the word could be changed from 'apologize' to 'regret'. This compromise offer was accepted. They were then told that they had to agree not to sign a contract with any would-be employer without first obtaining permission from the Pakistan Board, and that they should at all times 'put Pakistan first'. They replied that they had contracts with Packer until 1980. The Board replied firmly that this was not good enough.

The story was given another important twist by the attitude of the England team. For some time the possibility of the Packer players taking part in the Third Test had been openly discussed in the papers, but whereas Pakistan cricket blew up during the Second Test in Hyderabad with the meeting in Rawalpindi, the discontent within the England party did not manifest itself until they returned to Lahore for the third one-day international.

The four England players who had turned down Packer, Boycott, Willis, Old and Randall, were to the front in the general feeling of hostility within the England side to the return of the three Pakistanis to their Test team. Bob Taylor and John Lever were two more who felt strongly. While Brearley on his own would almost certainly have stopped short of pulling out of a Test Match he wrote in his book *Return of the Ashes*, 'I was against the ban on players, but I was never in favour of Packer's players coming in and out of Test teams as it suited them (or him).' In his role as captain Brearley tried to dissuade the players from taking such drastic action, but he could not prevent them. With most of the leading players so firmly against the return of the Packer trio, the younger members of the party went along with their seniors.

The team arrived in Karachi on Saturday 14 January. There

they held another meeting, and drafted a statement which Brearley was to read out the following day. Both these meetings were among the players only, and Ken Barrington was called in for short spells only and in a purely advisory capacity. As manager he was of course the representative of the TCCB, and so in a difficult situation. Obviously he could not condone rebellion by his players, wherever his sympathies lay. After the statement had been drafted some of the players spoke by telephone to Doug Insole. He tried hard to persuade them to play, but told them that they were in order to make a statement as long as they made it quite clear that it was theirs alone, and did not in any way represent the views of the TCCB.

These telephone calls went on throughout the night. The next day, the 15th, events moved with even greater speed. Attention was diverted from the main issue when Mike Brearley broke a bone in his forearm in the fifth over of an unimportant one-day game on a poor pitch on the charming Gymkhana Club ground. It was decided that he should fly home to England that night to have an operation to ensure that he regained the full rotating movement of his arm. So, by default as it were, Boycott achieved his life-long and oft-stated ambition to become England's captain. A replacement was sent for, and at about eight o'clock that night Barrington and Brearley held their last joint press conference of the tour in the team room, Brearley with his arm already encased in plaster. Barrington announced that the replacement would be Clive Radley. He was flying in from Sydney, where he had been coaching at Cranbrook School, and where with a number of other county cricketers he was involved in an elaborate scheme set up by none other than Mr Kerry Packer. Radley was not in any way directly involved with World Series Cricket but there was a strong element of irony in his choice – although I do not think that any of those who authorized his selection were aware of his winter employer. When Barrington was asked what he thought about Radley being a Packer employee he said he did not know that he was; but they knew at Lord's.

In his last official act as England's captain on the tour Brearley then read out the players' statement. It read simply: 'The England touring team are unanimously opposed to the principles of players contracted to World Series Cricket being considered for selection for official ICC Test Matches' – a bald statement of fact which left no one in any doubt as to what the players thought. After the statement had been issued I did not come across one player who was unhappy with all that had happened. They had come through eight hard weeks in Pakistan and had struggled to survive on the field of play; it is not surprising that they should have taken the line they did, and there was no mistaking the overall distrust of Packer and his associates.

It was unprecedented for a team to take matters into their own hands in this way – although several of the leading Australians had refused to come to England in 1912 for the Triangular Tournament because the Australian Board refused to give them the manager they wanted. Brearley stressed that the statement was issued at the wish of the players, that it had nothing to do with winning or losing this one Test Match, and that the players were particularly concerned with the approaching series between Australia and the West Indies in the Caribbean, for the West Indies Board had already said that they would play their Packer representatives.

The following morning the England party had nets, while team meetings went on for much of the rest of the day. Feelings hardened still further against the inclusion of the Packer players who were nearby practising with their Pakistani colleagues. That evening the entire party, players and press, went to the British Consul-General for a cocktail party, and from what I gathered there it was clear that the players were considering a further protest if the Packer trio should play. The next morning there were more nets; in the afternoon, more meetings. A press conference had been arranged for five o'clock. In the middle of the afternoon I went up to see Barrington on another matter, and as I went into his room I could see from his face something of what he was going through. The players were still in conference in the team room, and Barrington had been in to give advice. Frequent telephone calls were being made to Lord's. The press conference was put back an hour, for the players were still talking, and at six o'clock the press went into the team room where Barrington and Boycott met us with stony faces. As the rest of the players left the room they grinned sheepishly but said nothing. The two men then revealed that no side would be announced until the following morning – a crop of minor injuries was the cause, they said – and they refused at first to say anything at all about what had been going on. They finally admitted that calls had been made to Doug Insole, but they said that they could say nothing beyond this until an announcement had come from the Pakistan side. This presumably was the announcement of their team, which would reveal the Pakistan Board's intentions over the Packer players. Barrington then told us that there would be no more news that evening from the England party.

We left the room to make up our minds about the implications of what we had heard. The Pakistan selectors were said to be announcing their side later the same evening, but in the circumstances it seemed likely that that too would be delayed, probably till the morning: neither side wanted to make the first move. The situation was made even more confusing by the fear we all had that the public in Karachi, who had been made only too well aware of the arrival there of Mushtaq, Imran and Zaheer – Majid was needed in Australia – would riot at the National Stadium and disrupt the match if their three heroes were not selected. Karachi has a history of disturbed Test Matches, and since there had already been two days' rioting in the Lahore Test Match when Mrs Bhutto and the Pakistan People's Party had used the Friday of the Test Match for political ends it seemed highly likely that there would be more riots in Karachi. Another great danger was that neither side would announce their team until they arrived at the ground, when many thousands of spectators would already be there. If the Pakistanis announced then that they were including the Packer players and the England players decided to pull out the crowd might take hideous retribution.

To say the least, it was an uneasy situation that evening in Karachi. When I left the team room I had no doubt in my own mind that there would not be a Test Match the next day if the Packer trio were in the Pakistan side. I wrote accordingly for the next day's paper in London and filed my story from the cable office at half past nine that evening. On my return to the hotel I went up to see Michael Melford, who had just heard that there was to be a press conference at a quarter past ten that night in the room of the President of the Pakistan Board, Chaudri Mohammed Husain. Michael also said that Husain was going to read a statement saying that the selectors would not pick the Packer players. My first story, which I hoped was already going over the telex to London, was thus already out of date. The England players would not now pull out, but the Packer camp had suffered a defeat. Their three players had been returned to Pakistan having been guaranteed a place in the Third Test, but now they, along with Packer himself, had been made to look stupid.

At 10.15 about twenty-five of us squeezed ourselves into the President's bedroom – press conferences are seldom comfortable affairs – and a minute or two later the President and an aide emerged from the adjoining room. The President had laryngitis, so his aide read out his statement at dictation speed while we all scribbled frantically.

Chaudri Mohammed Husain said pertinently that the Board felt that the future of Pakistan cricket should be linked with cricketers in Pakistan and that it should not be dictated by those who lived abroad for most of the year and who came back to Pakistan only when it suited them. He stated his Board's total opposition to Packer and said that they did not intend to pick players who had given their first loyalties to Packer, now or at any time in the future. They were willing to welcome back any of the Packer players to Pakistan cricket, however, provided that they acknowledged the authority of the Board and made Pakistan their first loyalty.

It was a statement which should have left no one in any doubt that no Packer players would take the field the next day or come to England with the Pakistan touring side the following April, or indeed ever again while under contract to Packer. Of course, it greatly angered the opponents of the Board, who were probably much nearer to victory in this issue than one realized at the time. It was also interesting that both Ken Barrington and Bernard Thomas his assistant were in the room to hear this statement, and significant too that through the door in the adjoining room was Hafeez Kardar. The General had summoned him to Karachi and, having given his advice, he left the next day for Lahore or Rawalpindi and did not see any of the cricket. Kardar has become even more of an enigma in Pakistan cricket because he is not any longer in an official position and yet throughout these troubles his influence was both seen and felt. He said several times during England's visit to Pakistan that he had finished with cricket and would never again take any part in it; but I could not help remembering that excellent dinner at Salloos in Lahore where he was our host, and the important people in Pakistan cricket who were also guests. If anyone had the power and influence to control events in the world of Pakistan cricket it was still Hafeez Kardar.

I later learned that that same afternoon the General had agreed that in the circumstances the Packer players should not be selected, and that it was then that the statement later issued by the President of the Board was drafted. My informant stressed that the Board was at no time put under pressure by the likelihood of the England players refusing to take part in the match if the Packer trio were included. This would be easier to believe had Ken Barrington and Bernard Thomas not been present in the President of the Board's hotel room when his statement was read to the press later that night.

As it was the statement sent us all scurrying back to our typewriters to rewrite or amend our earlier stories, and although Pakistan has a five hours' time advantage over England the sheer weight of copy that was lodged at the cable office that night caused long delays, and several first editions were missed. For a journalist it had been a nightmare of a day. The President's unequivocal statement, however, was not quite the end of the story. Its long-term implications were abundantly clear, but in the light of all the other conversations and promises one could not be certain what would apply beyond the Third Test Match. The Test was duly played without the Packer trio, and ended in the dullest of draws, and while the public were apparently entirely unmoved by their absence there was much full-hearted discussion in the members' and press areas as supporters of both sides tried to justify their positions. Although he came only briefly to the National Stadium Omar Kureishi found himself under more pressure than anyone, and one morning early in the match he tried to vindicate his own actions by publishing in a Karachi paper the letter he wrote to Colonel Zafar as Secretary of the Board telling them of his intentions to bring back the players from Australia. By now Kureishi had made himself unpopular with Packer, while the General cannot have been too pleased with him. Yet had Kureishi been successful in his plans and succeeded in bringing down the Pakistan Board he would have been a most powerful figure in the next administration – one which surely would have recognized World Series Cricket.

In fact the General himself came to watch on the Friday, the third day. Arriving at the entrance that morning was like driving through an army about to join battle. The security was tight, and inside the ground the atmosphere was electric as members of the Board checked that everything was in order for the visit. The General, a small man with a gentle, moustached face and, according to those who know him, a delightful sense of humour, watched some of the cricket before lunch, and during an extended interval met the teams and presented the players with commemorative gold medals. He had lunch in the tent at the back of the pavilion by the main entrance. A rumour circulated in the press box that he was going to meet the three Packer players during the day. At the start of the lunch interval the General did meet the two teams and immediately afterwards I ran into Mushtaq and Zaheer (Imran had gone to Lahore to see his family) at the back of the pavilion. We had just begun to talk when an official came up, spoke quickly in Urdu, and all three, players and official, went off eagerly towards the lunch tent to meet the General. I heard about the conversation from two people who were in the tent at the time. First one of the ADCs asked the General if he would be prepared to see Mushtaq and Zaheer, and the General asked his aide if either player were related to him. When told they were not the General said that he would be prepared to see them – this showed that the General had his wits about him, for officials will do all they can to arrange for members of their own families to receive favours. The conversation between the three men was brief and to the point. The General spoke first.

'Why do you want to see me?'

'We were brought back to play in the Test Match,' Mushtaq answered. 'Why are we not playing?'

'That is your bad luck,' the General replied. 'Why are you not available to play cricket for Pakistan all the time? I have raised the fees of Test cricketers and I will guarantee that you will get good jobs.'

'We are professional cricketers, and have lived abroad for a long time. And Packer is promoting cricket.'

'What Packer is doing,' the General said quietly, 'is *prostituting* cricket.'

There the conversation ended. Two days later all three Packer players returned to Australia.

When the news first broke in Australia that the Packer trio would not be selected for Pakistan it was an hour or two before the start of the first Super-Test at the Sydney Showground between the Australians and the Rest of the World, and eight hours before the start of the Third Test in Karachi. An Australian journalist who reported the first two-thirds of the Packer season told me later in New Zealand that the Packer organization had two high moments while he was with them. The first came with Mr Justice Slade's High Court judgement, the second with the news that the three Pakistani players would be in their national side. They saw such a selection as a tremendous breakthrough. When the news finally came through that they would not play after all, this journalist spoke to Lynton Taylor, an executive of Channel Nine, Chris Forsyth and Tony Greig, and they were so confident about the outcome that Greig laughed when asked for a comment, saying, 'You want to wait and see who runs out on to the field.'

While the General was at the cricket on that Friday he asked Geoff Boycott if at the close of play he would come round to the State Guest House where he was staying and have tea with him; there were certain subjects on which he would like to hear the England captain's views. Boycott left the ground that evening for the guest house, and had more than half an hour's talk with the General. Their discussions were confidential, and all Boycott would say afterwards was that he had found his host charming, that he had been extremely impressed by his knowledge of cricket – and that he had been given an excellent tea. One gathered that the General had been thoroughly briefed; certainly he did not give the impression of being a man who would be easily persuaded by others into making a hasty decision. This meeting might have hardened the General even more against the Packer players, because Boycott was of course by then a committed opponent of Packer, and would have expressed his own views forcefully.

Events moved at a remarkable rate on those few days in Karachi, and one evening in my room at the Sind Club I remembered something which Benaud had said to me on our meeting just before I left Melbourne. As I was about to leave his room he asked me if it had occurred to me that one day when I was watching England play Pakistan in Lahore Australia might be playing the West Indies in Karachi at the same time – the WSC Australians and West Indians.

I have only been able to give an imperfect story of all that

happened in a remarkable week, and it may never be possible for
anyone to say without fear of correction what really happened.
My information all came from people who were personally
committed one way or the other. I am not accusing any of them of
deliberately distorting what happened, but because of their own
involvement they may have interpreted the same events differently.
In Hanif's version of the story the General is said to have realized
that he had made a bad mistake when Kardar went up to Rawalpindi to see him. This implies that he had given Kureishi his
blessing and instructed him to bring back the players from
Australia. I do not believe this, for in such a delicate situation it
was inconceivable that a man of the General's diplomatic stature
should have gone over the heads of the Board of Control to
Kureishi. I also find it hard to believe that the General needed
Kardar to point out the damage that could be done to Anglo-
Pakistan relations by playing the Packer players.

Then, three days before the match, the selectors announced
that Mushtaq, Zaheer and Imran would be considered for selection.
They most certainly would not have said this if they had not been
instructed to by some higher authority. It looks as if three days
before the match the Packer players were indeed going to be
selected, and the 'higher authority' would first have been the
Board of Control and then the General. Yet if the General had
realized that he had made a bad mistake he was now about to
perpetuate it. Then, on the day before the match, the three were
summoned before the Board and asked to apologize and to
promise allegiance to Pakistan cricket. By that time they had
already been practising with the Pakistan squad for some days
and now, less than twenty-four hours before the start, they were
asked to make a declaration of good faith which it would be
obviously impossible for them to do. By then the decision not to
play them had already been taken – for there can only ever have
been one outcome from that particular meeting. During those
forty-eight hours someone, presumably the General, had made a
decision. It does not mean that he necessarily changed his mind,
however. The events at Rawalpindi on 5 January have been so
sketchily told that one can be sure about nothing. It seems that
the position of the Packer players was discussed, and that either
privately or at the full meeting Kureishi indicated that he thought
he would be able to secure the return of the Packer players. I

would be surprised if the General made any definite pronouncements on the Packer situation then other than being asked to be
kept informed. He would have been greatly concerned about the
welfare of Pakistan cricket, and if the three could have been
brought back honourably and legally from Australia he probably
did not then think that it would have done any harm. The meeting
in Pindi must have broken up with the General having established
a watching brief for himself, and by then he would have had a
better understanding of the problems in Pakistan cricket. He
would have had seen, too, the squabbling over the Packer players,
although perhaps without realizing its full significance.

He must have been kept informed about the events of the next
fortnight and have heard that Kureishi had contacted Packer
and the three players were returning. At this point the General
would have wanted to be more thoroughly briefed on the Packer
situation. Kardar would have done this, although his opponents
would always argue that no one could have done it from a position
of greater personal prejudice. The General followed Kardar's
arguments, but was not yet prepared to make up his own mind.
By the time he arrived in Karachi he must have realized that a
decision had to be made, and he would by then have been fully
briefed on all that was happening. I do not believe the General
said that the players would be available for selection three days
before the match, but the Board and the selectors felt that in the
absence of any instructions to the contrary it was logical, now
that they were in Karachi, that they should play. Also, this
announcement would have kept the public happy.

When the General arrived the situation was tense, and after
discussion he made his decision and by then he would have been
made fully aware of the double-dealing of Omar Kureishi and
also of the opposition of the present Pakistan side to the inclusion
of these three. The likelihood of the England players pulling out
of the match must also have been an influence. Once the General
had made up his mind the Board President had to draft the
statement he had made to the press and the rest followed on. It
was a deeply confused story which mercifully had a happy ending.
There was a Test Match, albeit one of the dullest I have ever
watched – I discuss the series in some detail in Chapter 12.
There were no riots, and there were no Packer players either,
and I could not help feeling that for once, in spite of the mistakes

along the way, the right decision had been taken.

Nine weeks earlier the possibility of World Series Cricket catching up so dramatically with England's series in Pakistan had seemed remote. But now it was interesting to return to Perth in Western Australia and to see if the end-product of WSC had shaken down into a more acceptable form. And now, of course, there was the question of how the Packer organization had reacted to the setback they had experienced in Karachi. Already Greig had been extremely critical of Boycott in his weekly newspaper column in Sydney. He said that Boycott's ability to be where there were no fast bowlers was common knowledge in the game. Those comments caused Greig to be sacked from the Sussex captaincy and to be fined and suspended at the start of the season by the disciplinary commitee at Lord's.

◆

Cricket in Contention

IN THE NEXT ten days I was able to make some significant comparisons, for after watching two days of Super-Test cricket in Perth I was going on to Adelaide to watch the last four days of the Fifth Test between Australia and India. My second visit to Australia was not a matter of looking at the general outline of World Series Cricket and getting a blanket impression, for I had already done that in Melbourne. I tried now to see how WSC had settled down and to discover specific impressions from the players and others closely involved either with Packer's cricket or with the established game. Much of this was done hobnobbing over drinks or the dinner table, but it was a worthwhile ten days; and the information I acquired presented a very clear picture in spite of the seemingly disjointed way I was able to piece it together.

I arrived in Perth at four o'clock on the morning of Thursday 26 January after a journey which had lasted for twenty-seven hours, two days before the start of Packer's fifth Super-Test, to be played between the Australians' first side and the Rest of the World. The venue was to be Gloucester Park – nothing more than about eight to ten acres of rough, unkempt ground. In 1928 a piece of swampland on the edge of Perth Water had been reclaimed and turned into a trotting track. Nearly fifty years later the area, by this time known as Gloucester Park, was rented by Packer who set about converting the ground inside the track into a cricket arena. The transformation was astonishing, for when I first saw the park the day after I arrived in Perth it had been converted into an attractive cricket ground with the boats on

Perth Water at one side giving it a pleasant atmosphere.

Packer's matches at Gloucester Park a month before had been a relative success, and as many as 13,000 had come to one of them, but I was assured by several people in Perth that it was an open secret that at least half of these had been given complimentary tickets, distributed in places as far away as Rottnest Island and Albany, some distance to the south, a holiday resort off the coast of Western Australia about half an hour from Perth by aeroplane. Nonetheless WSC had made some sort of an impact in the city. On my first evening there they held their second successive night game at the VFL Park in Melbourne. These matches started at 2.30 p.m. and were played on under the floodlights through twilight until late in the evening. The first of these games had been played soon after I left Melbourne in December, had been an outstanding spectacle and had obviously caused great interest. Six thousand people had gone to watch – at the time a record for any WSC match.

The two night matches, held the day before and on the day I arrived in Perth, were even more successful – some 24,000 spectators watched the first and 17,000 the second. I watched a few overs of the second match on television before jetlag caught up with me, and it was extremely interesting. The floodlights made the cricket seem unreal, to the extent that I found it difficult to believe that I was watching cricket; but it was marvellous television, the colours were exciting, the crowd brought the VFL Park to life and the game itself provided splendid entertainment. The white ball was obviously extremely effective, and the white crash helmets of Barry Richards and Greig gave added excitement – in effect being a licence for fast bowlers to bowl a constant stream of bouncers, to the great delight of the crowd. The atmosphere was gladiatorial, and the cricket as much as anything a night out for the young and the curious. The crowd was very far from being the kind one would normally see at a cricket match: most would probably have gone to a drive-in cinema had they not made the journey out to VFL Park. While the presentation and the commentary had seemed contrived during the five-day Super-Tests they both now matched the occasion.

Night cricket may have come in time without the help of Packer, but he hastened its arrival, and it may be that it will fulfil a social need in Australia if not elsewhere. It has a number of pluses.

It is much more comfortable for spectators to watch in the cool of the evening than in temperatures which may be into three figures in the daytime; there is the instant excitement of one-day cricket, with the certainty of a result by the end of play; and as presented by Packer it made spectacular entertainment. It gives the younger generation a night out and it enables the office worker to see live cricket when his working day has finished. If floodlighting had been available and the fifth Super-Test at Gloucester Park had been played at night I am sure that more people would have come and watched. Packer and his advisers will want to develop this idea, but whether in a couple of years' time a new form of television spectacular will have arisen from what was once a game of cricket or whether the game will remain within traditional boundaries remains to be seen.

Packer's limited successes during his first season of World Series Cricket have all come from the one-day game, which has never been fully exploited in Australia. It has obvious public appeal, and if it produces a new audience this will not concern Packer or his advertisers, for in the final analysis they are concerned with the number of bottoms on seats and television sets switched on. It will be interesting to see if Packer continues to try to challenge Test cricket, or whether he will be content in the future to concentrate increasingly on the one-day game. It would seem to make the greatest financial sense to do so; but Packer may have other and conflicting motives which take priority even over this.

The same morning that I arrived in Perth I went to Gloucester Park, and the first dreadful irony was that the ground was only the width of a road from the Western Australian Cricket Association ground. During the match itself I was able to look out of the windows on the WACA at the back of the press box and see a club game in progress. It only underlined the strong 'them and us' feeling which had grown progressively stronger since the WSC matches had begun.

Gloucester Park was not ideal, but it was nonetheless remarkable how Packer's money and his workmen had transformed it in such a short time. The trotting track seemed to isolate the playing area from the stands, although wooden seats had been set out all round the ground on the grass between the track and the boundary rope, so producing an inner and an outer ring of spectators. The outfield was a lush green and extremely smooth. I walked out to look at the pitch, operations again being supervised by the bearded John Maley, who was himself on the heavy roller. Maley's remarkably successful wicket preparations in such a short time single him out as perhaps the main hero of the Packer revolution. This pitch did not look quite as good as that at the VFL Park in November, being well grassed in patches and bare in other places, and I wondered then if it would hold together for five days.

While I was looking at it two figures emerged from the big stand at cover point – which combines restaurants with most of the betting areas for the trotting. As they crossed the track I saw from his silvery hair that one of them was Richie Benaud and the other, from his tousled mop of thick black curly hair, Austin Robertson, one of the two originators of World Series Cricket. When they were about ten yards from me I greeted Richie, who raised his hand in acknowledgement and mumbled something about enjoying Pakistan. He passed by me in silence. The following week when I was in Adelaide I discovered that I had written something which had upset Richie. This accounted for his shortness, although at the time I was surprised. Once he had decided to work for Packer, Benaud did all that he could to promote the success of World Series Cricket. He ran the cricket side of things and was, like his wife Daphne, a tireless worker. In spite of his outward enthusiasm for Packer's type of cricket, however, and the admission he made soon after joining that he had been hoping to set up a similar full-time professional circuit himself in two or three years' time, I cannot believe that he did not several times during this first WSC season have serious misgivings about the whole project. For all that, his loyalty to WSC was unquestionable and he never gave the slightest outward hint that everything was going other than according to plan.

I arrived at Gloucester Park about forty-five minutes before play began on the Friday morning, eager to see how the cricket had developed, and made my way to the press stand, sited behind the trotting track and therefore some distance from the play. The changing rooms for the players were in a small round building at the back of the press stand. I was interested to talk if only briefly to several of the players who were probably well aware of the stance I had taken, and was also able to sound out their opinions about the progress of WSC and their feelings about events in Karachi.

I first talked to Tony Cozier, a Barbadian, who was employed by Packer's Channel Nine to commentate on the first season of WSC cricket. He was surprisingly rational in what he said, and told me that he thought that Packer's cricket had a future, although he felt the emphasis should be more on the one-day game. The Australian public were at last beginning to accept this form of cricket, he said. A few days later in Sydney Tony Cozier told another friend that he did not think there was a long-term future for Packer as long as the traditional authorities made sure they had blocked his lines of supply by tying their own players up with tight contracts. I sensed from talking to Tony, who has been a friend of mine for many years, that the official series in the Caribbean between the Packer West Indies and the Australian Board's eleven was likely to produce some extremely bitter cricket. As Cozier agreed, both sides had points to make, and those with the fastest bowlers the bigger ones.

I also had a long talk with Mike Denness who was managing the Rest of the World side. He was very much hoping that there would be a compromise, and went so far as to say that he thought Doug Insole, the Chairman of the Test and County Cricket Board, realized this. He told me that he thought that county cricket in 1978 would also be a bitter affair, especially after the line which the England players had taken in Karachi – considered by the Packer people to be the principal reason for the three Pakistanis not being allowed to play in the Third Test Match. The hatred directed at Boycott was intense, for he had taken a 'holier-than-thou' attitude in his weekly newspaper column in Sydney when he himself had opted out of Test cricket for three years, while during one winter, 1976/77, he had made a considerable amount of money playing Grade cricket for Waverley in Sydney, at the same time as England were touring India, Sri Lanka and Australia. I tried to explain to Mike Denness how the anti-Packer attitude of the England players had hardened considerably in the last few weeks, and that Greig's arrogant attitude, shown in comments he made to newspapers and in his own weekly column since the final decision taken by the Pakistan Board, had turned them even more against World Series Cricket. Denness found it surprising that players like Brearley, Edmonds and John Lever, who had all voted against the ban at the meeting of the Cricketers' Association in September, had changed their minds. But then the Packer players generally were surprised to find such solid opposition from other cricketers. They expected it from the administrators, and from the press too, but after the High Court judgement they seemed to think they would be welcomed back as of right. Mike Denness also spoke of the tremendous dedication and enthusiasm of his Rest of the World side, and he told me how the Australian public, after first looking warily at Packer, were now beginning to accept him. Prospects were tremendous.

Denness had been Greig's predecessor as captain of England and he had not had a particularly happy reign. Since Greig had taken on the captaincy, at Lord's against Australia in 1975, Denness had gone to Essex from Kent. His appointment as manager of the Rest of the World, which was announced at the time of the High Court hearing, must have come about at Greig's suggestion. Greig had felt sorry at the way in which Denness had been treated as England's captain, most of all by the press, and his support for Denness now may have been an attempt to make amends.

I talked briefly at different times to Derek Underwood, Alan Knott and Bob Woolmer, all of whom asked me about Pakistan and who then assured me with great enthusiasm that they were having the most wonderful winter of their lives. This constant enthusiasm became rather predictable, and I even heard the suggestion that Rudi Webster, the doctor from Barbados who once played for Warwickshire and was now managing the West Indian eleven and who used hypnosis professionally, had gone so far as to use a hypnotic technique on some of the players!

I had a drink with Mike Procter, whose view was, like Denness's, that there had to be a compromise. He was convinced that Packer would be successful in the long run, and deplored the money that had been wasted in the courts fighting WSC. That was a sane enough view, but on the second day at Gloucester Park I sat with Ian Redpath for more than an hour, and he went so far as to tell me that the Showground in Sydney was a better ground than the Sydney Cricket Ground, with a better atmosphere. As the SCG is in every way a very close second to Lord's, I laughed at him and told him to come off it.

'No, Blowers,' he said, 'I'm telling you,' his voice serious and convinced, an evangelist's delight. While I was talking with him Kerry Packer walked past, and Redpath asked whether I had yet met his boss. Packer smiled briefly at this, for by then he knew I was an opponent, but we shook hands – for maybe the seventh time. On this occasion Packer had the last word. As he turned away he said over his shoulder, 'You'd look better with your zip done up.' He was right.

The most rational and interesting of all Packer's lieutenants was Chris Forsyth, who had made that unfortunate statement after the first Super-Test in Melbourne. When Packer had asked him to become his public relations director Forsyth had told him that he would later write a book about it. It was, according to Forsyth, even written into his contract, despite his employer's protests, that Packer would not be allowed to read the proofs. Chris told me that he had twice been sacked by Packer who each time had rung him up and asked him to come back. Unlike most of Packer's employees Chris was in no way a sycophant, and nor for that matter was Richie Benaud. They both fought Packer on certain issues, and won.

Forsyth was positioned at the back of the press stand at a table surrounded by telephones, and was always delighted to talk – inevitably with a half-smoked, half-chewed cheroot in the corner of his mouth. He told me that he was sure Packer's future lay with one-day and night cricket, and maybe some three-day exhibition matches, but that five-day matches and therefore Test Matches should be left to the traditional authorities. He felt too that Packer was himself in many ways a handicap to the organization, and should get out of it as quickly as he could. Chris was as appalled as I had been with Packer's reaction to some of the press the day after the High Court judgement, and he told me that when Packer was in America playing in the Bing Crosby Pro-am tournament the difference in the atmosphere back home among the players was astonishing. The players enjoyed themselves more, it was all much more relaxed, and everyone concentrated on the cricket. When he returned there were photographs of him in all the papers and it was Packer, not the cricket, which attracted most attention. He was never relaxed when watching the game, and if crowds did not turn up was constantly demanding to know what had gone wrong and wanting to change the formula. Chris thought that the success in Melbourne might improve him.

He also said that it was important that World Series Cricket should be depersonalized, then run by a permanent committee. He spoke of the dedication of the West Indians and the Rest of the World Players, but apparently the leading Australians had failed to live up to the image of Caesar's wife. Some of the senior players had been motivated by self-interest and had not been prepared to join in the promotional activities with any enthusiasm, or to help the younger players, and Packer had had to pull them into line. Forsyth agreed that Tony Greig's utterances had harmed Packer's cause and said that although no one was more dedicated on the field of play Greig sometimes got his priorities wrong off it. The day before the start of the first Super-Test between the Australians and the Rest of the World in Sydney Greig had been asked to make a personal appearance not directly tied to the promotion of WSC for a considerable fee some twenty or thirty miles out of Sydney. He went, missing the team practice that afternoon, and had to have a net at seven o'clock that evening while John Spencer and one or two of the other English players involved in Packer's coaching scheme at Cranbrook School bowled to him.

Greig's Test record as an all-rounder is second only to that of Gary Sobers, yet in sixteen innings for the Rest of the World up until the end of the Perth Super-Test he only passed 40 once. Chris made the point that this was an eloquent indication of Greig's psychological approach to this form of cricket. In Test cricket he had always been a 'big occasion' player: now he seemed to feel that the occasion was not big enough.

The response to WSC had been so poor at the Football Park in Adelaide that the WSC had decided to transfer the remaining matches there to the Showgrounds in Sydney. Chris told me the story of Packer himself standing forlornly in the car park at his football stadium there one morning of the Super-Test, counting the few cars which came in.

The day before the Super-Test began a friend of mine in Perth whom I had met on a previous tour of Australia rang me to say that two extremely wealthy businessmen in Perth had decided to form a group of professional cricketers of their own. They were to be called the 'West Coast Professionals', and sixteen players were going to be approached. As captain they hoped to recruit Ian Brayshaw, who had played for many years for Western

Australia and while I was in Perth was in the middle of his testimonial year. These two businessmen had obviously been attracted by what they considered to be the potential commercial value of all that Packer was doing, and their object was to challenge the Packer teams to one-day matches played in groups of three on successive days for prize money of A$33,300, and in front of television cameras. They would be prepared for their side to go anywhere in the world to play in front of television for money. They had already spoken to the Packer organization about the possibility of transferring players from one group to another along the lines of professional football. If this happened the West Coast Professionals could in time hope to match the strength of WSC. They warned Packer that if he wanted too much money for playing against them they would simply look elsewhere for opponents.

I was also told that two equally rich businessmen in Sussex, both of whom had supported Greig against the Establishment, were planning to set up a similar group within the county. They had been guaranteed the use of 'a county ground in central southern England', and it was intended that their side should also challenge Packer for money in front of television. Trident Television, a conglomerate which includes Tyne-Tees and York-shire Television, had apparently agreed to televise their matches in England. Packer is one of the conglomerate's directors. At the time of writing nothing has come of either of these stories: it may be that they were put around by Packer's organization for publicity purposes, or even that they could still happen – although the rich men involved may well have had second thoughts.

At first these ideas seemed too far-fetched, but the more I thought about them the more logical they seemed. There was nothing that Packer wanted more than a worthwhile opposition, for that would help remove some of the sterility from his cricket. The forming of another group would mean that his ideas were thought to be succeeding, and this would impress potential sponsors. It would also mean that Packer would no longer have sole responsibility for the type of cricket he had produced. I could foresee a situation where he might secretly finance a rival organization.

Packer also wanted to find a way into England. He had said that now his players had not been banned from county cricket he would not export his circus there, but the superstars had still not been whole-heartedly welcomed back to county cricket, and if Packer needed the excuse to come to England it was there. But if a group of professionals were already in existence in England with a ground at their disposal it would provide him with a marvellous means of entry. As soon as other professional troupes set up in opposition the development of an eventual professional superleague would be that much nearer, with dangerous implications for the first-class game.

I spent most of that Thursday evening and the next day, the first of the match, trying to check my story out without giving it away to anyone else or alerting anyone who did not want it published. I talked to several cricketing friends in Perth and then to various Packer players, not telling them what I knew but giving them the chance to tell me that this sort of thing might happen. As it was in Packer's interests that it should, I thought they might hint at it if they knew, but the Packer players had been warned by Ian Chappell in November how 'unprofessional' it was to talk to the press, and one never heard more than the official party slogans from the players. The next day I talked to Chris Forsyth again and got the feeling that he knew about it. We were watching the cricket at the time, but later I asked him straight out if what I had heard was true. He implied strongly that it was, although it may have suited WSC for this to be written, as the ICC were meeting in London at the start of February and this news would hardly have helped the nerves of the delegates. Just then Chris's telephone rang. He spoke for a minute or two, then replaced the receiver and turned to a colleague on his right. He said quietly, 'Kerry has said in an interview with the *Sunday Independent* that he is going to bring an English side over next season.'

This was a logical move. He already had the services of six English players in Greig, Knott, Underwood, Amiss, Snow and Woolmer, and therefore only needed seven or eight more. Mike Denness was managing the Rest of the World side, and most of the eight county players taking part in the coaching scheme at Cranbrook were said to be Packer supporters, or at any rate Greig supporters. If need be they could make up the numbers, but with the money at Packer's disposal it would have been surprising if he had not been able to attract other players from English cricket. As Packer had himself suggested on his first meeting with the Australian Board, 'We all have our price,' and since then he had found that this was true of a great many cricketers. I had talked to Richie Benaud at Swansea during a wet Gillette Cup semi-final the previous August and had asked him if he thought that the Packer cricket could hope to compete with an Ashes series in the 1978/79 season in Australia. He replied that if it were partially successful in the first winter it would be a tremendous success in the second, but would go no further. Maybe it was at that time Packer's intention to sign up eleven Englishmen before the start of his first season, in order that he should have an England side available for the following winter. In that context it would have been a bigger setback for him than it may have seemed that Boycott, Willis, Old and Randall turned him down. If Packer were to have an English side playing under his colours while England were playing Australia for the Ashes it would cause considerable confusion in the minds of those Australians who were not full-time cricket supporters. It may also have been in Packer's mind to have staged his own World Cup in Australia during that season, and when I was in Lahore I spoke to Sadiq Mohammad on Christmas Day who told me that he had had a letter from his brother, Mushtaq, and he had said that Packer was planning the following season to bring a team to Australia from each of the Test-playing countries. In any event, signing up eleven English players in the early stages would have been a useful investment for him.

During those three days in Perth I came across a further example of bad PR by one of Packer's main administrators. It occurred during dinner with John Inverarity and his wife Jane. John had played several times for Australia, was now captaining Western Australia, and was a strong opponent of Packerism. There were eight of us at dinner, and one of the others was Austin Robertson. He was an old friend of John's, but when he had heard that I was going to be there his inclination was not to come. He was persuaded otherwise, however, and when he arrived he presented us all with WSC ties. It was plain that he was still uneasy about me, and Jane very sensibly sat us at opposite ends of the table. I had a splendid evening talking to Jane and one of the other wives on my left, while at the other end of the table Austin talked intensely about Packer's plans to John. I heard very little of what was said until I heard Austin talking about the diabolical stuff that I had been writing for the *Guardian* and that other English journalists had been sending home. He complained that we had not given World Series Cricket a chance.

I had told the BBC where I was spending the evening, and in the middle of dinner they rang to arrange for me to record the story for Tony Lewis's Saturday sports programme the following morning. I carefully shut both doors between the dining-room and John's study, in which I answered the telephone, acutely aware of the irony that I was discussing a controversial Packer story while one of his main aides sat at the dinner table two rooms away.

I was the first to leave because I had to get back to the city to receive another call from London, and when I got up from the dining table I told Austin that I was not in the least surprised that he had found some of my writings about WSC intolerable. I said that I felt as strongly against what Packer was trying to do as he was in favour, but that I could see no point in hating each other to the point of refusing to communicate. Surely it would be more sensible if he were to discuss his point of view with me and to see if there were any common ground? I suggested that he came up to the press area the following day and that we had some beer and sat down and talked. I said I thought that he had little chance of changing my mind, but at least he might make me understand his motives and his reasoning more clearly. He agreed, but at four o'clock the following afternoon I received a message to say that his mother and father were with him in the VIP area and that he would be unable to come across. It never ceased to amaze me that the public relations work by the people at the top of World Series Cricket was so bad.

I watched the first two days of the Super-Test in Perth, and what I saw was riveting. The Rest of the World won the toss and batted, and at the start the crowd was no bigger than it had been on that first morning at the VFL Park. John Thicknesse, writing in the London *Evening Standard*, had described the few spectators in Melbourne as being 'scattered round like confetti in a grave-yard', a phrase which still rankled with WSC. With the wooden seats all round the ground just behind the boundary rope, Glou-cester Park had a far more intimate atmosphere than the VFL Park. During the first day the Rest of the World made 433 for one, Barry Richards made 207, Gordon Greenidge retired hurt for 114 and Viv Richards got 72 not out. Together they produced as

formidable a display of batting pyrotechnics as one could hope to
see in a lifetime. The Australians had decided to play only four
bowlers, of whom one, Lillee, was not fully fit, but they wanted
him as a drawcard in his home town. The other three soon seemed
jaded too, and even Max Walker had 115 runs hit off him in 15
overs.

It was an unbelievable exhibition of strokeplay, and it was one
of those days when Barry Richards could have done anything he
liked with every ball which was bowled to him. As an exhibition
it had been tremendously exciting, but once again the unimportance
of the result made it appear as cricket in a vacuum. The WSC
people pointed out several times that the rivalry between the
teams was intense because of the size of the prize money. Even
if the teams had been playing for A$330,000 a match and not
A$33,300 there would have been no greater involvement among
the spectators.

Before the start of this Super-Test the WSC organization was
brimming with confidence after the two floodlit games in Melbourne, and although the crowd at Gloucester Park was at best
just under 3500 the batting display seemed a great advertisement
for the holiday week-end. Even Chris Forsyth was confidently
expecting that there would be 10,000 spectators on the Saturday.
Only 3500 turned up. On the next two days, both of which were
holidays, there were slightly less. It was rejection at a bad time for
WSC. During dinner with the Inveraritys Austin Robertson had
said that it made him angry to read about the prospects of Western
Australia in the next Sheffield Shield match all over the back
page of the *West Australian* when the scores and report of the
Super-Test made about half a dozen paragraphs on the inside
back page. However, Rupert Murdoch had instructed all his
papers in Australia to give Packer's matches big coverage, so
that in certain papers Packer was receiving plenty of space. Yet
for all the publicity and the complimentary tickets for the one-day
games in Perth the public had shown what they thought when
asked to put their hands in their pockets.

To be fair to WSC, there were other factors working against
them that week-end. First, it was extremely hot, with the temperature hovering around three figures. During the second official
Test Match against India the temperature had been even higher,
and in spite of a thrilling game of cricket, won by Australia by

two wickets, the largest crowd of that match was 5000. Second, the Super-Test was being played over the holiday week-end, when a great many people leave Perth for the beach. Finally, the match coincided with the Fifth Test Match in Adelaide, with Australia and India balanced at two-all in the series. Many people must have stayed at home to watch the game on television, relayed from the Adelaide Oval. It was a measure of the arrogance of the WSC organizers that they decided deliberately to take on the official series against India, and the dates of five of their Super-Tests coincided with Test Matches against India. Significantly, the most successful of the Super-Tests was the first against the Rest of the World in Sydney, the only one which did not coincide with an official Test Match. It was there at the Showground that they had their only crowds of five figures for a Super-Test. More complimentaries were given away then, but not on the same scale as in Perth. During my two days in Perth I could not help remembering Greig's remarkably unprophetic words on the Indian series at that first press conference in Hove. 'No one,' he had said, 'is going to want to see an Australian second eleven playing India at the Melbourne Cricket Ground while the Rest of the World are playing Australia's first eleven just down the road.' He may say that they never played their matches at the same time in the same cities, but I do not think there can be any doubt what would have happened if they had.

On the second day of the WSC match Viv Richards took his score to 177, and Greig even sent Gordon Greenidge and his pulled leg muscle into bat again when seven wickets were down. Greig himself went in as Greenidge's runner; Ian Chappell complained, but the umpires allowed Greig to remain. Greig and Ian Chappell were constantly at loggerheads, but it was hard to tell whether this was genuine or whether it was just good box office – which of course it was. The Rest of the World were eventually out for 625, and by the close the Australians had lost four wickets. On the third day, in front of another crowd of 3000, Greg Chappell made 174 and on the fourth the Rest of the World won by an innings and took a two-nothing lead over Australia in their three-match series. During the first three days of this match the three best batsmen in the world, Barry Richards, Viv Richards and Greg Chappell had all scored more than 150, and yet the total attendance for the four days was only just over 13,500.

I had planned to see the last four days of the Indian Test, and thus duly left Perth for Adelaide at midday on the Sunday. The next day I was in a different world. I took the charming walk down the hill from North Terrace past the theatre on the left and over the Torrens River with the parkland stretching away on either side. After crossing the bridge I turned left past the memorial to those two pioneers of the air, Keith and Ross Smith (after whom Keith Ross Miller was named) and into the Adelaide Oval by the Memorial Drive tennis courts which have seen many Davis Cup matches. Young bronzed Australians in T-shirts or bikini tops, carrying 'eskies' (insulated containers full of cold cans of beer), chattering away as they stood in the queues, told of a big crowd. In fact more than 19,000 people watched each of the first two days, and more than 17,000 came on Australia Day.

The Adelaide Oval is the most beautiful Test ground in Australia. One looks across the ground from the main stand, past the wrought-iron Victor Richardson Gates, over the trees and shrubs in the parkland round the Torrens River and over the roofs of the houses to the foothills of the Mount Lofty Ranges at the point where Adelaide runs out of houses. Each year the scars left in the hills by the quarriers seem to have grown bigger, but they have become friendly scars. To one's left there is the huge scoreboard on the hill in front of the thick Moreton Bay fig trees which, at some time or other, seem to provide a perch for just about every starling in the country. Behind the fig trees the twin spires of the cathedral look down over the ground, and if they do not bestow a divine blessing upon the Oval they at least add to its tranquil atmosphere. The Adelaide Oval itself is a strange shape. It has the longest straight boundary of any Test ground in the world, measuring 208 yards from end to end, and one of the shortest square boundaries, only 138 yards across. All the time the ground is being circled and dive-bombed and landed upon by a never-ending flock of seagulls. In all it made a perfect setting for a wonderful game of cricket.

While I watched the Fifth Test Match I realized how crucial the decision had been not to allow Packer to use the established Test grounds. People who might not have approved of what Packer was trying to do would probably have gone to watch some of his matches if they had been played at the traditional cricket grounds. It may be possible to fit a new order into a traditional background, but a journey to any of Packer's grounds meant breaking new territory, and at the end of the journey there was not the favourite seat or the familiar bar or that shady corner just under the scoreboard – and maybe a white crash helmet as opposed to the familiar, baggy, dark green Australian Cap. Even when Packer had his biggest crowds they were not a traditional audience.

While in Adelaide I heard that an attempt had been made to bring the Australian Board and World Series Cricket together, with David Lord, who was still Jeff Thomson's agent, the self-appointed mediator. He had talks with Greig which lasted in all for fourteen hours. It came out later in the papers that Kerry Packer, John Cornell and Richie Benaud knew of the meeting, although as soon as it became public knowledge Packer denied this. It was impossible to say who was right.

Lord and Greig had tried to work out a new series of international matches which would incorporate both Packer and non-Packer players. During their talk Greig had stressed that Packer was there to stay, no matter what the cost. Lord for his part wanted to bring the two sides together, but one knows how plausible Greig can be, and it may be that Lord had allowed himself to become too optimistic about a compromise. During the last few weeks of 1977 Lord had several times flown between States to speak with members of the Australian Board emergency committee, Sir Donald Bradman, Tim Caldwell and Bob Parish. They had told Lord that they had no objection to his working towards a settlement but they also made it clear that he was not representing them officially. Packer for his part is said to have given Greig permission to talk to Lord on the condition that he was kept fully informed on all that took place. After Lord's meeting with Greig the Board were given copies of the proposals which had been worked out, and Parish then reiterated that if WSC had any desire to reopen talks they had to do so through the ICC in London.

This story confirmed my impression that at around this time the Packer side were eager for a compromise, but the negotiations were conducted in secrecy, as any admission of weakness, which the full details of the talks might well have revealed, would have harmed the Packer image. Packonian views are the enigma here, for not long afterwards in the West Indies compromise could hardly have been further from his mind. It may have been that

Packer himself was never behind this rather strange peace initiative. A statement was later issued from Packer's headquarters in Sydney which said:

Mr Packer stated that he had no interest in any discussions which involved Mr Lord, and he did not anticipate having any discussions with Mr Lord except before the High Court of Justice in London. Mr Packer saw no purpose in dealing with Mr Lord, who, as far as he was aware, had no official standing.

These unofficial meetings made it clear that there was no common ground between the two sides. Apart from Bob Parish, who was in London for the meeting of the ICC, the Board members were all in Adelaide for the Fifth Test. Even in those friendly surroundings whenever two or more discussed the Packer situation a solicitor sat with them to make sure that they were not unwittingly giving Packer a hostage at some future date. On those few days in Adelaide, however, traditional Test cricket needed no legal advocate. It defended itself in a brilliantly coherent and unanswerable way.

The authorities of course were extremely lucky that a series which did not have much potential should have built itself up in the way that it did. Australia had won the toss and had made 505, with Yallop and Simpson both making hundreds. India were then bowled out for 269 which gave Australia a lead of 236, but Simpson did not enforce the follow on, for he was without Thomson, who had pulled a hamstring in India's first innings, and it was also more than half-way through a very hot day. In any case it was only the third day of the match; by the sixth day (the extra day granted for this, the decider) the pitch should have been more worn and would not therefore be playing so well.

Australia made 256 in their second innings, and Simpson's 51 gave him an aggregate for the series of 539, more than anyone else on either side. India were left to score 493 in the final innings in almost two and a half days. They lost their two openers in the last two and a half hours of the fourth day, and were 101 for 2 at the close. The next day, the fifth, was fascinating. Mohinder Amarnath, Viswanath and Vengsarkar batted beautifully, but they each got themselves out just when it began to seem that they might go on and take India to an incredible victory. No side in the history of Test cricket had ever scored as many as 493 in the

fourth innings to win a Test Match. But without Thomson the
Australian bowling was hardly penetrating, and the pitch was
still extremely good. The Adelaide Oval has destroyed the hopes
of many better bowlers than Australia were fielding that day
against India.

At the end of the fifth day India were 326 for 6, needing 131
more runs to win. In the last 45 minutes Vengsarkar, who had
played well enough for his 78 to suggest that he would become the
leading Indian batsman of the next generation, had been caught at
long-on from a lofted-on drive, a dangerous stroke with fielders
back and with such a long boundary. Then Gaekwad had driven
without getting to the pitch of the ball and had been caught and
bowled. These two wickets effectively destroyed India's chances.
Kirmani and Ghavri were the only two batsmen left, but they
stayed together the next day for another 80 minutes, taking the
score to 415 for 6, when only 78 more runs were wanted. Simpson
then took the new ball, and in the second over Ghavri drove at
Callen and was beautifully caught in the gully by Hughes, who was
Thomson's substitute. Two runs later Kirmani, who had reached
a fine fifty, appeared to lose concentration and he drove much too
soon at a slower ball from Clark without moving his feet, and was
bowled.

India still did not give up. Prasanna and Bedi swung their bats
cheerfully, and with so relatively few runs between the two sides
the Australians were obviously apprehensive. But at 442 Bedi
played back to Callen – who had been so ill the night before that
a nurse had to be sent for – and Cozier held a splendid catch in
his right hand low at second slip. When Simpson had Chandrasekhar caught behind three runs later, trying to cut, India had
lost by 47 runs. This last wicket had been a notable forty-second
birthday present for Simpson. The match had been watched by
more than 70,000 people and Simpson said in a speech afterwards
that for sheer excitement and drama the series had matched
Australia's against the West Indies in 1960/61 which had included
the Tied Test at Brisbane. The standard was clearly much lower
now, but with two evenly balanced sides desperately wanting to
win and the spectators just as involved the players did not have
to be the best in the world to attract big crowds. Traditional Test
cricket could not have stated its own case more eloquently.

♦

CHAPTER 12

Cricket in Four Moods

NEW ZEALAND came as a welcome relief. Packer had scarcely crossed the Tasman Sea since World Series Cricket began, and his version of cricket had made little impression on lovers of the game in New Zealand, since he had not acquired the services of a New Zealander. The papers printed only the abbreviated scores of the final Packer Super-Test, and not every day at that. Walter Hadlee, the Chairman of the New Zealand Cricket Council and father of two of New Zealand's present side, Dayle and Richard Hadlee, exerted a calming influence on the game in his country, and the change in atmosphere at last enabled me to look rationally at the state of world cricket in the immediate aftermath of the Packer invasion. In Pakistan and Australia I, like the other journalists there, had been so much involved with minute-to-minute events that it had not been easy to look carefully at the new generation of Test cricketers who were growing up and who had mostly been given their chance by Packer. I arrived in Christchurch from Melbourne on Saturday 4 February when England began their three-day game with Canterbury, and now at last I had the chance to reflect on all the cricket I had seen.

The immediate threat had been to Australian cricket, and here the country's Board had responded by picking a side full of non-Packer players for their series against India. My first encounter with the new generation of Test cricketers was in Lahore on 14 December, the first day of the First Test Match between Pakistan and England. Two very unfamiliar sides took the field. England had lost Greig, Knott, Underwood and Woolmer (Amiss would

not have been selected for the tour), while Pakistan were without
Mushtaq, Imran, Majid and Zaheer. Asif might also be included
here, depending on how one views the announcement of his
'retirement' before Packer's plans were announced. Every country
involved – India and New Zealand being as yet untouched – had
its leading recruiters for Packer, and Asif was to Pakistan what
Greig was to England, Derryck Murray to the West Indies and
Ian Chappell to Australia.

The previous summer Mike Brearley's England side had regained the Ashes in the most convincing manner. Now they had to
find a new side. As Brearley led England out at the Gaddafi
Stadium that morning there followed behind him Boycott, his vice-
captain, Rose, Randall, Roope, Miller, Old, Taylor, Cope, Lever
and Willis. The only truly experienced Test cricketers were Boycott, Old and Willis, but even with these three the team lacked the
inspiration which Knott, Greig and Underwood always brought
to any side. The batting was poor, and although Willis had
developed into one of the best fast bowlers in the world he was not
going to be much of a factor on the Pakistani pitches. The spinners
were all very inexperienced. Nonetheless, with Hendrick,
Edmonds, Gatting, Botham and Downton the other five, there
was no obvious omission when the touring party of sixteen was
announced. It was reasonable to say that this was about the best
side that England could produce at the time.

This tour was a jumble of intrigue off the field, some depress-
ingly dull cricket on it. Conditions in Pakistan make cricket a
difficult and confusing game for an experienced side, let alone a
young one. The pitches are made of baked mud and are flat and
slow and completely lifeless. Survival is reasonably simple, but for
all but the best players strokeplay is difficult. Fast bowlers might
as well wear handcuffs, while the spinners wheel away for hours
getting sore fingers on pitches which turn too slowly to be dangerous. Further, play is constantly interrupted and delayed, and
nowhere else in the world does a game of cricket progress at such a
miserable rate. Pakistan is the only country in the world, too,
where a day's Test cricket lasts for only five and a half hours as
opposed to six, so that a game stretches over twenty-seven and a
half hours against the usual thirty. In Lahore there is some excuse
for this, as the dew does not allow a start before ten o'clock, and by
half past four the light is already fading. But six hours would be

perfectly possible in Hyderabad or Karachi.

During each day's Test cricket the game was held up by crowd interruptions, as spectators ran out to congratulate batsmen or threw oranges at policemen – a favourite pastime – or at boundary fieldsmen. On other occasions they would break up the stands, or pull down the fencing, or tear up the advertising boards. Interminable discussions took place between the umpires, who seemed ever unable to take a decision without running to their colleague at square leg. Often they would bring back the players after an interval anything up to ten minutes late, for no good reason, except perhaps that the players themselves seemed reluctant to keep the game moving. I have never before watched cricket which was so dull for such long periods: one wonders why they bothered. Even though most of the bowling was done by spinners the over rate hardly ever rose above twelve eight-ball overs an hour, and was often less than that. Although the Pakistani spinners frequently beat the batsmen in the air the ball came off the pitch so slowly that batsmen were given time to adjust. Another problem was that on these pitches lower-order batsmen were able to bat on unproductively for hours, and on these occasions the game seemed to come to a complete standstill. The pitches were so slow that bad strokes were hardly ever penalized. At the start of the Third Test in Karachi England lost their first five wickets for 107 and the last five wickets then held out for another six hours, scoring 159 more runs. I cannot remember watching a more excruciating piece of batting.

Yet another handicap is the Pakistani obsession in their own country with the fear of losing, tantamount to a national humiliation. Captains and players are terrified of taking even the smallest risk if there is the slightest chance it might lead to defeat, and they lose sight of the fact that to take a calculated risk can sometimes be the best and only way of winning a match. In the Second Test in Hyderabad Wasim Bari probably cost his side the series when he made one of the most ludicrously delayed declarations I have ever seen. Pakistan had made 275 in their first innings and Abdul Qadir had spun out England with his leg-breaks for 191. Pakistan began their second innings towards the end of the third day, the pitch was wearing and Abdul Qadir, who had bowled his leg-breaks round the wicket, had caused complete disarray in the England batting – there was never the remotest chance that England could do more than save the match. When tea arrived on the fourth day Pakistan were 198 for 4, 282 runs ahead with seven hours of the match remaining. Wasim Bari allowed his batsmen to continue until eighteen minutes before the close, when he set England to score 344 in 340 minutes. There was only time for two overs that night and in the second, bowled by Abdul Qadir, Boycott was twice all but LBW. I have never seen a side as relieved as England when Wasim Bari delayed his declaration so long. If he had allowed England an hour or more batting I have little doubt they would have lost. As it was, Boycott and Brearley saved the match with great skill the next day.

Pakistan were obviously likely to be a less attractive side without their Packer players, all of them formidable Test cricketers. As it happened, though, Pakistan had no cause for immediate worry. There appears to be an almost limitless amount of natural talent in that country, all the more astonishing when one realizes that only about two per cent of the population have the opportunity to play organized cricket of a standard that can lead to first-class and Test cricket. Pakistan had the better of a drawn series, and by the end it looked as if they had a side which might develop into the best in the world over the next three or four years. In each of the last two Tests eight of the side were twenty-five or under.

The most impressive of all the young Pakistani players was Haroon Rashid, who seemed altogether more composed than his twenty-four years would suggest. He had toured Australia and the West Indies the year before, and had apparently played a particularly impressive innings of 57 against Lillee in the Test Match at Sydney. He had made some useful runs in the West Indies too, but his place in the side was only made sure after the defection of the Packer players. In these three matches against England he showed that a batsman of the highest class can score runs quickly and entertainingly even in Pakistani conditions. In the second Test at Hyderabad he made 108 in three and a half hours with a wonderful piece of batting. The Niaz Stadium is a small ground, but unlike any of the Englishmen Haroon was never afraid to hit the ball in the air, striking six sixes during this innings. Barry Richards, Viv Richards and Greg Chappell are three modern batsmen who could have played a similar type of innings, but few others could have batted in such commanding fashion as Haroon that day. Yet on the tour in England in 1978 he scored 33 runs in five Test innings.

7.   Unmistakably Barry Richards in spite of the crash helmet. He pulls Bob Bright for six during his innings of 207 in the second Super-Test between the Rest of the World and the Australians at Gloucester Park, Perth. His helmet was to be seen later in the winter in the established Tests when Richard Yallop followed suit against the West Indies, and they were common in county cricket in England the following summer. Behind Richards, both on the pitch and on keeper Rodney Marsh's shirt, the symbol of World Series cricket can be seen.

8. Packer's World Series cricket gets under way. One of the pitches prepared in a greenhouse outside the ground is lowered into position by crane and lorry at the VFL Park, Melbourne. It was hoped that they would be floated on a cushion of compressed air and taken from the greenhouse by hovercraft, but this was not possible. A local dog tries out a section of the pitch for size.

9. The glare of the floodlights illuminate the VFL Park at Melbourne, the only ground where night cricket was played in Packer's first season. Here over 24,000 spectators turned out one evening to watch World Series Cricket, the largest crowd of all their games in Australia.

He has a striking appearance, with facial features which are more European than Pakistani. He was born and bred in Karachi, although he has the build of one who comes from the tribal areas in the north of the country. He might be a Petan, for he is tall and enormously strong with big arms and broad shoulders. He is, for all that, charming, gentle and unassuming, and unfailingly courteous and friendly. His father is one of Pakistan's leading film producers and Haroon fits easily and unselfconsciously into the style of life which comes from a well-to-do background. It is not surprising that the batsman he admires more than anyone and from whom he learned most about the game is Majid Khan. They come from similar backgrounds and play the game in a comparable way, although while Majid regards success seemingly as a divine right and is much puzzled when it eludes him Haroon is a harder worker, a more deliberate batsman and marginally the less elegant of the two. I doubt he will ever be quite the same player as Majid. I talked to him in my hotel room in Hyderabad and he continually produced that marvellously perplexed expression which comes over the faces of truly natural athletes when they are asked how they play as they do. They do not know.

As a batsman, Haroon prefers to come on to the front foot and most of his runs are scored in the arc between extra cover and mid-wicket. He hooks well and when in Australia he learned to play off the back foot. He is a natural timer of the ball, although with his strong shoulders he puts plenty into his strokes. On his tour in Pakistan it seemed only a matter of time before Packer approached him and when he arrived in England the following April it was to persistent rumours that he, Javed Miandad and one or two other of the Pakistanis had agreed to sign for WSC at the end of the tour.

Another central figure in this series, although of a different kind, was Mudassar Nazar. His father, Mohammed Nazar, had played for Pakistan and his rather fragile-looking son was another who had been given his chance by Packer's World Series Cricket carrying off the established players. He is slightly built and rather shy, and at the crease looks almost as if a strong gust of wind might blow him away. This is an illusion, for his adhesive qualities became a byword in the First Test. In his side's first innings he batted for nine hours and 51 minutes for 114 and had the somewhat dubious distinction of breaking the record for the slowest-ever Test hundred, previously held by Jackie McGlew of South Africa.

In this first match Nazar batted as if he were all too conscious that this might be his last chance in Test cricket. Yet every hour or so he produced a stroke handsome enough to show there was no need for him to bat in this way. He hooked Lever and then against Willis square cut and drove him off his back foot for four in fine style. This mammoth innings did wonders for his confidence, for in the next two Tests he looked a far better player, and his 76 in the Third was an excellent innings.

On the second day of the First Test, Mudassar had the misfortune to be indirectly responsible for the start of the first of the riots which held up play on successive days. Don Mosey and I were doing live ball-by-ball commentary for the BBC on Radio 3, and I had just taken over for a spell in mid-afternoon when Mudassar turned Cope to long leg for a single, taking his score from 98 to 99. The crowd had been patiently awaiting his hundred, and now about thirty or forty of the younger members could restrain themselves no longer – they may have thought that the batsmen would go for a second run. Anyway, they jumped the fencing and ran out to congratulate Mudassar. The civil police, who were in constant conflict with the public, duly took off after them. The boys ran off, but a policeman caught one a nasty blow with his lathi stick, and this infuriated the crowd, who now poured over the fencing and gave chase. The police – there must have been well over a hundred – fled across the pitch, disappeared through the members' area in front of the pavilion, and regrouped outside the ground at the back. Satisfied with their victory the crowd withdrew to the other side of the ground, but when the civil police returned the crowd again chased them off, and for a time stayed in front of the pavilion throwing all manner of objects into the enclosure. The military police now appeared, complete with khaki uniforms, red armbands and rifles. There was a state of martial law in Pakistan, and their presence was immediately respected by the rioters who again withdrew to the far side of the ground. It was now that Colonel Zafar, the secretary of the Board, and some other local officials went across to talk to the leaders of the rioters, and soon the people on the ground, some several hundred, began to clear the debris which had been left on the playing area by the angry crowd, and order was restored. Meanwhile the players had taken tea, and only 25 minutes playing time was lost. It made marvellous running commentary for listeners in England, while being never in the least dangerous, for the policemen were well out of harm's way and the rioters were making no attempt to harass the players. The England side were nonplussed initially and raced back to the pavilion, but then, realizing they were in no danger, saw the funny side of it. Most stayed in the dressing room, although one or two joined the press on the pavilion roof in order to obtain a better view.

The riot the following day was much more sinister. Under the terms of martial law public meetings are not permitted, and a crowd of between 35,000 and 40,000 at a Test Match was a great incentive for the unscrupulous to cause trouble. At that time the leader of the Pakistan People's Party, Mr Bhutto, was in prison undergoing trial for committing a political murder for which he was later found guilty and sentenced to death – at the time of going to press his appeal is still being heard. Lahore was his party's principal stronghold, and on the third day of the match Mrs Bhutto and her daughter, recently President of the Union at Oxford, and who had returned to Pakistan to fight for her father's cause, visited the ground. No one could remember ever having seen them at a cricket match before, and it seemed a deliberate attempt to stir up trouble. At first they walked round the back of the stands, and one could follow their progress from the roar of the crowd, who were now pressed against the back of the terracing looking out at the empty ground at the back of the stadium where Mrs Bhutto and her daughter were walking, surrounded by noisy supporters. The trouble started in the stand at square-leg, where the ladies all sit together making a colourful splash in their Punjabi clothes – there were ladies' stands in most of the grounds, but some sat with the men and were not compulsorily segregated. Suddenly some youngsters burst into the enclosure and began to throw the ladies' chairs – together with any other movable object they could find – out on to the field. The ladies themselves fled. The youngsters seemed to be supporters of the Pakistan National Alliance, the party that wanted to eject Mrs Bhutto and her daughter, and the opposition party to the Pakistan People's Party – Bhutto's party. Soon the rival political factions were fighting, and there was chaos. The military police were again quickly involved, and had to use tear-gas to break up the fighting sections of the crowd. This was the second time I had smelled tear-gas at a Test Match, the first being at Sabina Park, Kingston, in 1968 when the match between Cowdrey's side and the West Indies was badly interrupted by bottle-throwing and rioting.

Mrs Bhutto and her daughter escaped from the ground and were driven away in a cavalcade of cars. During the afternoon Mrs Bhutto had received a cut on the face, probably from a stray stone, but that evening her daughter gave a press conference and read out one of the most ludicrous statements I have ever heard, saying that her mother had been deliberately struck by a police lathi stick. Mrs Bhutto drove to the residence of the Martial Law Administrator of the Province who offered to have her driven to the military hospital. She refused this, sure she could obtain greater publicity elsewhere. It was a shameful way to use a cricket match, but indicative of the troubles there were in Pakistan at that time.

Another young Pakistani to make an impression for the first time in this series was Abdul Qadir, the leg spinner. He is a beautiful bowler who really spins the ball. He is a small man, always cheerful, with a bouncing six-pace run-up which matches his temperament. In these three matches he yet again showed the Englishman's innate weakness against this type of bowling. In the second Test in Hyderabad he took 6 for 45 for the first innings and, but for his captain, would have won the match for Pakistan. He is in all ways a most engaging cricketer, constantly smiling and both friendly and talkative. He was given excellent support by Iqbal Qasim, an orthodox slow left-arm spinner who already has astonishing control and twice during the series, at Lahore and at Karachi, pitched a ball on Boycott's middle stump and turned it sharply enough to hit the off. Of the other batsmen Javed Miandad, who had already made an impression for Sussex, showed that he is an excitingly wristy player even if his constant appealing from silly point shows that he has been brought up under Greig's tutelage. Wasim Raja is another who batted well, and like Javed is a useful leg spinner. In the last Test Mohsin Khan came into the side, and from his innings of 44 looked as if he might become the most elegant and graceful of all these young batsmen. He is a lovely fielder in the covers and an almost completely effortless batsman; he showed again how wonderfully lucky Pakistan are to have such a wealth of talent at their disposal.

Mohsin Khan's entry into Test cricket broke a remarkable family sequence. He took the place of Sadiq Mohammed, who had had a poor series, and this was the first Test Match that Pakistan had ever played without one of the Mohammed brothers in the side. Sadiq, Mushtaq, Hanif and Wazir had between them played in all ninety Test Matches.

England's successes on the tour were fewer. Of course, Boycott was successful, but he saw every innings as an interminable defensive operation, and after Brearley had broken his arm and he became captain, batting became an obsession with him. His efforts were so often counter-productive to the needs of his side that there were times when one could only question his motivation. In the First Test his 63 took 332 minutes, and while he was there the innings was hopelessly bogged down: only Miller's strokeplay later on took England out of trouble. Boycott's innings of 79 and 100 not out at Hyderabad were masterpieces of defensive batting in their own way, but both innings had to be played at the pace which Boycott nowadays chooses for himself, whatever the situation. In the Third Test his 54 took three and three-quarter hours. Yet he regards himself as one of the finest batsmen in the world.

In the First Test Miller made 98 not out and had the bad luck to be deprived of his maiden first-class hundred when Willis was given out caught at backward short-leg when the ball did not seem to touch his bat. Hyderabad ended in that dull draw, and was mainly made memorable by the batting of Haroon and Javed and Abdul Qadir's bowling, while Boycott's batting and Brearley's in the second innings, when the English captain approached the problem of Abdul Qadir with great sense, retrieved the situation for England. Karachi was then the dullest match of the three, and 176 runs was the most scored on any of the five days. Edmonds's bowling was an encouraging feature for England in this match, and in Pakistan's only innings he took 7 for 66 in 33 overs. Edmonds has for a long time been a cricketer with an enormous amount of talent, but without the determination or the concentration to make the most of it. During this tour Ken Barrington had worked hard to make him concentrate while bowling, for this is as important for a bowler as for a batsman; he had also tried to get him to follow through more. Now, for the first time, it all began to come together.

The other great success on the tour was Bob Taylor, who showed, as most players had thought for some time, that he is probably a better wicket-keeper than Knott, if not such a good batsman. He is a much less ostentatious performer, but his hands are remarkably safe and for one who is 37 his reflexes are astonishingly quick. The wicket-keeper's job should be his for the next two or three years. As a whole, however, the tour of Pakistan did not produce over-much encouragement for England, and when the day after the Third Test ended they flew via Singapore to Auckland to start their tour of New Zealand not many questions had been answered.

I left the England party in Singapore and flew on to Perth, in order to have another look at a Packer Super-Test and to see how his cricket had developed: cricket in the second of its moods. I felt I might have been unfair on that first occasion in Melbourne, but I soon decided most emphatically that I had not. I then went on to Adelaide to watch the last four days of the Fifth Test between Australia and India. This had been the series which had been most affected so far by the Packer intrusion, and which ironically was to do a great deal of harm to the impact of World Series Cricket, for Australia and India showed that nothing Packer had yet devised could compete with the competition and the challenge of Test cricket.

The Australian Board had made an inspired choice when they asked Bobby Simpson back to captain Australia, and now under his control an entirely new generation of Australian cricketers were growing up. It was a shock to arrive on the third day when the Australians were in the field and to be able to recognize only Simpson, Cozier and Hughes (fielding substitute for Thomson). It was not long, though, before the flowing fair hair of Darling in the covers, the almost Chaplinesque moustache of Yardley, with his cop-on-the-beat walk, Clark, who at seventy yards away might have been a slightly smaller Thomson, the angular enthusiasm of the moustachioed Callen, the neat left-handedness of Yallop beneath his dark hair, the precision of Wood and the class of Toohey were happily identifiable. These were the successors to the Chappells, to Marsh, Lillee and the others, who seemed to spend much time in their weekly newspaper columns in the local press, syndicated around Australia, firing off broadsides at the new Australian side and most particularly their captain.

When Simpson led Australia out at Brisbane in the First Test he and Thomson were the only two members of the team to have played in as many as ten Test Matches. The Australian selectors had been ruthless, and not only in the matter of Test selection. They had refused to approach the Packer players in any way and indeed they were not selected for their States in the Sheffield Shield competition. Those who were playing Sheffield Shield cricket had to sign contracts with Benson and Hedges, the official sponsors, promising not to promote any other goods, which inevitably excluded the Packer players. Most of the WSC Australians were not allowed to play club cricket either, which comes under the ultimate jurisdiction of the Australian Board. In Perth Dennis Lillee was not even allowed to park his car at the WACA (although John Inverarity, the Western Australian captain, refused to obey the instructions of the committee when he and his players were told not to talk to Lillee); in Melbourne Max Walker, eager for practice, was unable to find any team to play for at all, and Richard Robinson walked into the Victorian dressing room during a State game to see his former colleagues and was very quickly shown that he was not a welcome visitor.

Simpson's young players had all been given their chance by Packer, and here they were fighting him in the most brilliant way. The Indians, too, played their part magnificently. If they had faced the best side Australia could have produced India would probably have been well beaten, and would soon have grown disillusioned. In the previous three years no side in the world has been able to withstand the formidable Australian bowling combination of Thomson and Lillee – with Walker and Gilmour in support. As the situation was, the Indians realized that they had an excellent chance of winning their first-ever series against Australia, and no side could have gone more whole-heartedly about their job. In so doing they entertained the public to the extent that they attracted record crowds for an Indian series in Australia.

Thomson's speed gave Australia their best chance of beating India, while the spin of Bedi, Chandrasekhar, Prasanna and Venkatraghavan, as it had for a number of years, gave India her best hope of victory. After five days of fascinating cricket at the Woolloongabba at Brisbane Australia finally won by 16 runs after India had only just failed to make 341 in the fourth innings. One of the new Australians, Peter Toohey, came to the fore straight away with two fine innings, and in the second innings Simpson made 89 for Australia after they had lost three wickets for seven, showing that he was still a marvellous player of spin bowling.

In Australia television ratings are not usually taken after early December, as by then it is the holiday season and the hot weather takes people to the beaches. However, because of World Series Cricket and its importance as far as television advertising was concerned, the normal independent ratings surveys were continued. In Sydney, the Australian city most likely to be attracted to Packer's American way of seeing things, 16 per cent of viewers watched the Davis Cup at the start of December, 6 per cent looked at the First Test between India and Australia at Brisbane, and 5 per cent the first Super-Test at VFL Park, Melbourne.

On Sunday 18 December the Melbourne public had the opportunity to watch the Second Test in Perth, the second Super-Test in Sydney and the New South Wales tennis championships. Tennis had 16.6 per cent, the Second Test 12.6 per cent and the Super-Test 7.2 per cent. On Saturday 31 December the Open Tennis Championships attracted 19.3 per cent of Melbourne's viewers, 9.2 per cent watched the Third Test against India and 5 per cent saw the third Super-Test. There were no official ratings published in January.

The Second Test was played in Perth during a heatwave which kept the crowds well down, but it was another thrilling game of cricket which Australia won by two wickets after being left to score 339 to win. Gavaskar, Mohinder Amarnath and Chauhan all made runs for India, the first two making hundreds in the second innings while Simpson (176) and Mann (105) scored runs in Australia's first and second innings respectively. Bedi was the most successful bowler in the match, taking a total of ten wickets. The sides met for the third time over the New Year in Melbourne, and now Chandra's leg spin, giving him 12 for 104 in the match, and Gavaskar's third hundred of the series enabled India to win by 222 runs. Viswanath and Mohinder Amarnath also scored useful runs for India, while Serjeant batted well for Australia and Clark picked up four wickets in each innings. India confirmed this sudden superiority at Sydney, where they won the Fourth Test by an innings and two runs. This time Gavaskar, Chauhan, Viswanath, Vengsarkar and Ghavri made the runs while the three spinners, Bedi, Chandra and Prasanna, took sixteen wickets

between them. While Thomson badly missed a fast-bowling partner of any real pace, the young batsmen had for the second match
running been made to look extremely vulnerable to high-class spin
bowling. It was also remarkable that the Indians, far from falling
apart when two-nil down in the series, kept their confidence and
came back as strongly as they did.

So to the exciting climax at Adelaide. By the time the game
began the transformation of the new Australian side was complete. For several years the image produced by the Chappells,
Marsh and Lillee had grown progressively more ugly. There can
have been few if any worse-behaved sides than those presided over
by the two Chappells. A combination of thongs, shorts and shirts
open to the navel, T-shirts, track suits and hardly ever a coat or
blazer was the aggressive dress of the Chappell era. Punctuality
was negotiable, the players did only what suited them, and
the wishes of a succession of tour managers were ignored. Now,
under Simpson, the players were always smartly turned out.
Ties and blazers were again in fashion, the length of hair was
orderly and the language was respectable. 'Sledging' on the field,
the habit of swearing at and insulting batsmen, had stopped – the
word 'sledging' is an Australian invention – the players looked as if
they were enjoying their cricket and not in the self-conscious
manner of the World Series players, and were not outwardly
indulging in a hate campaign against the other side. Of course,
they were not as good as the side they had succeeded, but they had
potential. When, soon after he took over, Simpson said that he
would not tolerate the behaviour and the general deportment of the
Chappell sides it brought down on him a torrent of abuse in the
newspaper columns from the Chappells and from Lillee, who all
gave the impression, for the last few years at any rate, of being
convinced that they were bigger than the game itself. They denied
Simpson's own criticisms of themselves and said that now he was a
hired hand of the Australian Board he was being told what to say
about the WSC players.

A new era of Australian cricket had begun. But they were about
to face the stiffest test of all in modern cricket. Ten days after the
Fifth Test in Adelaide Simpson was going to take his side to the
Caribbean, where these young and inexperienced players were to
take on the full strength of the West Indies who were going to
include their Packer players. It was an enormous task for anyone,

let alone a side with such limited Test experience. Almost certainly, too, there would be strong pro-Packer and anti-Packer
feelings expressed during the series, and with the fastest bowlers
playing for the West Indies Australia were not going to have an
easy time. Their victory in Adelaide was just the send-off they
needed, but it is one thing to beat an attack based almost solely on
spin and quite another to take on a fast-bowling combination of
Roberts, Holding and Daniel – to say nothing of Garner and Croft.
It was against this highly involved background that the England
players flew from Karachi to New Zealand where cricket is a
different, more naïve game largely unaffected by outside influence.

In New Zealand preparations were under way for the first-ever
series against a full England side not just tacked on to a tour of
Australia. Packer had weakened England to the point where New
Zealand had probably never played them with such a good chance
of winning, and now, further reduced by Brearley's injury,
England were even more beatable. India had found themselves in
an identical situation to New Zealand when they had played
Australia and lost so narrowly. In the circumstances, therefore,
this was an extremely important leg of the tour for England. They
needed to win, they needed one or two of the younger players to
come through, and they needed to show that at least a beginning
had been made to the job of replacing their Packer stars.

There were other problems, too, for tours to New Zealand are
not always as easy as they sound. The pitches are often incon-
sistent – perhaps hardly surprisingly as they are churned up each
winter by rugby players. All the Test grounds are huge rugby
stadiums except for the Basin Reserve in Wellington, which is
used for soccer. For this series the only pitch that was really
satisfactory was at Eden Park, Auckland, where the last Test
Match was played. New Zealand had had a long dry summer, and
this was no doubt part of the reason, but several grounds looked as
if they had not had enough work done on them at the important
times of the year, and were underprepared as a result. Poor
pitches are irritating for touring sides, and they work against the
development of the home country's cricket too. In New Zealand
cricket is very much a secondary sport to rugby, and it relishes its
amateur image. This is all very well until it comes to winning
Test Matches, which must be the ultimate object for a country's
cricketers. There is not much money in New Zealand cricket, and

it is important that that which there is should be used to produce the best facilities possible. The net wickets on most grounds were also inadequate, something which it would have been easy to overcome. Ironically and with no excuse they found the net wickets in England as unsatisfactory in 1978.

Over the years New Zealand have produced some extremely able cricketers and they have won a handful of Test Matches, but they have never been able to maintain any consistency. The amateur nature of their cricket is one of the main reasons for this; most of their players are unable to get leave of absence from their jobs as and when they want, and so are forced to miss certain tours, thereby spoiling the continuity when New Zealand have a good Test side. It is a chicken and egg situation, for the only way in which significantly more money will come into the game is when sponsors are made to realize the commercial possibilities of cricket. For that to happen New Zealand must win more Test Matches. As it is, the media show great interest in Test Matches and games against touring sides, but Shell Series matches raise extremely little interest. They have a strongly insular approach to the game which probably helps explain why they were relatively unconcerned about Packer. This may change if he should obtain the services of a New Zealander who might then become unavailable to represent his country.

The New Zealanders do not play enough first-class cricket, and this too holds up the development of their players. However, the situation has been helped in recent years by the few who have been signed by English counties and have had the experience of playing county cricket six or seven days a week for four and a half months. Players like Turner, Parker, Howarth and Wright have thus learned to become efficient and better-disciplined cricketers. The New Zealanders themselves, especially some of the older Test players, feel that this experience of English cricket has not been all for the good. As commercialism creeps into the game the incidence of gamesmanship and what is wrongly called 'professionalism' increases. The introduction in England of one-day cricket in the early 1960s saw more money come into the game. Bonuses for winning and other financial incentives developed a strong win-at-all-costs attitude, and suddenly umpires found themselves under greater pressure. Appealing increased, rules were stretched to the limit, 'sledging' began and all kinds of ploys developed to un-

settle batsmen, bowlers and umpires alike, ploys which had little
to do with cricket.

In New Zealand there were definite signs that modern-day
gamesmanship was creeping into their cricket. Their leading fast
bowler, Richard Hadlee, behaved throughout the series with
England as if he had watched Dennis Lillee at his worst and had
decided that the only way to be fully accepted as a fast bowler was
to behave in similar fashion. There were rumours during the tour
that Hadlee had been approached by Packer. They were quickly
denied, but they made people aware how easily Packer could
break up the present New Zealand side.

Another weakness in New Zealand cricket is their umpiring.
When one criticizes a country's umpires there are those who react as
if one is doubting the national integrity. Umpiring, quite simply,
is bad in New Zealand; and there are several reasons for this.
Probably the main one is that relatively little first-class cricket is
played so that the experience of their umpires is extremely limited.
Another is that the game does not attract retired first-class
cricketers to umpiring with the result that a group of umpires
have grown up who are word perfect as far as the rules are concerned but have little feeling for the game. This is something
which the rule book cannot teach. I have seldom seen such officious
umpiring as there was in New Zealand, and there is nothing that
irritates players more than this. I have also never seen umpires
who are so obviously unsure of themselves, and who waste a considerable time each day in unnecessary conferences in mid-
wicket. These discussions go on endlessly and serve only to slow
up a game which needs all the encouragement it can be given.
This was one of my complaints about the umpiring in Pakistan,
but one feels that it should be much more easily avoidable in New
Zealand.

In this series weak umpiring, as it always will, introduced
tension and bitterness into the cricket. The New Zealand umpires
interpret some rules differently to any other umpires in the world.
In their domestic cricket batsmen are very seldom given out LBW
to the point where an off-spinner is rendered almost impotent.
Cope did not play in any of the three Test Matches in New
Zealand for the umpires do not give batsmen out LBW when they
are sweeping, they are almost never given out on the front foot and
often, too, when right back on their stumps the umpire remains

unmoved. This may be a tradition in New Zealand cricket, but if so it is one which can only harm their chances at Test level. When New Zealand sides tour overseas their batsmen will find themselves being given out when they would always receive the benefit of the doubt at home. The New Zealand interpretation of the LBW rule might be acceptable – 'home rules' as it were – if only it was consistent. During the England series the umpires were put under pressure by both sides, and after, say, two days in which no appeal was upheld one would then find that batsmen would be given out LBW in the strangest circumstances. This obviously encourages bowlers to appeal, so putting umpires under as much pressure as possible in the hope of winning a decision. It is desperately important for the development of New Zealand cricket that something is done about the umpiring standards. Many of the leading administrators arc aware of the problem but have few ideas about how to solve it. I would like to see the Cricket Council take charge and talk strongly to the local umpires' association. There was trouble during this series about bowlers following through on the pitch. The law states categorically that the danger area starts four feet out from the popping crease and runs straight up the pitch a foot either side of the leg and the off stumps. In the First Test in Wellington the damage done within this area was obvious, and yet the umpires said that the directive in the law was only there as a guideline. Their failure to interpret this law at Wellington had a definite effect on the match. I got the impression that the umpires were frightened of making what would appear to be an unpopular decision; a stronger support from their own association might be a way of rectifying this.

Having criticized New Zealand on several counts, all of which are, I believe, holding back their cricket at international level, I can only say that I have made three tours there and have enjoyed them all enormously. It is a beautiful country full of delightful people, but it would be marvellous for cricket if New Zealand became a Test side which won often, and not just occasionally. The greatest moment their cricket has known came during the First Test Match in Wellington when they beat England for the first time – after 39 years of trying. Boycott put New Zealand in to bat on a green pitch which had one or two curiously bare patches at one end. Willis bowled the first ball of the match with a fierce wind behind him and John Wright played back and survived one of the most confident appeals for a catch behind I have ever heard. This set the tone for much of what was to follow. New Zealand struggled to 152 for 3 on the first day, and a fine spell by Chris Old had them out for 228 the next day. Old took 6 for 54 in 30 overs and bowled as well as he had done in the Centenary Test Match in Melbourne the year before.

England's first innings made extremely painful watching. The ball was coming through at different heights and moving around off the seam, and Boycott took it upon himself to play an interminable innings of 77 which lasted seven and a half hours. When he was 39 the entire New Zealand side thought that he had been caught at second slip off his glove from a short ball from Hadlee. Boycott stood his ground, the umpire said not out and Hadlee and Boycott had words. Boycott was as lucky as Wright had been on the first day. England were bowled out for 215, and the next day on a pitch which had grown worse, a fine spell by Willis destroyed the New Zealand second innings, and they were dismissed for 123, thus leaving England to score 137 to win. In the last two hours of that day England lost eight wickets for 53. The pitch was bad, but so too was the batting. The England side panicked after Boycott had driven all round a half-volley in the second over, and one could not help but feel that if Knott and Greig had been there 137 would not have been an insurmountable problem. As it was, Richard Hadlee bowled at his fastest, which is quick without being in the top bracket. Collinge was always accurate in support, and both were helped by batsmen who were not able or prepared to move behind the line of short deliveries. Short-pitched bowling that evening was overdone, but in the circumstances one cannot blame the New Zealand bowlers for taking advantage where they could. The following morning the last two wickets went quickly, and Hadlee finished with 6 for 26 in 13.3 overs. It had been a wonderful piece of bowling, and New Zealand deservedly won their first Test Match against England.

This game revealed all too clearly Boycott's approach to his own batting now that he had become England's captain. He saw it as his sole duty to remain at the crease, regardless of anything. It is true that the state of the middle-order batting gave him an even greater responsibility as the side's leading batsman, but his approach to the problem was remarkably short-sighted for one who is a deep thinker about the game. His fellow batsmen needed all the encouragement they could get, and yet Boycott's introspective batting had exactly the opposite effect. In the first four hours of the third day's play he scored at an hourly rate of 10, 12, 6 and 12. The other batsman could be forgiven for thinking that if such a fine player as Boycott could only score at this rate batting must be impossible for them, and when their turn came they would not have approached their task with much confidence. Nor did Boycott ever appear to understand the importance of the quick single as a means of keeping the scoreboard moving, as well as giving the opposing bowlers and captains a problem. When asked about his rate of progress at a press conference on the rest day of the match Boycott declared that he and John Wright were the only two batsmen in the game with the character and the ability to bat on in these conditions. I wanted to ask him if he did not regard himself as a better batsman than Wright. During the three Tests against New Zealand Boycott batted for five minutes under fourteen hours for 166 runs, and when England made 400 in their last two Tests neither innings built up its momentum until Boycott had been out. One of the reasons I felt that the captain's job should return at the first possible opportunity to Brearley was that Boycott's understanding of his role as captain prevented the side from getting the best out of him as a batsman.

There were other reasons too. Boycott was an extremely un-relaxed captain, and this affected his team-mates. He seemed to make every move, whether repositioning gully to backward short leg or putting back a third man, as if his whole reputation depended upon it. Having watched him in four Test Matches as captain I was unable to find any aspect of his captaincy which was significantly better than Brearley's, whose more gentle and relaxed leadership brings out the best in his side. Boycott also showed himself to be a singularly undiplomatic captain off the field. He has a deep suspicion of the press, and although he was grudgingly prepared to accept the likelihood of not being let down by the British correspondents all of whom he knew, he several times told the New Zealand press that he was not sure he could trust them. Often he seemed deliberately to keep the press waiting before a conference, having previously agreed on a definite time. On a number of occasions he was extremely abrupt with officials in New Zealand concerning matters like practice pitches and cars to take the players home after a day's play, and once at a press conference in Wellington he was extremely offensive to Ken Barrington. He has a disturbingly abrasive manner. Boycott was late for a press conference when the England team was to be announced the day before the First Test in Wellington. In his absence Barrington read out the twelve from whom the team would be chosen saying that the final place would be between Lever and Hendrick and if Hendrick was fit he would play. When Boycott eventually arrived Barrington told him what he had said and was immediately abused in no uncertain terms for giving advance information to the enemy about the last place. Boycott was lucky that he was not in Australia where the press would have hounded him unmercifully. If he had been significantly better than Brearley on the field maybe these things would not have mattered so much. As it was, they did.

The defeat in Wellington was the low point of England's tour. In the last two Tests they not only scored runs but Botham emerged as a formidable Test cricketer, Greig's natural successor. He played a brilliant innings of 103 coming in at number seven in the Second Test at Christchurch, took eight wickets in the match and held on to three good catches in New Zealand's second innings. Edmonds also had a good match, and began to look as if he should retain the left-arm spinner's place for a number of years. He is a fine natural cricketer who showed now that his haul of wickets in Karachi had been no fluke. Miller was out for 89 in England's first innings, having had to retire hurt when he was hit in the face hooking at Collinge, and this innings was another stage in his development into a regular England cricketer which sadly was checked in England in 1978. The last Test in Auckland was played on the best wicket of the series, and Botham again took five wickets in the innings as New Zealand made 315. Geoffrey Howarth made his first Test hundred, and a rotund stroke-maker called Jock Edwards hit an entertaining 55. When England batted Boycott made 54 in three and three-quarter hours, while Radley, after an agonizing start, batted for ten and three-quarter hours in making 158: although he does not seem the obvious answer to England's middle-order batting problems it was a relief to see someone make a big score. He could do a useful job for England for a year or two. When New Zealand batted again Howarth completed his second hundred of the match and Edwards made another engaging fifty, but the game ended in the dullest of draws.

10. In January three of the Pakistanis playing for Packer flew back to Pakistan to make themselves available for their country's third Test against England. The England side were on the point of refusing to play in the match when the chief Martial Law Administrator declared that Packer's cricketers should not be picked. One of the three, Mushtaq Mohammad, had to make his way back to Australia, his clothes and his suiting revealing conflicting loyalties.

11 On the eve of the third Test Barrington and Boycott hold a tense press conference at six o'clock in the evening. The England players are threatening not to take part in the match if Pakistan include their three Packer players. At this conference the position is still not clear for the Pakistani selectors have not announced their side. The journalists sitting on the far side of the team room in the Intercontinental Hotel are Jon Henderson of Reuters, myself, Alex Bannister of the *Daily Mail*, Peter Laker of the *Daily Mirror* and John Woodcock of *The Times*. The debris on the two tables is evidence of the lengthy team meeting that directly preceded the conference.

12. At 41, Bobby Simpson came back to captain the young Australian team. In this first Test against the West Indies in Port of Spain he found himself bowling under the watchful eye of Packer umpire Douglas Sang Hue, who so upset the Australians with his decisions that they asked the West Indies Board that he should not be picked again during the series.

13. The West Indian side, containing its full complement of Packer players, outclassed the Australians in the first two Tests. Peter Toohey was one of the victims of Andy Roberts's pace in the first Test at Queen's Park Oval, Port of Spain. *From the left:* Croft, Roberts, Kallicharran, Richards (summoning help), Greenidge and Lloyd. Later in the match Toohey had his thumb broken by Roberts.

During this Third Test Match the non-Packer Australians played their first game against the West Indies at Queen's Park Oval, Port of Spain, and lost comprehensively inside three days. The England party left Auckland on 12 March having gained more from their tour than seemed likely when they left Pakistan. I began a journey which was to land me in England for two days and then deliver me to Barbados on the afternoon of Tuesday 14 March, two days before the start of the Second Test Match between West Indies and Australia at Kensington Oval. The vested interests of the two sides promised to make the series the worst-affected and most bitter of the four I had watched during these months. It was a promise to be frightfully fulfilled, but I did not anticipate the disruption that the influence of Packer was to cause and which led to the break-up of the West Indies side.

◆

CHAPTER 13

The Weak Link
in the Chain

DOWNTOWN AUCKLAND to the West Coast of Barbados in three and a half days, two of which were spent in London, was an exhausting journey. By the time I arrived in Barbados there was a feeling of great apprehension surrounding West Indies cricket. The authorities were now distinctly uneasy about the influence of Packer and his players, and the chain of events, which was to culminate in the Packer players pulling out of the West Indies side in Georgetown in late March, had already begun. I had therefore to pick up the threads of the story as and when I could on those first few days in Barbados. As so often with events surrounding Packer, it was like having to fit together a jigsaw puzzle.

Before going to bed that Tuesday night I discovered that the West Indian players had told their Board of Control on the eve of the First Test at Port of Spain, Trinidad, that if they did not receive more money they would not play. The Packer players – five were selected for the West Indies in this match – were behind this, with Derryck Murray their spokesman. Unwillingly, the Board had given them a substantial increase.

In the First Test Simpson's Australians had had the bad luck to be put in to bat on a wet pitch and had no chance against the West Indies fast bowlers, losing by an innings and 106 runs. During this match the Australians had been so dissatisfied with the umpiring of Douglas Sang Hue, a Jamaican who had for a long time been the best umpire in the West Indies and who had been standing for WSC in Australia in the months before this tour began, that they asked the Board that he should not be appointed for any of the remaining four Test Matches.

In 1977 Sang Hue had umpired in England throughout the county season, and it was while he was there that he was approached by Benaud on behalf of World Series Cricket. In this First Test he gave several doubtful decisions against the Australian batsmen while the West Indies batsmen received the benefit of the doubt when the Australians felt that none existed. During the match Sang Hue also expressed doubts about Clark's bowling action to various members of the West Indies Board. Ralph Gosein, the other umpire who comes from Trinidad, said that he had seen nothing wrong with it.

On my second day in Barbados I learned that during the time of the First Test in Trinidad the five non-Packer players in the West Indies side, Kallicharran, Croft, Haynes, Austin and Parry, had met the Board and had given the President, Jeff Stollmeyer, a verbal undertaking that if they were approached by Packer they would not sign before 31 March, the start of the Third Test in Georgetown, by which time the Board would have come forward with some much-improved financial proposals for these players. The West Indies Board had not been directly threatened by Packer before, but they were already feeling the effect of Packer upon their players, and soon the problem they hoped they would not have to face would be upon them: in November 1978 the West Indies were to tour India and Sri Lanka. The Board and selectors thus wanted to know officially whether their Packer players would be available for this tour. During the first one-day international in Antigua at the start of the Australian tour Derryck Murray had unofficially told a representative of the Board that they would not be available. The West Indies Cricket Board was the only Board of Control which had gone against the wishes of the majority of the ICC and which had still been prepared to pick their Packer players for Test Matches – and, indeed, realizing the poor financial returns for players in their country, they had done all that they could to accommodate their Packer players, even to the point of straining relations with the rest of the world's authorities. All their Packer players were available for the series against Australia, however, and the West Indies Board had at an early stage announced that it was their intention to play them. Public feeling in the West Indies remained very much behind the Packer players.

On 9 March Stollmeyer rang up Derryck Murray, who is the

secretary of the players' association in the West Indies besides being Packer's representative among his West Indian players, and asked that those players who had signed for Packer should state their availability for the forthcoming tour of India by 23 March at the latest. This telephone call was confirmed by letter on 15 March. After talking to Stollmeyer, Murray immediately contacted the World Series Cricket organization. The Board had said that if they had received no answer by 23 March they would be forced to assume that the players were not available. The Packer organization should have foreseen this moment, but perhaps they did not expect it to come so soon. In any event, it must have caused a stir in Australia, for on the first evening of the Second Test Match two of Packer's representatives flew into Barbados – Austin Robertson, who had acquired a near-Afro haircut, and Michael Turnbull, a solicitor. Over the next two days they spoke at length to the West Indian players and in particular to Lloyd and Murray.

I spoke to Jeff Stollmeyer on the third day of the match, and he was worried about Robertson and Turnbull's presence but confident that the five non-Packer players in the West Indies side would not sign. The West Indies administrators were beginning to find out all that Australia, England and Pakistan had already discovered, but they were still unaware of the lengths to which the Packer organization would go, if it suited them.

It was in an atmosphere of suspicion and uncertainty that the Second Test Match was played out. Until teatime on the second day it was a wonderful game of cricket, with little to choose between the two sides, but in the end the West Indies' fast bowling proved too much for the young Australians. On the first day Australia were put in to bat by Lloyd and bowled out for 250. Roberts, Croft and Garner took nine wickets between them, while Wood, the small 21-year-old left-handed opening batsman from Perth, showed that he was already an outstanding player, batting against the fast bowlers with great skill. He made 69 in the first innings and put on 92 with Yallop, who also batted well, for the second wicket. After that only Yardley – who relies more than anything on a good eye – made a significant contribution, hitting 74 important runs towards the end of the innings.

The day before the match began Jeff Thomson had said to Allan McGilvray, the Australian commentator covering the tour for the ABC, that if Australia were to get anywhere he would have to do it. The West Indies had seventy minutes' batting that evening, and in this time Thomson produced one of the greatest spells of fast bowling and one of the most absorbing pieces of cricket I shall ever see. He did it on his own, too, for he no longer had Lillee to help him, and well though Clark bowled at the other end he was inevitably a respite for the batsmen after an over of Thomson. That evening, bowling from the pavilion end at Kensington Oval, Thomson took 3 wickets for 40 in 6.5 overs. These figures may not seem out of the ordinary and they do not hint at the effort and the pace Thomson generated and the confusion he caused to some of the greatest batsmen in the world. He would not have been flattered if he had taken five or even six wickets in these overs. It was a heroic piece of bowling and, to say the least, luck was not on his side. Thomson at full stretch is as inspiring a sight as any fast bowler I have seen. He comes to the wicket like a tidal wave, surging forward, gaining in momentum with every stride, his lightish hair bouncing up and down in time with his feet. When the arm comes over it is as if he is hurling down a thunderbolt with some primeval force.

In his first over he appeared to hit Greenidge hard on the glove and the ball flew to Cozier in the slips, but Greenidge was given the benefit of whatever doubt existed in the umpire's mind. It was all Greenidge could do not to shake his hand in pain. A similar ball, which rose sharply from only just short of a length, accounted for Greenidge in an identical fashion in Thomson's third over. Later in the same over Richards, before he had scored, shuffled across his stumps, was beaten for pace and must have been perilously close to being leg before. Soon after this Haynes, who had moved unflinchingly into line, hooked and survived an ebullient and unanimous appeal for a catch behind. The crowd were alternately stunned and exhilarated.

An indication of the pace Thomson achieved that evening was given by Richards, arguably the best batsman in the world. He hooked and drove and flailed at Thomson in sheer desperation, yet he played one or two strokes that were streaks of pure gold. It was a truly magnificent battle which would have been a credit to any jousting contest from the Middle Ages. Richards might have been out two or three times before he reached double figures. Then, when Thomson pitched right up – and he scarcely bowled a short ball in those seventy minutes – Richards drove him off the back foot, over mid-off and first bounce for four. Next he went back and hooked Thomson into the Kensington stand at mid-wicket for six. This was a prodigious stroke, but nonetheless that and its predecessor were the strokes of a man who had panicked. Being such a wonderful player, Richards's sole preoccupation that night should have been to stay there until the morning when Thomson might have been unable to find quite the same blistering pace. When he had made 23, however, he aimed another wild hook at Thomson and was brilliantly caught by Clark down by his ankles at long-leg. Then, off the last ball of the day, Kallicharran could only fend away another lifter with his glove to backward short-leg, who duly took the catch. It had been the most wonderfully inspiring piece of fast bowling and no one who saw it – and they know their fast bowling at Kensington – will ever forget it. Thomson was Australia's vice-captain in the West Indies, and his performances throughout the tour, both on the field and off, could not be faulted. No captain could have asked for more support from his principal player. If Thomson has one trouble it is that he has an extremely physical bowling action which puts a great strain on his body, and he suffers increasingly from injuries.

The next day, the second of the match, Haynes showed that he will one day be another fine West Indian strokeplayer; in some ways strongly reminiscent of Seymour Nurse, another Barbadian, he made 66 in fine style. Then, as he has so often done in similar situations, Derryck Murray played an invaluable innings of 60, assuring the West Indies of a total of 288 and thus a first-innings lead. Thomson finished with 6 for 77, having spent some time off the field with an injured leg muscle. When Australia batted a second time just under two and a half hours remained, and although Wood made his second fifty of the match and was 55 not out at the close of play Australia had lost five wickets for 96 and the match was virtually over. It finished in the middle of the next afternoon when the West Indies, needing 141, won by nine wickets. There was nothing more to be said about the West Indies side: with their Packer players they were undoubtedly the best in the world.

During this match there were clear signs of conflict on the field of play. The tour regulations stipulated clearly that a maximum of three bouncers could be used every two overs, with not more than two in any one over. There were overs in this match when

Garner, Croft and Roberts bowled as many as four, and yet they were not warned until late on the first day when Garner twice hit Yardley on the upper part of the body with successive balls.

In the years before the advent of Packer cricket had become increasingly a game of physical combat, and too much fast, short-pitched bowling had been allowed. If the members of both sides in this match had belonged to Packer, and his lieutenants had not been present in the pavilion, would there have been the same number of bouncers bowled by the West Indians at the young Australians? I could not help wondering too if the superiority which several of the players seemed to think that World Series Cricket had given them made it even harder for the umpires to keep them in check. They gave the impression that they were playing a form of cricket which was almost beneath their dignity, and Bobby Simpson told me that he also had this reaction. World Series Cricket was primarily designed for a television audience, and batsmen avoiding or being struck by bouncers makes better television than spin bowling. It is interesting that Packer's first 55 signings did not include any member of the best spin attack in the world – Bedi, Prasanna, Chandra or Venkat.

A match which had promised so much for most of the first two days ended all too predictably in victory for the West Indian fast bowlers. The following day rumours began to circulate that Packer's two emissaries had been far from idle during their short visit to Barbados, and that Croft, Haynes and Austin, three of the players who had given the Board a verbal undertaking that they would not sign before Georgetown, had done precisely that. At a hastily-convened meeting at the team's hotel the following morning Peter Short, the Chairman of the Barbados Cricket Association and a member of the West Indies Board, asked the three players if the rumours were true. Two admitted that they were, but the other denied it – and then changed his mind on the telephone an hour later.

With hindsight, Packer's and his advisers' reasoning for what they had done is simple to follow. The WICBC's request to the Packer players to state their availability for the tour of India had precipitated WSC's action. As I have tried to show, Packer has continually tried to split his opponents. At the beginning of February it had been unanimously agreed by the ICC at their meeting at Lord's (at which Lance Murray, the father of Derryck, had been the West Indies representative) that no member country would negotiate with or talk to Packer on a unilateral basis, but that if he wished to talk it would have to be to the full Conference. By signing these three players Packer had brought his number of West Indians up to eighteen. He probably thought that the Board would now have to go to him and ask him to release some, if not all; otherwise they would not be able to send a touring side to India. He may also have hoped that the Indian Board would have put the West Indies Board under pressure to bring their star players to ensure big gates. As soon as the WICBC had talked to Packer they would have gone against the ICC agreement and they would at the same time have abdicated their control of West Indies cricket, in effect passing it over to Packer. The WSC camp might argue, as Packer did himself when he came to the West Indies, that they needed more West Indies players; but I cannot believe that WSC would have signed Richard Austin if their only intention had been to bring up their numbers, for as yet he is a limited player who would have been unlikely to have kept his place in the West Indies side, with or without World Series Cricket.

Robertson, if not Packer, would have known that the three men had given the Board a verbal undertaking not to sign for WSC before the start of the Third Test, and while the players concerned might have wanted to respect this they were put under considerable pressure by their Packer colleagues. I do not think there is any reasonable doubt that one of the motives behind the signing of these three was the wish to be disruptive. It had been a tremendous blow to West Indies cricket and must, in some ways, have been even more sickening for a Board who had gone a fair way to accommodate World Series Cricket. Yet it is still surprising that Packer acted in this way, for the West Indies was the one country where there was sympathy for him among the authorities, and an action of this nature could have killed whatever goodwill existed. He was lucky in one respect, for the West Indian public were badly misinformed in the papers and on the radio about the real issues involved. Cricket is the only sport at which the West Indies lead the world, and anyone who prevents the public from watching their heroes is considered a public enemy. The West Indies public were persuaded that it was the WICBC who would be responsible for such a possibility, and were never clearly told that it was the fault of the players for joining WSC.

Whether a cricketer can serve two such totally different masters at the same time, and whether he should be allowed to play for his country only as and when he and Mr Packer decide, are questions that have not yet bothered many people in the West Indies. Nor has the likely effect of WSC on their domestic Shell Shield competition, which has produced all these fine cricketers. The main West Indies players will at best be fitfully available for the competition, and as soon as a young player comes through WSC will be waiting to sign him: the result will be that the standard will fall, and the interest with it, and so the sponsors at present involved will be likely to pull out.

The Australians' arrival in Georgetown found the whole West Indies in a high state of indignation, and was to the background of a rumour that Packer himself would be in Port of Spain for the Fourth Test Match. The three West Indies selectors, Joey Carew, Clyde Walcott and 'J.K.' Holt, together with the captain, Clive Lloyd, met after dinner on Sunday 26 March to pick the side for the Third Test in Room 702 at the Pegasus Hotel. This happened to be the room next to mine, but unfortunately the soundproofing had been done much too well! The Australians were meanwhile in the middle of their match against Guyana. The selectors' meeting was held three days after the expiry of the deadline for the Packer players to state their availability for India, and before picking the side the selectors decided that in view of the continuing uncertainty about this tour they would use the last three matches in the Australian series to give some young players the chance of Test Match experience. Some of the older, established players would therefore be left out. Clive Lloyd agreed with this principle. By the time their deliberations came to an end – in the early hours of the morning – the selectors had decided to drop Derryck Murray, Haynes and Austin. Lloyd found that he was unable to go along as far as this, but was outnumbered. He could not agree to the dropping of Murray, who had been a central figure in WSC and had many times helped and guided Lloyd, both on and off the field. It was almost three o'clock on the morning of the 27th when Lloyd told the selectors that he had no alternative but to resign the captaincy. For the rest of that morning the selectors remained silent, but Lloyd revealed his intentions to Johnny Comber of Australian Associated Press in a telephone conversation.

That same day Joey Carew, the chairman of the selectors, flew back to Trinidad, presumably to talk to Stollmeyer. Still there was no confirmation from the Board that Lloyd had resigned, or that his resignation had been accepted. The rumour about Packer now said that he would arrive in Georgetown in the next two days. Lloyd himself spent part of the Monday with the Minister for Sport, Shirley Field Ridley, who helped him draft the eminently reasonable statement which he issued to the papers that evening. In the most diplomatic terms, he asked the Guyanese people to support the new Test side just as they had done the old one. The Guyanese Government handled the situation extremely well, for although they were closely involved and were determined that there should not be trouble, they kept a low profile, saying openly that it was not their problem but that of the West Indies Board.

The selectors were perfectly entitled to look ahead to India and to play some young players, but they made two tactical mistakes. The first was not to explain in more detail to the public why they had omitted Murray – and perhaps add a public 'thank you' for all he had done for West Indies and that he might continue to do in the future. Second, Haynes had scored fifty in each of his first three Test innings, and it was not the psychological moment to drop a young player: one necessarily asked why they had not dispensed with Greenidge instead. The dropping of Haynes was thus made to look the direct result of his having broken his word to the West Indies Board. Austin's departure made sense anyway in cricketing terms, but Croft, the third new signing, was retained. In fact they should have dropped him too, for they would have won more respect had they done so. Their argument was that they had kept the basis of the side the same – that is, their leading fast bowlers – and made changes around this nucleus. I am quite satisfied that the Board did not instruct the selectors whom to choose, but equally I am just as sure that Board members would have spoken to one or more of the selectors. Carew is himself on the Board, and with such a ferment going it was impossible for him or indeed the others to spend as long as three minutes a day in one another's company without discussing Packer. After a meeting of the Barbados Cricket Association at the end of this tour, when an attempt to sack Peter Short and Keith Walcott as their representatives on the WICBC failed, CANA, the Caribbean Associated News Agency, fierce opponents of the Board, reported that Clyde

Walcott, the selector, had said that the side for Georgetown had been selected under Stollmeyer's guidance. This was hotly denied by Walcott, and CANA were forced to retract and issue an apology.

Lloyd wasted no time in getting in touch with Murray in Trinidad and with Packer, and it was probably his telephone call that prompted Packer to come to Guyana. Lloyd later said that Packer had told him to act in whatever way he thought fit, and he never faltered in his intention to resign. Murray, who for some reason refused Lloyd's request to come over to Georgetown, said in Port of Spain that he expected the other Packer players to refuse to play – in effect to come out on strike in sympathy with Lloyd. Meanwhile Croft made his presence felt playing for Guyana against the Australians with one of the most despicable pieces of fast bowling I have seen. He bowled a constant stream of bouncers, breaking Yallop's jaw in three places in the first innings and then, on the last day, almost knocking out Yardley, who fortunately had to have nothing more than three stitches in the back of his head. At that moment the cricket resembled gang warfare. It was a vicious display by Croft, who was never once warned for intimidation.

By the Tuesday evening there was no word from Trinidad, and stories were now coming through that Packer was in London and was flying to Georgetown from Miami in a private jet the day before the match. On the Wednesday morning I talked with Clyde Walcott by the swimming pool of the Pegasus Hotel. He was in a difficult situation, for he was a selector and not a member of the Board. He and 'J.K.' Holt were the two selectors in Georgetown, and they were powerless to say or do anything: all news had to come from the Board itself. Clyde told me that he had spoken to Jeff Stollmeyer on the telephone that morning and had impressed upon him the importance of coming to Guyana; Stollmeyer said he would be arriving that evening. As we talked we were joined by Fred Bennett, the Australian manager, Bobby Simpson and later still by Alan McGilvray. After several minutes of animated conversation it was clear that the Australians, whose own Board had themselves acted in the most forthright manner, feared that the West Indies Board would not act until after Packer had arrived in Georgetown, and that the likelihood was that Packer would manipulate the West Indies side by telling his players to take part in the match in spite of their feelings. They felt it was a distinct possibility that Lloyd would lead the West Indians out on Packer's instructions. Their feelings were, simply, 'We don't mind who we play against as long as it is a team chosen by the West Indies selectors and not by Packer.' There was a feeling, too, that if the West Indies allowed themselves to be manipulated by Packer he would himself receive great publicity as the saviour of the series in both the West Indies and Australia, and that the Australian Board, having taken a firm stand on a point of principle, would be badly let down.

Rumours abounded throughout the day. Allan Shiell, who was ghosting a column for Clive Lloyd in Australia, was told by the West Indian captain that he was sure the Packer players would pull out. At the time I was surprised, for I felt that Packer would have wanted to keep his players in Test cricket. He had gone to great lengths to infiltrate his three Pakistani players back into their national side for the Third Test against England, and it seemed too that his prime motives in signing Croft, Haynes and Austin were, first, to take over West Indies cricket; to be seen by the authorities elsewhere to be giving a display of strength; and to show the Board that he, Kerry Packer, was indispensable to them and someone with whom they had to negotiate in order to take an adequate side to India. If his players pulled out in support of Lloyd the sympathy of the West Indies Board would have been finally alienated, and all chance of negotiation in the immediate future would have gone.

Packer had in fact left himself a different option. Having gained control of eighteen West Indian players he was planning to return to the West Indies with his World Series Cricket and play a series of matches there, leaving the public in no doubt as to which were the best players, and that the villains of the piece were the WICBC. His problem was to get the grounds on which to play: hence his presence in the Caribbean.

That evening, 2 March, I had dinner with Sir Lionel Luckhoo, the famous Guyanese advocate in his fifties who holds the world record for gaining the acquittal of accused murderers. (It stood then at 209, although I gathered that he had twelve new clients on his hands at that particular time; it may now be more. He has not had one conviction in this time.) His brother Lloyd was there, and so too were Fred Bennett, Bobby Simpson, Alan McGilvray and several others closely involved with cricket. Berkeley Gaskin, the president of the Guyanese Board of Control, came in for a short while before going to the airport to meet Jeff Stollmeyer, who was flying in with Peter Short from Barbados. At about eleven o'clock the telephone rang, and shortly afterwards we were all ushered out and driven home. I gather that Stollmeyer, Short and Gaskin had gone round to the house and discussed the issue with Lionel Luckhoo until the early hours of the morning. I do not know if anyone else was at the meeting, but because of their concern about likely civil unrest the government would have been kept in touch. The male members of the Luckhoo family are all considerable advocates in Guyana, and over a question of law and order, with which the Third Test Match was now closely tied, it was not surprising that Lionel was in close touch with the Prime Minister's office at such a critical time.

I was dropped at the Pegasus Hotel by Lloyd Luckhoo, and immediately I ran into Allan Shiell. With him was another journalist, Graham Eccles from Melbourne. Both asked at once, 'Have you heard the news?' It had been announced half an hour before that the other five Packer players had definitely pulled out of the West Indies side in support of Lloyd. I waited until almost three o'clock for a call to the BBC in London, and shortly before it came through I was in the lobby when Stollmeyer and Short came into the hotel. Packer was meant to be arriving later that morning: the WICBC had cut it fine.

The following day, the day before the match, was if anything even more confused. It began in the Pegasus Hotel at nine o'clock in the morning in a small conference room on the ground floor by the lifts, where Lloyd, Greenidge, Garner and Croft, four of the West Indies Packer players picked for the Third Test, had a meeting with representatives of the WICBC, led by Stollmeyer. Richards and Roberts had not made the journey from Antigua to Guyana. Croft turned up late, carrying his crash helmet as if he feared that Jeff Stollmeyer was going off his long run. After about half an hour the players emerged, and Clive Lloyd told the press in a strained voice that he had been glad to have the opportunity to meet the Board, was willing to talk with them, but that they had come along with their minds made up and that there was no chance of compromise. Soon after this meeting broke up Stollmeyer let it be known that he would hold a press conference in the same room at midday. At the conference he was flanked by Peter Short and Glendan Gibbs, both Board members, and he spoke with great feeling. First, he announced that Lloyd had resigned the captaincy and that the other five Packer players had pulled out of the coming Test Match in sympathy. He then read out the names of the new West Indies side: Alvin Kallicharran, Alvin Greenidge, Basil Williams, Larry Gomes, Irving Shillingford, David Murray, Sew Shivnarine, Norbert Phillip, Vanburn Holder, Derek Parry and Sylvester Clarke. He added that although the selectors' recommendation for the captaincy had gone to the Board it had not yet been confirmed, and that the Packer players would not be considered for the remainder of the series.

Stollmeyer then said that he intended to give the press the background details to what had gone on in the last few days. There was no doubting his anger or the resentment he felt at the way in which he and the Board had been let down by the Packer players. First, he reiterated the original position of the West Indies Board with regard to their Packer players, and their own position compared with that of the other three countries so far involved, Pakistan, England and Australia. Unlike these three countries the West Indies Board had agreed to keep their Packer players in Test cricket as long as they were available to play for the West Indies when needed.

He went on to say that, with the tour of India and Sri Lanka scheduled to begin in November, it was important for the selectors to know the availability of the Packer players, for if they were not available there was still time to give some young players Test Match experience in the last three Test Matches in the current series. Accordingly, on 9 March, Stollmeyer had telephoned Derryck Murray and asked that the Packer players should inform the Board of their availability by 23 March. This conversation was followed by a confirmatory letter dated 15 March. In spite of the amount of time the players were given the Board had not received a firm answer by 23 March.

Murray wrote a letter to the WICBC on 22 March which in effect asked for a deferment of the deadline and made another request for the WICBC to talk to Packer. In that letter Murray had written that he had been informed that at the suggestion of the WICBC the World Series Cricket organization had sent a telegram to the Indian Board regarding rationalization of dates for the forthcoming tour of India by the West Indies. Stollmeyer was adamant that the statement in Murray's letter was a fabrication. Packer had wanted the tour brought forward so that his players could go to India and then be in Australia in time for his matches. In February he sent the WICBC a telegram urging them to discuss the dates of the Indian tour with him. The Board had cabled that the WICBC would not under any circumstances deal unilaterally with World Series Cricket.

On the following day, 24 March, the Board received another letter from Murray in which he wrote, 'I have been informed that the Indian Board of Control for Cricket has been in contact with the World Series Cricket and a confidential meeting has been arranged for early April.' On receiving this Stollmeyer rang up Jack Bailey at Lord's, who was able to confirm that this was completely untrue; no arrangement was to be made by the Indians either then or in the future to negotiate with WSC. Stollmeyer had also been annoyed by a statement which had been made by Lloyd during the Bridgetown Test, when he had said that two WSC administrators were present in Barbados and would make themselves available to the WICBC for discussions. Stollmeyer asked how any WSC official could expect to have discussions with the WICBC after the cable which the Board had sent to Packer in February.

Stollmeyer went on to say that the players representing the West Indies in the Third Test would have to sign contracts guaranteeing their availability to West Indies cricket for a two-year period to prevent Packer signing any more players. He reiterated the Board's determination initially to do all they could to help the West Indian players who had signed for Packer, as they were well aware of the poor financial rewards from the game in the West Indies, and this was why they were prepared to continue playing them in Test cricket. He then gave a detailed explanation of the peculiar financial problems facing West Indian cricket, which in a sense had made them the weak link among the various international Boards standing up to Packer. All the other Test-playing countries had made money out of their home series and then played overseas on a guarantee which did little more than allow them to break even. With the West Indies the situation was different. Three of the four Test grounds, Bourda, Kensington and Sabina, were so small that a full house did not come to much more than 13,000 or 14,000 and there was obviously a limit to the amount which the inhabitants of poor countries could be asked to pay at the gate. Queen's Park Oval in Port of Spain held 35,000. The expenses of a tour of the West Indies were very high because of the distances which had to be travelled by the two teams and because the tourist hotels in which they stayed were expensive. The result was that the WICBC made little if any money out of their home series, and as they had to work within the same guarantee system which applied to other countries when they toured the West Indies Board hardly ever had any money at its disposal.

Stollmeyer and the Board were anxious that when the West Indies visited England and Australia they should be guaranteed expenses and then a worthwhile percentage of the overall profits, especially as the West Indies had for a long time been one of the biggest crowd-pullers. They would then have the money to make better offers to their own players and therefore be able to compete with Packer. This problem is to be discussed at the annual meeting of the ICC in July 1978 and all counties expressed their sympathy with the West Indies who should receive better treatment when they arrange future tours. Although big crowds are attracted in India and Pakistan their foreign exchange problems make it extremely unlikely that they would be able to help in similar fashion. When the West Indies have tried to raise this problem in the past they have been told by the ICC that it is something which must be worked out between the countries concerned when the details of the tour are finalized. As can now be seen, this was a woefully short-sighted approach. The ICC had tried to present Packer with a united front, and members had been annoyed by the West Indian decision to play their WSC players in Test cricket. If they wanted a united front they had no alternative but to help the West Indies financially.

Stollmeyer took his press conference well. Probably because he was angry, for the first time he left no one in any doubt about his feelings on this issue. Our next visit to the conference room came at about twenty minutes past seven that evening, for Kerry Packer had finally arrived from Miami, accompanied by Rudi Webster, the Barbados doctor who managed the WSC West Indians in Australia. After microphones and tape recorders had been draped around him, Packer assured everyone that he had never had the chance to see Guyana and that he also wanted to see some cricket. Packer and I were on opposite sides of a large round table. When these opening exchanges had finished I asked him, 'Would your visit to Georgetown and the West Indies be connected with the fact that the WICBC have asked your players to state their availability for the forthcoming Indian tour?' He replied, 'You always know more about my movements than I do myself. I have just heard you say on the BBC that I am intending to play at the White City before the World Cup in 1979.' 'No,' I said. 'I said that I had heard that you were going to.' 'It didn't sound like that to me,' came the reply, and conversation ceased. I walked out of the conference soon afterwards, for I had heard most of what he had to say several times before.

The Test Match began the next morning, and by midday Packer had not appeared. There had been some discussion as to where he would sit, for he would hardly have been welcome in the pavilion or in the members' stands. News reached Bourda at lunchtime that Packer was flying to Barbados that afternoon where he was to host a gathering of all his West Indian players, their wives and girl-friends at Sandy Lane Hotel. Packer later said that because he liked Barbados so much he had decided to stay on an extra day, but that may not have been the only reason.

It is not too difficult to interpret his visit. The pattern of the fortnight, culminating in Packer's return to Australia, indicates that WSC had a change of policy. Robertson and Turnbull came to Barbados and signed Croft, Haynes and Austin in open contempt of an undertaking these players had given to the WICBC. In Georgetown the West Indies selectors picked a side for the Third Test and dropped three players, including Derryck Murray. Clive Lloyd resigned in protest, the other WSC players backed him up and refused to play, and Packer, who had been seen for some time to be trying to get his players back into Test cricket, threw up his hands and said to Lloyd, 'Do as you think fit'. It was roundly reported in the West Indies that the Packer players had been sacked by the Board. If Packer's main hope had been to persuade the WICBC to talk to him he now realized that he had failed, and the back-up plan came into operation: to go it alone in the West Indies. Packer had plenty of advisers who understood the political and the cricketing situation there, and also the amounts of foreign exchange which might interest impoverished governments. I have no doubt, too, that before he arrived in the West Indies his employees were finding out surreptitiously about the availability of the main grounds for use by WSC at the start of 1979, and the amenability of the politicians. The new West Indies side would then be in India, and by bringing forward the dates of his own series in Australia Packer could bring his WSC West Indian and Australian sides to the West Indies when there was no other cricket being played. New Zealand had agreed in principle to tour the West Indies early in 1979, but not before the middle or end of February. The West Indians never get enough cricket, and if Packer's West Indians played his Australians over seven or eight weeks there would be a huge public response. How discriminating the public would be after the first game or two remains to be seen, but if the West Indians kept on winning their games maybe for some time.

Packer's main problem had been to get the grounds. He himself runs an extremely complex business, and would only make a trip to the Caribbean if he thought he stood to make an important gain from it. He knew by late March that the traditional authorities would do everything there to block him, and thus his only alternative was to negotiate at government level. He visited three countries, Guyana, Barbados and Jamaica, all of whom hold Test Matches and have grounds that Packer would need. During his visit to Guyana, short though it was, he made contact with a member of the government and they discussed the likely reaction to a visit by WSC. Packer was probably told that there was no objection in principle, provided his South Africans were left behind, but if there was any trouble permission would be withdrawn. The Guyanese economy is bankrupt and Packer's dollars would have been a useful bait.

In Barbados he made similar political contacts, maybe through Wes Hall, who used to be a senator, or through Gary Sobers. Barbados as an island is strongly pro-Packer. There must be a strong likelihood that WSC will come to Barbados at some stage but it is not certain that Packer will be allowed to use Kensington Oval, though the athletics track half-way between Bridgetown and the airport has been discussed. It is a small ground and a pitch would have to be laid: maybe John Maley, the WSC groundsman, will be one of Packer's next representatives in the Caribbean.

Packer flew on to Kingston to talk with Michael Manley, the

Jamacian Prime Minister, in order to find a way into Jamaica and Sabina Park. Foreign exchange again played an important part in discussions, for in Jamaica too the economy is struggling and Manley may have seen an opportunity to win popularity for himself by trying to act as a mediator between Packer and the Establishment. In July 1978 the administrators of WSC undertook an extended tour of several of the West Indian islands during the course of which details of the WSC's visit in 1979 were worked out. It looks as if all the major grounds will be available to Packer except for the Queen's Park Oval in Port of Spain and Bonida in Georgetown. The best fifteen West Indians contracted to WSC will play four Super-Tests against the best fifteen Australians in Barbados, Guyana, Jamaica and Trinidad. One-day and two-day matches are likely to be played in the smaller islands of Antigua, St. Lucia and Dominica. There are many details in fact still to be resolved, one of which may be the way in which Channel Nine will treat the television coverage; cricket in the West Indies takes place in the middle of the night in Australia. The only concession is that Packer is going to call his West Indian Eleven 'a Caribbean Eleven'. At the end of it all, though, if Packer's WSC plays in the West Indies in 1979 I have an uneasy feeling that the presence of Packer's WSC will have made a mockery of all that went on in Georgetown in March and April 1978. But almost certainly those who made the decisions then will have had nothing to do one way or the other with the decisions which affected Packer's coming to the West Indies.

For me there was a sickening similarity between the events in Karachi and those in Georgetown two months later. Packer used his time in the West Indies to do some excellent public relations. There were photographs in the papers in Barbados of him in high good humour, signing dollar bills for the journalists employed at the local news-agency, CANA. And he told the West Indies public that if he came to the West Indies he wanted to cover only his expenses, and that if he made a profit it would be set up in a trust fund to be used for the development of young cricketers in the Caribbean. Yet the WICBC is unable to make any money on a home tour; how will Packer make any profit with considerably higher expenses?

Perhaps Kerry Packer should be allowed the last word. While in the West Indies he allowed himself to be interviewed by several papers and the following long interview appeared in Trinidad's *Sunday Express* on 9 April.

Sunday Express: Why are you in the Caribbean at this time?

Packer: Well, I was always going to come over and have a look at one of the Tests, and I was hoping to come over for the Fourth Test. Then it became fairly apparent that it was probable that it would be a little too late to see my boys in action, and so I decided to come over for the Third Test – though even that was a little too late. So that was the basic reason why I came over; and then I wanted to meet Colin Croft and the others who had just signed up and whom I had not met before.

Sunday Express: So you are not interested in the engagement at Bourda, between Australia and the West Indies?

Packer: I think that is a matter for the West Indian Board and the Australian Board. It does not involve me except in relationship to the players, and I think that it has been a great mistake to do what has been done to the players and what has happened to Clive Lloyd in particular. It is absurd.

Sunday Express: Do you believe that the press could usefully talk to you at the end of your stay in Barbados? Will there be a lot for us to hear?

Packer: No, I am not here for any ulterior motive. I am not here for anything tricky. I thought it was a good thing not to be in Georgetown at this time, to come here to what people tell me is the most beautiful island in the Caribbean and lie here in the sun and see the players and get some good Barbadian hospitality.

Sunday Express: Why is it that you have taken such an active and personal role in all aspects of World Series Cricket? Why is it that you are seen examining the grounds and the wickets and talking to the players? Is your interest in cricket that consuming?

Packer: My interest in cricket is no greater than if we were bringing out a new magazine. I would be doing exactly the things in any area in which I am involved at the outset. I'd be doing the same thing for a new magazine, except that it would not be so visible or public. Any new venture which the company gets involved in is a venture which is going to get a lot of my attention to start with. We have now appointed an excellent man as managing director of WSC, and he will be doing more and more and I will be doing less and less. When you have the responsibility in an organization for starting something you should take an active and personal interest in it.

Sunday Express: Do you hold out any hope for reaching a compromise with ICC?

Packer: Of course I would like a compromise if it is possible. But as we had said already a compromise will only come along if they treat the players the way they should treat them, and not victimize them. This is an example of victimization inspired, I think, from elsewhere than the Caribbean.

Sunday Express: To what extent do you plan World Series Cricket beyond the three-year period?

Packer: The fact that we signed some players recently and they were all signed on three-year contracts and one year has already gone on the original three-year contracts with the initial players means that we are here to stay. Three years seems like a good period to sign players for. It is a good time for them to decide if they want to be involved, and there will be many players who will be re-signed. There are young players there whom I think will be re-signed in three years – and be re-signed three years after that.

Sunday Express: Are you going to bring WSC to the Caribbean?

Packer: We would like to bring WSC to the Caribbean and show the people of the Caribbean the best cricket that they will ever see. Next year I don't think you have any international tours. I don't think that you are playing any cricket, and if the people of the Caribbean wanted to see WSC we would be delighted to bring it. The only thing we would have to get is the grounds. If you can give us the grounds you have the team . . . right now.

Sunday Express: Are you planning to extend your cricket to England?

Packer: I do not know anything about that.

Sunday Express: If your players are unable to play county cricket in England would you not consider going into that country?

Packer: There may be a chance of it now. Whereas we said before that the players would be available and we would not go and interfere with their season if our players were properly treated there must be a chance that we will end up going to play in a place like England eventually.

Sunday Express: There are persons who accuse you of having no regard for Test cricket. How do you respond to that criticism?

Packer: Test cricket is regarded with a certain reverence today, but it is only regarded with that reverence because the best players are involved in it, producing a high standard of the game. The image of Test cricket will be destroyed in the minds of the spectators once the Boards continue to play boy scouts in Test Matches. If you don't pick your best teams then the standard and prestige of Test cricket will very rapidly evaporate. The very meaning of the word 'tests', which is 'the highest standards between nations' will be destroyed by those who have built it up over these hundred years or so. Whereas people now talk about these boys not being able to play Test cricket again, and feel that that is the highest standard of cricket, you will have a new higher standard of cricket in the future.

Sunday Express: Are you really as confident of the future as you come over as being?

Packer: When the people who run traditional cricket see that we are
a fact of life and that we are going to succeed in providing the most
exciting cricket they will want to be involved, and at that time I am
sure that compromise will come about.

It was interesting that before he left the West Indies Packer also
said that Test cricket badly needed his players, just as he needed
the challenge of Test cricket. This was the first time that Packer
had admitted that his own form of cricket was not totally self-
sufficient and that he needed some aspect of Establishment cricket
in order to be ultimately successful. In the meantime his influence,
let alone his presence, was causing great anxiety in Georgetown.

The drive to Bourda on the first morning was tense, for none of
us knew what would happen; it seemed more than likely that there
would be disturbances. Only about three thousand people were
present at the start of the match, and the smart police horses
mounted at the various vantage points round the neat ground
looked as if they would not even have a crowd to control, orderly
or otherwise. However, by the early afternoon the ground was
almost full, with at least 12,000 watching the game. In the end
there were good crowds for all five days, about the best behaved
and fairest I have seen in the West Indies. There was never a hint
of trouble, and good cricket was appreciated, no matter whether
it was played by a West Indian or an Australian. The crowd also
had the disappointment of seeing their new young side lose after
they had seemed to be in an invincible position, yet they took it in
wonderfully sporting fashion.

Throughout the game I sensed a strong feeling of unreality, as
if it were an anti-climax to be watching cricket after all the drama
of the previous few days. It had taken a match or two to get to
know the Australians, but now a group of strange West Indians
were practising in front of the pavilion. Kallicharran, appointed
captain for the rest of the series and now before his home crowd,
won the toss and batted, but his young side allowed themselves
to be bowled out for 205. This was partly due to nerves and partly
to the strangeness of the situation, for most of them had come into
Georgetown secretly, not knowing whether they would be needed
or not. Once picked, they had no time to practise together as a
team – a team that included five cricketers who were playing for the
West Indies for the first time.

Australia were bowled out for 286 in their first innings, Wood and Rixon making competent fifties and Simpson, never a particularly glamorous batsman, a painstaking 67. By the time they batted a second time the West Indians had recovered enough to make 439, leaving Australia to score 359 to win in two days. The home side looked as if they had won the match in the first forty minutes of the fourth day when Clarke dismissed Darling, Ogilvie and Simpson for 22. Wood was now joined by Serjeant, who had been having a dreadful tour, and both playing innings of great character they put on 251 for the fourth wicket, taking the score to 273. However, in the last hour of the day Serjeant was out for 124, caught at long-leg hooking, Cozier played lazily back to Phillip and saw the ball roll back on to his stumps, and then in the last over Wood, momentarily losing concentration, started for an impossible run after Rixon had driven Clarke to mid-on, and was thrown out for 126. At 290 for 6 Australia needed 69 more on the last day, and Rixon, Laughlin and Yardley saw them home with some ease. Australia's final margin of victory was three wickets. It had been a wonderful game of cricket, and had, one hoped, done something to defuse the situation round the West Indies. The series was now poised at 2–1 with the West Indies still in the lead, and having blooded some excellent new players.

Of the batsmen the two openers, Alvin Greenidge and Basil Williams, both tall and thin, showed that they were typically instinctive West Indian strokemakers. Greenidge (like Gordon also from Barbados, but no relation) hit a good fifty in the first innings and Williams a hundred in the second. Larry Gomes, wearing ageing, yellowing pads which he might have just borrowed from Lord Hawke, also made a hundred in the second innings. Shivnarine made an attractive fifty in each innings, and though chosen for his bowling looked as though he may end up a better batsman than orthodox left-arm spinner, while Parry made a useful fifty as a nightwatchman. The tall Sylvester Clarke from Barbados bowled well at fast medium, and when he has thickened out will be pretty fast. Norbert Phillip will never be of top pace. He is tall with a high action, but he wastes these advantages by bowling too short, always making batsmen play off the back foot. Parry, the off-spinner, and Shivnarine did not bowl well on a typical slow and lifeless Bourda pitch, but Vanburn Holder did a steady job as the West Indies third seamer. Kallicharran did not have a particularly impressive first match as captain, especially when Australia recovered from 22 for 3 in the final innings to win. His spin bowlers did not help him, but he went on the defensive much too soon.

In Trinidad where the Fourth Test was to be played matters returned to their previous poor state. The local rabble-rousers had formed 'CIDWIC' (Committee in Defence of West Indies Cricket), and they set out to organize a boycott of the Test Match. It was remarkably successful: hardly 10,000 watched the four days' play. The stands were empty throughout, and for the first two mornings angry demonstrators gathered behind the commentary box and shouted so loudly that it was difficult to commentate. They roundly abused the West Indies Board and Jeff Stollmeyer, a Trinidadian, in particular. They sang a rhythmical first line of an impromptu calypso which may make its mark in next year's carnival, Trinidad's all-involving pre-Lenten festival, 'Everybody like Packer'. They made it sound rather good. But had there been a demonstration against the neutron bomb the following week, the basketball authorities the week after and the Hilton Hotel the week after that the same people would have been making the noise. It was an unpleasant demonstration, but ephemeral.

The Fourth Test promised much for three days, then folded on the fourth day when Australia batted extremely badly on a typically slow turning Port of Spain pitch. Simpson had won the toss and put the West Indies in on a damp pitch. However Thomson, their likely match-winner, did not bowl well that first morning. Then, after the West Indies had lost a couple of early wickets, Williams batted splendidly for 92, a better innings even than his hundred in Georgetown. Gomes gave him good support for a time, and then Kallicharran made runs as he usually does at Queen's Park Oval, so that the side finally reached a total of 292. When Australia batted Toohey, in particular, Yallop and Serjeant all batted well, and for a short time Simpson gave a masterful demonstration of how to play spin bowling; but Vanburn Holder took five wickets for ten runs with the second new ball with a splendid piece of controlled swing bowling against some poor batting, and finished with 6 for 28. Australia were all out for 290. When the West Indies were 151 for 6 in their second innings it looked as if Australia might win. But Greenidge made a good 69 and, like Williams, looked a fine prospect, and then Parry made 65, coming in at number eight. With further help from Phillip the West Indies reached 290.

The first three innings had all ended within two runs of each other. Could Australia repeat their earlier performance? In fact their batting on the last day against the orthodox left-arm spin of Jumadeen and the off-spin of Parry was dreadful. They were bowled out seventy minutes after lunch for 94, Yallop achieving the highest score with 18, and the West Indies had won by 198 runs. Parry, who bowled with better control in this innings, took 5 for 15, although he still looked some way short of a Test off-spinner. With this anti-climax the game came to an end, and the West Indies regained the Frank Worrell trophy, having taken an unassailable 3-1 lead in the series.

Although I now returned to London the Australians flew to Jamaica for the island match and the Fifth Test Match. When they played Jamaica Sang Hue was one of the umpires and during the course of the match he called the off-spinner, Bruce Yardley, for throwing and reopened the old wounds. He had been one of the umpires originally chosen to stand in the Fifth Test but when the Australians objected the West Indies Board replaced him with Wesley Malcolm who stood in what was his first Test Match. Ralph Gosein was the other umpire.

The final Test of the series ended in complete turmoil as the Kingston crowd rioted when Australia were about to win. The West Indies were asked to bat through the last day to save the match or to score 369 to win. They collapsed to 88 for five by mid-afternoon and then recovered through a brilliant innings of 126 by Kallicharran. He was then LBW to Higgs, and Holder was soon afterwards given out caught behind by Malcolm and the last pair of Phillip and Jumadeen would have had to survive the last 38 balls of the match. Holder was clearly unhappy with his decision and he had scarcely reached the pavilion before a hail of bottles and stones and other missiles were thrown on to the ground from the eastern side – the same part of the ground where the riots began when Cowdrey's side were winning in 1968. The Australians remained on the field for twenty minutes in the hope that play would be able to continue but they were eventually forced to return to the pavilion.

After lengthy consultations the West Indies Board announced that the match would be played to its conclusion on an un-scheduled sixth day – this had happened in 1968 when 75 minutes' cricket was played on the sixth day in which England almost lost a match they had earlier seemed to have won. Amazingly neither of the umpires was consulted or informed initially about the Board's decision on this latter occasion. As a result Gosein had to be hurriedly brought from his hotel to Sabina Park only fifteen minutes before the match was due to restart.

Gosein then said that there was no provision in the Laws or the playing conditions for the match to be extended and he refused to take part, as did the standby umpire, Johnny Gayle. The Board therefore had no alternative but to announce that the match had been abandoned. Allan Rae, one of the two Board representatives in Jamaica, said that the decision to play an extra day had been taken because of the prevailing circumstances and because there was a precedent and the playing conditions did allow for extension of time in the case of time lost to circumstances other than acts of God. Gosein replied that the match was of five days' duration and that the playing conditions made it clear that the only way it could have been extended was if more than an hour's play had been lost in circumstances other than acts of God. As it happened, there were 6.2 overs, or twelve minutes' playing time before six o'clock which was the close of play when the troubles began. To make confusion worse, umpire Malcolm said that he would be willing to continue and the Board said that the game would have been played to its conclusion had another umpire of first-class status, acceptable to both teams, been available. None could be found.

In many ways it was perhaps an appropriate end to a tour in which for the most part the actual cricket had been of secondary importance to the turmoil caused by the Packer situation. It was nonetheless sad for the Australians that they were deprived of a victory which would have helped their morale after losing the series. They had held the initiative from the start. They batted first making 343 and Toohey made his first Test hundred. Gomes then made his second hundred of the series and the West Indies were out for 280. In Australia's second innings Toohey was three runs short of his second hundred of the match when he was stumped off Jumadeen, and Wood also made ninety before Simpson declared at 305 for 3 leaving the West Indies the last day to score 369 to win. They had reached 258 for 9 when the riot began.

♦

CHAPTER 14

Summary of Play

I LANDED AT HEATHROW on Saturday 22 April, 351 days after that fateful occasion in Hove when news of Packer's plans first broke. In this time I had not only seen Packer's cricket in action but had experienced its effect on the established game all round the world. On Sunday 8 May 1977 no one could be sure what would come of Packer; by 22 April 1978 he and his World Series Cricket had become an established fact of life in the cricket world. He had made a considerable impact – even if it was not always in the way he wished. In May 1977 the main question had been: would Packer's proposed form of cricket ever make a start? A year later that had been answered most emphatically, and by then it was clear that Packer and World Series Cricket were not going to fade away. After this first year, however, a new set of questions has come to take its place.

First, is compromise possible – or even desirable, considering the positions taken up by both sides? The events of the year left the two sides in positions even more polarized than they were originally; it is now harder for either side to make the first move towards compromise for fear it will be interpreted as weakness. The established authorities had hoped to prevent Packer from ever making a start, but the situation has been reached where he will continue, probably for a number of years. Contact between Lord's and WSC was re-established during the summer of 1978 when David Clark and Jack Bailey met with Packer's representatives in New York. They discussed the possibility of compromise and Packer's demands were put to the ICC at their meeting at the

end of July. Packer and his allies had worked out a formula
whereby WSC would be in operation for ten months of the year.
It was so clearly unacceptable that even the representatives of
Pakistan and the West Indies who had been hoping for compromise voted with the other countries in rejecting this plan.
The ICC decided to set up a committee to monitor the progress
of WSC and said that it would be prepared to keep a dialogue
going with WSC. Two days later Packer representatives, who had
come to London, produced an entirely different set of suggestions
for the future of WSC involving considerably less cricket. In
which case why the first set of proposals?

When the High Court judgement was announced Kerry Packer
said that there was nothing the Establishment could give him. He
amended this later in the West Indies to say he needed the challenge of Test cricket. This must be true; if his players continue to
take part in Test cricket it will keep them in the news. He has nonetheless taken up a position of total hostility to the Establishment
and he has tried to embarrass them at every opportunity. When
WSC's plans for 1978/79 were announced in Sydney he said he had
tried 33 times to talk with the established authorities, and then
said it would be more accurate to say he had tried 66 times. Yet
in the events of World Series Cricket it is impossible to find even
one conciliatory gesture by Packer. The Establishment opposed
him with equal vehemence; they tried to prevent him using Test
grounds, they tried to ban his players from Test and first-class
cricket and by the end of these twelve months none of the countries
involved, England, Australia, Pakistan or the West Indies, was
selecting their Packer players for Test cricket. In Australia
World Series cricketers were even unable to play Sheffield Shield
cricket.

For all that, there are several possible means of compromise if
both sides genuinely wish it. WSC might confine its activities to
one-day and night cricket and leave Test cricket to the established
authorities, and a compromise could then be worked out over dates
which would leave both types of cricket with a certain amount of
the Christmas and New Year period in Australia. It might be that
Packer would agree to confine his activities to a six-week period at
the start or the end of the Australian season. Packer could also take
a side each year to a country which had no Test series of its own.
The two sides could sit down and work out their dates so that there

would be no conflict over the major matches. The Australian authorities might change their mind about exclusive television rights and Packer might then accept the five points he was given by the ICC at Lord's. Other combinations are equally feasible.

Many of the participants in WSC would welcome a compromise, and I know that some members of the Establishment feel that for the good of cricket an effort should be made to see if it is possible to find a solution which would satisfy both sides. In February this year Raman Subba Row, a member of the TCCB, wrote a letter to *The Times* to this effect, and in this he was supported by Bernie Coleman, another member of the TCCB. The main obstacle to compromise could be Kerry Packer himself. For all his talk he seems – as I have suggested – to be more and more determined to settle for nothing less than outright victory; the established game is no concern of his, and he has no interest in it. Is he interested in any form of compromise which would not in effect be forcing the authorities to give up a large measure of their control, if not to sell their birthright? Here I am pessimistic. Packer now has plans to play in New Zealand, in the West Indies and in America, and he may feel that having gone so far on his own there is no need to compromise, no matter what he is offered.

Of all the countries affected by Packer, England have suffered the least. Edmonds, Taylor and Botham have minimized the effect of losing the three Packer players, even if Underwood can never be replaced. With the exception of Thomson Australia have had to find a completely new side, and after beating India and losing an extraordinary series in the Caribbean they have the nucleus of a very good team, with Toohey, Wood and Yallop the best of their new players. Although the West Indies did not play their Packer players in the last three Tests against Australia strong public support for Packer remains, and since that series the West Indies Board have been forced to take a different line by the local associations who elect Board members and were urged to seek compromise. When Stollmeyer and Rae came to England for the ICC meeting in July 1978 it was with the intention to talk unilaterally to Packer if the ICC was not in favour of compromise. As it happened when they heard from David Clark the extent of Packer's demands they, like the other representatives, realized that they were not acceptable. Shortly afterwards the West Indies picked their side to tour India and the Packer players were all omitted. The effect on their future cricket is uncertain. When they played those three Tests against Australia without their Packer contingent they showed yet again the remarkable amount of natural ability there is in the West Indies. Players like Gomes, Alvin Greenidge and Williams made it clear that with a little more exposure they would soon fill the gaps left by the more illustrious players. As for Pakistan, after England had played three Tests there in December and January 1977/78 it did not look as though the home side would be too badly affected, judging by the way Haroon Rashid, Javed Miandad, Wasim Raja, Mudassar Nazar and Mohsin Khan played then. Six months later, however, this same side could hardly have fared worse in England, and none of these players did themselves justice. Their defeat in England was responsible for once again bringing out into the open the squabbles which had so bedevilled England's tour of Pakistan the previous winter. After the tour of England the Pakistan Cricket Board was disbanded and control was given to a group of four men with a general in the chair. The best known cricketer in the group was Javed Bulg, who played for Oxford and Pakistan and was a strong supporter of the opponents of the previous Board. He represented Pakistan at the ICC in July. Late in 1978 Pakistan and India were scheduled to play their first series for 18 years and Pakistan announced after their disastrous tour of England that they would choose their Packer players for this series and India said they did not object. It all made a mockery of the Karachi affair and was another example of a principle being sacrificed for expediency. One can only wonder who had the ear of General Zia-ul-Haq this time.

It would be idle to suggest that Packer's arrival has not affected the Test sides of all the countries concerned, but the disappearance of many well-known names from Test cricket has given young players the chance they would not otherwise have had. All these new players I have mentioned are exciting prospects, and represent a rising generation of Test cricketers from whom the famous names of the future will come. But one necessarily asks: will Packer and his colleagues try to sign these new players? Cricketers do not make their reputation in World Series Cricket; they make their names in established cricket. And it is this which qualifies them for Packer, who, if he is going to continue with World Series Cricket for any length of time, is going to have to replenish his personnel. The authorities of all the Test-playing countries are now contracting their players for a longer period than just one immediate series, but Packer has said that he will still get the players he wants. This could lead to yet more legal battles. Because of the relative poverty of their respective Boards of Control it may be that the West Indies, Pakistan and India will be his best recruiting grounds, but while Packer is still running World Series Cricket all Test-playing countries will be in danger of losing their best young players.

The first season of WSC was not as successful as its promoters hoped, but nonetheless it gained credibility. Packer lost more money than he expected, but that has not worried him unduly. His second season will be crucially important, especially as he will be competing against the oldest and most popular series of all, England versus Australia. His greatest success in his first season was with night cricket, and he has developed that considerably. Five Super-Tests are planned for 1978/79, and they will be played over four days, from 1.30 p.m. to 10.30 p.m., the last half of the day being played under floodlights. The players will wear coloured clothes – yellow for Australia, light red for the West Indies and light blue for the Rest of the World – principally to enable them to see the white ball more clearly. In the first year it was often lost for a brief moment against the white of the players' clothes. Also they will use a white ball with green stitches.

In his first year Packer invited competition by arranging his matches on the same dates as the official Test Matches, and lost. Significantly, he has ensured that the dates of his next round of Super-Tests do not coincide with the official Ashes Test Matches, save for one day, 1 February, when there is an unavoidable over-lap. There will also be a succession of one-day matches and a country competition. Two of the Super-Tests will be played at Melbourne, two at Sydney (where Packer has permission to use the Sydney Cricket Ground), and one in Adelaide, where he had so little support in his first year that he stopped playing there. It may be that he will be allowed to use the Adelaide Oval and also the Woolloongabba at Brisbane. This may be a sign that opposition to him is weakening in Australia, or that he has been able to by-pass the relevant cricket authorities. By the time his matches start more innovations will have been thought of, but it remains to be seen whether World Series Cricket will seriously rival the Ashes series.

It may even be that the lack of enthusiasm that some of the authorities show for compromise stems from the fact that they are sure that Packer will come off the worst – that by April 1979 he will not be in such a strong position from which to discuss compromise settlements. However, this fails to allow for one crucial factor. It was clear after World Series Cricket's first season in Australia that it should go overseas. The Australian public were reluctant to support Packer's version of the game, with so little sense of international rivalry, but as soon as WSC goes overseas its identity will become stronger and the television pictures flashed back to Channel Nine of the game being played in a foreign environment will be that much more likely to hold an audience.

Much of the activity which has taken place since the end of WSC's first season has been to arrange for the export of Packer's latest product. Ian Chappell went to New Zealand while England were there, ostensibly to play in a charity match in Wellington, but he also visited Christchurch; that the WSC Australians and West Indians are to play a series of four matches in New Zealand before the start of the programme in Australia in November 1978 will not have been entirely unconnected with his visit. WSC are not using the Test grounds for these matches. Packer's own visit to the Caribbean has been discussed in detail.

Before the decision had been taken by the WSC to tour the West Indies, the West Indies Board had already invited New Zealand to make their second visit to the Caribbean in late February and March 1979, after the West Indies had themselves returned from India and Sri Lanka. At first this seemed to be a move designed to present the West Indies public with an alternative series to Packer's. Now that WSC will be making their 'tour' the Board may feel that the public will support their old star players, almost all of whom play for Packer, and will not bother to watch the series between the young West Indies side and New Zealand – a series which would then make an enormous loss, the one thing the West Indies Board more than any other cannot afford. At the moment of writing this series is in the balance. New Zealand are prepared to send a side although not all their best players may be available, but are waiting for the West Indies to confirm their invitation.

Packer has made other ventures overseas, one of which has been central to his thinking. As we have seen, he is a friend of Mark

McCormack, and WSC has always been interested in taking cricket to the United States. At the start of the English summer of 1978 Greig went to America for ten days to talk to representatives of the major television networks, and he met with an encouraging response. A one-day game was arranged in New York for early September and many of the WSC players will be taking part although it is not being directly organized by Packer. At the time of writing this has not been played, but it is being used as an opportunity to gauge the response of the American public. If it is satisfactory WSC will, in some form, be visiting the United States in March or April 1979, soon after the West Indies. Greig has since spoken of the need to quicken the game up for an American audience, even to the point of changing the rules. The idea of a game which finishes in three to four hours is appealing, and would probably mean a contest over something like 25 overs for each side. Maiden overs may be outlawed in the same way that a baseball player is out if he fails to make contact with any of his three strikes. If the game is to be a success on television in America it might easily involve the wholesale rewriting of the rule book as it now stands.

To make WSC even more world-wide there is a plan for a world eleven to play games in Bombay and Karachi. The likely reaction to World Series Cricket in New Zealand remains uncertain, although the novelty value is bound to produce crowds when Packer goes there. In Pakistan he will have support after the beating Pakistan took from England in 1978, clearly in large part attributable to the absence of their Packer players. International matches in India traditionally draw huge crowds. Thus at the end of his second year Packer may not be any nearer to making a profit – for his expenses will still be vast – but he may be closer to becoming permanently established.

Initially, acquiring the grounds to play on was his biggest problem. Ingenuity overcame this in Australia, and in his second year the problem will not be so acute. His biggest worry now could be to get hold of new players. The Establishment's best defence against Packer is to dry up his lines of supply, and while England and Australia may be able to do this it will be surprising if the other countries can find the money to make established cricket as profitable as Packer's. Then there is South Africa.

Outlawed from Test cricket, South Africa should be the

natural breeding ground for WSC, yet the country has caused Packer difficulties. In Australia in 1977/78 the West Indian and Pakistani players refused to play against the two South African-based South Africans – Graeme Pollock and the leg spinner Denys Hobson – and Packer has several times said that he will not go to South Africa until such time as they are playing Test cricket against the West Indies, Pakistan and India. He has therefore to ensure that any South African who signs a contract with WSC is made respectable by taking part in county cricket in England – it is this that has given Barlow, Procter, Barry Richards and Rice a clean bill of health. Clive Rice's signing was announced just before the start of the 1978 season and Nottinghamshire sacked him as player and captain, but were forced because of the legal implications to reinstate him as a player. It has been rumoured that Keppler Wessels, who played for Sussex in 1977 before returning to South Africa for national service, has signed for WSC, and also that Garth Le Roux, a young fast bowler, is also on the WSC payroll. Le Roux came over to England during the summer of 1978 and stayed with Greig in Hove. He played for Sussex in their match against the New Zealanders, and one wonders whether Greig wanted him to do this in order that he too should gain respectability.

If all goes according to plan, Packer's World Series Cricket will have visited all the game's main centres round the world by April 1979, except for South Africa and England. He is not going to take on world opinion by attempting to go to South Africa, but England is a different matter. Packer has often said that he will not come to England provided that his players are not victimized for joining WSC and are allowed to continue playing county cricket. They all played for their counties in 1978 in accordance with the High Court judgement with the exception of Knott, who did not want to accept the one-year contract he was offered by Kent, and Snow, who could not come to a satisfactory arrangement with Sussex. Kent offered their four Packer players one-year contracts which they said would not be renewed. Warwickshire acted similarly with Amis, and in August 1978 confirmed that he would not be playing for them in 1979. On the other hand the Kent committee reversed their decision and decided to re-engage their four for 1979. With extraordinary timing this decision was announced on the eve of the ICC meeting and David Clark, the

President of ICC and for years a Kent Committee member, was forced to resign from the county committee for otherwise he might have laid himself open to charges of double dealing by the ICC representatives. He was another in the long list of casualties caused by the Packer affair. During the 1978 season Greig, Roberts and Barry Richards all opted out of county cricket. If Packer is looking for an excuse to justify a visit to England, I am sure he will find it. He has already sounded out the possibility of playing at the White City, at Stamford Bridge and at Villa Park in Birmingham. The English climate cannot be relied upon to make night cricket a success, or indeed to enable a ground used for football to be turned into a suitable cricket ground in a matter of weeks, but there is a large expatriate population in England which could provide Packer with his support. Finally, Packer may come to England simply to show the authorities at Lord's that there is nothing he cannot do if he wishes.

Already Packer has had a considerable effect on cricket, and if he were to disappear tomorrow his influence would remain. As it is, there can be no doubt that Packer will maintain a close personal involvement with the future of WSC. He has had to fight a hard battle to bring it this far, and not only is there a considerable financial investment hanging on its success but he also has his own sense of pride. I do not believe that he would attempt to find a face-saving formula to allow him to pull out of cricket. Meanwhile cricketers are being paid considerably more money for Test Matches, more money is filtering through at lower levels, the authorities have been forced to take a hard look at themselves and see if they are doing their best for those under their control, and have been shown that if they go out into the market-place and try to sell their product there is more money about than they thought. In short, Packer has increased considerably the gross world income for the game. The white ball, coloured clothes and night cricket have still to be evaluated; but it may well be that one or more of these innovations will stay.

In an early attempt to justify the amount of money he was paying his players Packer has said, 'There are certain people who are meant to perform skills which have a real time limit on them, on an honorary basis, for the glory, and ten years after they've stopped nobody even remembers or cares. These players, in a very short career, by normal standards, have to set themselves up for life,

and I don't think they are being outrageously paid on that basis.'
One cannot ignore that argument, nor deny that some good has
come from Packer's intervention into the game. Nonetheless
cricket on its own cannot afford this money, and Packer's intervention has also meant that the game has finally lost its inde-
pendence, to become controlled by big business. This is something which cricket has avoided longer than any other major sport,
and at root this is what the authorities were trying to stave off in
their wholehearted opposition to Packer.

By the time the England side reaches Adelaide in late October
1978 there will have been more developments from the Packer
camp. No side in the history of cricket will have gone overseas
under greater pressure with such huge responsibilities as this
England side. They will be upholding the honour of traditional
cricket and its greatest showpiece, the Ashes, to a deafening blare
of rival publicity. It is desperately important that England's
cricketers play attractive cricket. They must hold the attention of
the Australian public, but if they bat as they did in Pakistan and
New Zealand spectators may desert in their thousands to Packer.
It is a daunting challenge. I believe, though, that Test cricket, for
all Packer's innovations and gimmickry, will remain the most appealing of all types of the game. The sterility of Packer's cricket,
played between non-representative sides when the result does not
matter, will over the long term be an insuperable handicap. I do
not believe the public in Australia will want it for ever, and
although the arrival of WSC in other countries may generate early
interest it will not make a lasting impact. The Australians have
already shown that they do not see the Super-Test as the genuine
article. If I am wrong and World Series Cricket is still here in ten
years' time the game itself will have significantly changed. Crash
helmets, bouncers, coloured clothes and hidden microphones are
only a beginning; and the American market, so crucial to Packer,
will produce many more changes.

If the American market becomes a reality it is easy to see World
Series Cricket playing there more often than in any other country.
That is where the money is, and WSC has been principally designed to make money. In a few years the situation could arise
where a form of popularized, bastardized cricket, full of instant
appeal, is played to mass television audiences in the United States
and maybe Australia, while the traditional game continues as it

does today. It might become a Rugby Union/Rugby League situation, and whether the games could exist side by side is a matter of pure conjecture. They would not appeal to the same audience, but will traditional cricket then appear as antiquated as Real or Royal Tennis appears to Lawn Tennis devotees, and have a similarly limited appeal? I do not think so, for I believe that cricket as an international game has never been stronger. Another beneficial rub-off from WSC has been that the game can never in its entire history have been talked about as it has since 8 May 1977. People who have never shown the smallest interest in cricket have become fascinated by the Packer affair, and when cricket appears on television or on radio or in the papers their subconscious now makes them pay attention. Eventually they may even go to watch. And that can only be good.

Index

Owing to late changes made as a result of recent developments in the cricket world certain pages in the book have been revised, occasionally resulting in the reference appearing a page later than stated in the Index. Where this is likely to be the case a small 'f' is placed next to the entry in question.